2nd Edition

HOW TO PLAN
for Baby Boomers

Advisor's Guide to the New Retirement Model

Donald Ray Haas, CLU, ChFC, CFP®, MSFS, RFG

This publication is designed to provide accurate and authoritative information in regard to the subject matter covered. It is sold with the understanding that the publisher is not engaged in rendering legal, accounting or other professional service. If legal advice or other expert assistance is required, the services of a competent professional should be sought. – **From a Declaration of Principles jointly adopted by a Committee of the American Bar Association and a Committee of Publishers and Associations.**

Circular 230 Notice – The content in this publication is not intended or written to be used, and it cannot be used, for the purposes of avoiding U.S. tax penalties.

ISBN: 978-0-87218-923-2
Library of Congress Control Number: 2007926323

Copyright © 1998, 2007
The National Underwriter Company
P.O. Box 14367, Cincinnati, Ohio 45250-0367

2nd Edition

Printed in U. S. A.

Acknowledgements

Robert L. Spence for sharing with me his forty years of experience in the publishing business, for acting as my personal editor on all aspects of the development of the manuscript for this book, and most importantly, for being a good friend.

Carol L. Edwards for being my companion and best friend and for giving me both moral and physical support, not only in writing of this book, but in all of the activities in which I have participated during the past 30 plus years.

Neal E. Cutler, Ph.D. for sharing his expertise on gerontology issues and the editing of Chapter 9, The Boomers Are Retiring, Or Are They.

Lori A. Gilbert for her talent and creativity in design, layout, and development of all graphs and Power Point slides.

About the Author

Donald Ray Haas, CLU, ChFC, CFP®, RFC, AEP, MSFS, Registered Financial Gerontologist, is president of Haas Retirement Services, Inc., located in Birmingham, Michigan. He is a financial consultant in practice since 1956 and was cited by *Worth* magazine as one of the *"300 Best Financial Advisors in America."*

Haas, who served on the Society of Financial Service Professionals' National Board of Directors from 1991 to 1993, also served as its Detroit Chapter's president. He currently serves on the Board of Advisors for the American Institute of Financial Gerontology and serves on the Board of Governors of the University of Michigan Music Alumni Society. He is a 33-year member of the Million Dollar Round Table and has received the prestigious National Quality Award for 33 years. He has been an adjunct instructor in Financial Planning at Lawrence Technological University and served on the CFP® Board of Practice Standards. He served on a Curriculum Review Committee for The American College and on an Examination Review Committee for the CFP® Board of Standards.

Since 1986, Haas has authored a monthly client newsletter, *Money Monitor*, has articles published in the *Journal of the Society of Financial Service Professionals,* and served as author of the bi-monthly newsletter, *Financial Monitor,* from 1990 to 1997 for the Society of Financial Service Professionals. In 1999, he hosted the weekly two-hour CBS radio show, *"Financial Fitness with Don Haas."* He has also served as an expert commentator on local Detroit Fox-TV.

Haas is an international speaker on financial planning topics with special emphasis on retirement and aging issues. In 2000, he presented workshops across the United States and in 2003 spoke to an audience of over 2,000 at the Asia Pacific Life Insurance Congress in Singapore where his message was positively received. He has co-presented the popular workshop, *"Health and Wealth",* with Dr. Fred Stransky. This workshop's theme involves how and why to live a long time in relative good health, and how to make your money last as long as you do.

Additionally, Don has spoken to many professional associations, including the American Society on Aging, Million Dollar Round Table, Institute for International Research, Financial and Estate Planning Council, Financial Planning Association, National Association of Insurance and Financial Advisors, International Association of

Registered Financial Consultants, and more than 20 chapters around the country of the Society of Financial Services Professionals, as well as at its National Conferences, video teleconferences, and Keeping Current Clinics.

Haas was recognized for his multitude of contributions to the financial planning industry as the 2001 recipient of the Loren Dunton Award. Mr. Dunton is known as the "father" of financial planning. In 2002, Haas was inducted into the Michigan Insurance Hall of Fame, and in 2003 he became a Registered Financial Gerontologist. In 2005, the National Association of Estate Planners honored Don with the Distinguished Accredited Estate Planners Award.

After graduation from the University of Michigan, Haas joined the trumpet section of the Detroit Symphony Orchestra, a position he held for twenty years. During most of those years, he developed his financial planning career, and since retiring from the DSO in 1973, has devoted his full time to the financial services profession. He lives in Birmingham, Michigan.

He holds a Bachelor of Music degree from the University of Michigan, a Master of Education from Wayne State University and a Master of Science in Financial Services from The American College.

Table of Contents

Chapter 1

The Baby Boomer Market

Between news segments on CNN Headline News, a simple statement filled the screen of the TV. The white letters on a black background were displayed for no longer than 5 or 10 seconds, but the message they relayed was a real thought provoker. The simple statement was: "Each day since January of 1996, 11,000 Baby Boomers turned 50." Ten years later (2006), these 50 year olds turned age 60.

Who are these Baby Boomers and why are there so many? What are they like, and how can a financial adviser make contact with this huge supply of prospective clients? When an adviser makes contact, what special concerns, needs, and desires do these Baby Boomers have that the adviser should be prepared to address?

WHO ARE BABY BOOMERS?

Baby Boomer *noun*; anyone born during the years of 1946 through 1964, a member of a Baby-boom generation.

The above is a dictionary definition of Baby Boomer, but it does not even begin to describe this large, powerful, and not uncomplicated group of people. For example, have you ever wondered why there are so many Baby Boomers?

The number of Baby Boomers is impressive. They began to make their appearance in 1946, registering 3,288,000 births that first year. They continued to show up in the birth columns of the nation's newspapers until the end of 1964, the last year during which they managed to account for 4,027,000 births. To appreciate the significance of these numbers, you should take a look at the following graph that shows the annual births from early in the 20th century up through 1964.

What caused this rapid increase in the birth rate? Two historical events preceded the Baby Boomer generation. The first was the Great Depression, which began in 1929, and lasted through the thirties. Few couples felt they could afford more than one child. Some couples had none. Hence, the birth rate during these years was kept

Figure 1.1

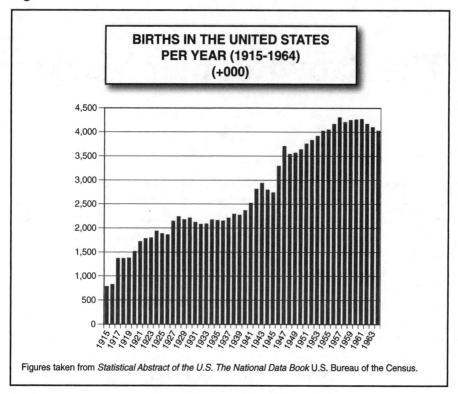

BIRTHS IN THE UNITED STATES
PER YEAR (1915-1964)
(+000)

Figures taken from *Statistical Abstract of the U.S. The National Data Book* U.S. Bureau of the Census.

relatively low. Next came World War II. Many of the men found themselves in parts of the world they had never heard about, and many of the women found themselves in jobs they never expected to have. This separation was not at all conducive to producing children.

Then came August 14, 1945, the day President Truman declared V-J Day. The war was over. The lights were on again all over the world. The boys came home, and the girls no longer worked the swing shift. A great feeling of optimism flowed over the whole country, and young people everywhere felt it was a wonderful time to raise a family. So, they started having children, and by the end of 1964, they had produced 76 million of them – the Baby Boomers.

As all these babies grew up, their numbers greatly affected each segment of the economy. The Baby Boomers currently represent about 33 percent of the nation's population, and so they will continue to have a great effect on the economy. In the last few years of the 20th century, many of these Baby Boomers have been very much involved in child raising and career interests. This entails a lot of toys and furniture, a lot of computer games and the accompanying hardware, and a lot of business suits and business travel. All of this consumerism is just starting to turn into *accumulationism*. It is not surprising that the economy has been booming because of these one-time babies.

When Baby Boomers turn age 50, an interesting phenomenon happens. All of a sudden they realize that their lifetime dream of retirement at age 55 simply isn't going to happen, and they become worried that they won't be able to accumulate enough to retire, even at age 65. Actually, one-half still plan to retire before age 65 – the younger Baby Boomers, for the most part – but many experts believe such plans are unrealistic for most Boomers. "It's time to realize that Boomers have not done a good job in planning for retirement, and that very soon, they are going to wake up to some harsh realizations. When it comes to Baby Boomers and retirement planning, the contrast between perception and reality is almost blinding." So said Dr. Robert Froehlich, Managing Director of Scudder Kemper Investments and an investment strategist.

The financial adviser (planner or consultant) will be well rewarded by seeking to serve this large group of people. Baby Boomers want and need the services of expert financial advisers. Because of what the Boomers know how to do so well – spend money – they want help in changing the direction of the flow of their money. They have had everything else, they think, so now why not have wealth? There is a lot of self-help information available to Baby Boomers, and Boomers have no lack of confidence in their ability to select proper investments. However, this takes time to study and apply, and patience is not one of the Baby Boomer's strong suits. Also, Boomers are busy climbing the success ladder in their careers. Thus, there exists this opportunity for a financial adviser to provide the assistance Boomers want and, according to reputable studies, know that they need.

The financial needs of Baby Boomers are quite extensive. Among the important motivations for these needs are, believe it or not, the babies of the Baby Boomers. There are 71 million babies of Baby Boomers to raise, educate, and provide some assistance getting a start in adulthood. Of the Baby Boomers who have children, about half have children under the age of 18, and 60 percent of Boomers provide financial assistance to their children, regardless of age.

These 71 million babies of the Baby Boomers are called the Echo generation, because their birth rates over a 19-year period – the same number of years as the Baby Boomers – have produced an echo effect that is evident when shown in graphs.

When the Baby-Boomer years – 1946 through 1964 – are isolated and compared with the echo-generation years – 1976 through 1994 – the echo effect is even more apparent.

Figure 1.2

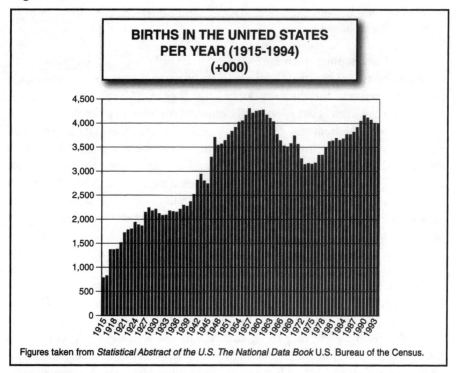

BIRTHS IN THE UNITED STATES
PER YEAR (1915-1994)
(+000)

Figures taken from *Statistical Abstract of the U.S. The National Data Book* U.S. Bureau of the Census.

Figure 1.3

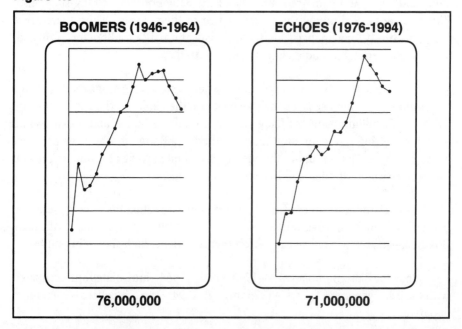

BOOMERS (1946-1964)   ECHOES (1976-1994)

76,000,000   71,000,000

Enough on the Echo Generation for now, but don't forget about them. Families are important to Baby Boomers, and many of their decisions will be influenced by their concern for their children. Also, the Echo Generation will eventually present their own unique characteristics, wants, and needs, and they might even require another book written to help financial advisers serve this new generation.

Baby Boomers want to learn more about their finances. They want to know more about how to manage money wisely. Retirement planning has changed drastically. Many Boomers must decide for themselves where to invest contributions into retirement plans, such as 401(k) plans. Boomers need a greater understanding of asset allocation. Many Baby Boomers know the word *diversification*, but some do not really understand the difference between having a diversified portfolio of CDs – different maturity dates and at different banks – and a diversified portfolio of real estate, stocks, bonds, and a mix of fixed dollar investments. Even among Baby Boomers who have a reasonably clear understanding of a diversified portfolio, about 60 percent have no idea how much money they should place in the different asset allocation categories.

It is important that the financial adviser teach those principles of financial management and wealth accumulation to Baby Boomer clients. Most Boomers want to acquire this knowledge, not only for their own use, but also to pass along to their children. Being a role model is important to Baby Boomers. However, the financial adviser must also teach Baby Boomers that the fabulous stock market that started in 1982 might be an anomaly. Most, if not all, of their investment life the stock market has been on an almost non-stop bull run. No bears in sight, except for 1987. The crash in 1987 is perceived by the Baby Boomers as a fluke, or just one of those happenings in the past. Of course, the wake-up call came in 2000 and continued into 2002. This stock market crash was significant and not only brought the reality that long-term bull markets come to an end, but substantiated that 20 and 30 percent annual growth rates are not sustainable. It is time for the financial adviser to get these people to accept the probability that if double-digit returns continue, it is more likely they will be in a range of 10 to 11 percent long term rather than the high teens.

Baby Boomers are just beginning to realize the potential difficulty of providing for life after work. In a study conducted for Scudder Kemper Investments by Dr. Christopher Hayes, Professor of Psychology at Southampton College of Long Island University and Executive director of the National Center for Women and Retirement research, 64 percent of Baby Boomers polled had no idea how much money they will need for retirement. He also found that 64 percent have resigned themselves to reduced or no Social Security benefits, with 40 percent expecting reduced benefits. Twenty-four percent do not believe they will receive any benefits from Social Security.

Another fact not properly attended to by many Baby Boomers when planning for their retirement is the fact that people are living longer, much longer in many cases. If Baby Boomer clients are not aware of the implications, both financial and physical, of a longer lifetime, then financial advisers need to accept responsibility for bringing this information to their attention.

Whatever a Baby Boomer's life expectancy was at birth, it is no longer that today. The amount of medical knowledge, both curative and preventative, discovered since the birth of a Baby Boomer is astronomical. Hardly a week goes by without the media reporting on another marvelous cure or preventive intervention for some illness, and many more such discoveries go unreported by the general media.

It is one thing to look at life expectancy in the year of birth, but an entirely different picture appears when a person has reached age 65.

Figure 1.4 shows that, in 1960, just four years before the last of the Baby Boomers were born, only 14 out of every 100 people 65 years old would live to see age 90. Today, this figure is approaching 50 percent. Figure 1.4 also shows that, in 1995, 60 out of every 100 people 65 years old will live to be 85, and eight will live to see age 100.

Figure 1.4

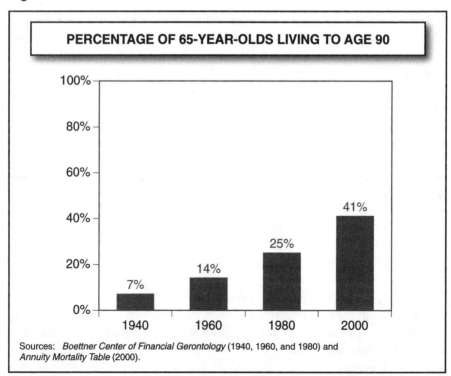

PERCENTAGE OF 65-YEAR-OLDS LIVING TO AGE 90

Sources: *Boettner Center of Financial Gerontology* (1940, 1960, and 1980) and *Annuity Mortality Table* (2000).

Figure 1.4 (cont'd)

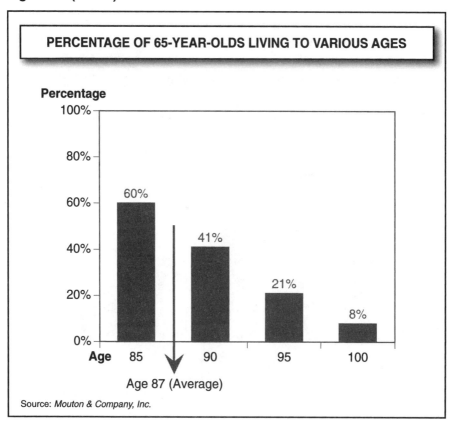

PERCENTAGE OF 65-YEAR-OLDS LIVING TO VARIOUS AGES

Source: *Mouton & Company, Inc.*

Since the majority of all species live in pairs, it is even more real, as well as enlightening, to look at the life expectancies of at least one of the two in a human couple from age 65 on.

Study Figure 1.5 closely. Not only does it indicate there is a 16 percent probability that one of a couple who live to age 65 will live to age 100, but an extrapolation from the data shows that the average life expectancy of one of each couple is about age 92.

At the present time, life expectancy trails off very fast after age 92, but for those who live a well balanced lifestyle with proper nutrition and exercise, the fast drop in life expectancy could be significantly altered. The tremendous amount of research in health and aging will produce significant future changes, maybe even generating life expectancies of age 120 or beyond. But even an average life expectancy of 92 means that any Baby Boomer who retires at 65 should have enough wealth to support a proper standard of living for at least 28 more years, if not longer. At the World

Figure 1.5

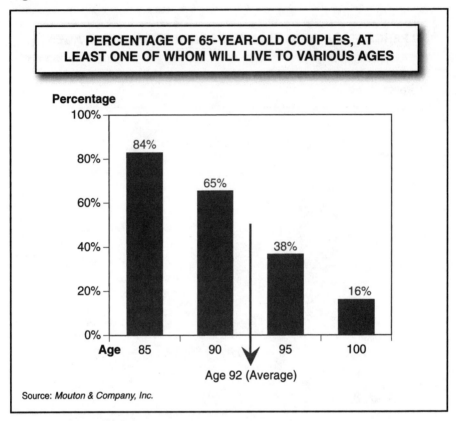

PERCENTAGE OF 65-YEAR-OLD COUPLES, AT LEAST ONE OF WHOM WILL LIVE TO VARIOUS AGES

Source: *Mouton & Company, Inc.*

Future Society annual conference (2006) in Toronto, the common belief among the attendees was that a life expectancy of 120 years will soon become the norm. One speaker (Ray Kurzweil) said that a girl alive today will live to age 150. Barrons (April 17, 2006) front page headline was "Live to 150."

The Baby Boomers will likely be the first large group of people to experience a life span in excess of 120 years. The results of extensive research today already promise that the aging process is not inevitable. Science and medicine will learn how to prevent it, fix it, or compensate for it, and the timetable fits the Baby Boomers very well. Of course, if age 120 is to become an average life expectancy, this will greatly affect all financial aspects for Baby Boomers. Just about all current planning for retirement income will prove to be grossly inadequate, and current government pension systems and employer plans will not be able to provide these extended payouts. Probably, our whole financial structure will require modification. This is not likely to happen over night, but it could be upon us over the next several years.

The financial adviser is not expected to be able to see clearly into the future, but it is incumbent upon all advisers to be aware of possibilities. Certainly, it would be a mistake to assume that client's life expectancy should be based on life-expectancy-at-birth tables, such as the following one, currently in use.

Figure 1.6

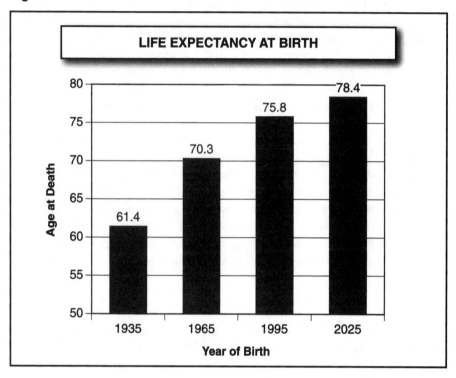

The numbers shown in the graph have already been surpassed. Over the next thirty years, as the oldest Baby Boomers embark on an extended life span, financial planners will serve clients well by putting this subject on the table. Financial planners must encourage their clients to start early in their wealth accumulation, and must project the future needs of their clients both with inflation adjustments and by planning for life expectancies that go beyond current life expectancies.

Yes, the financial adviser may be killing off the Baby Boomer client's wonderful thought of retiring at age 55, but that thought would never have become a reality for the vast majority of Baby Boomers anyway. Most of them already suspect or know this. What they want now is help in accumulating the wealth required to retire at a reasonable age. The wise adviser knows and informs clients that even if retirement at 65 is possible, the accumulated wealth must be sufficient to support a much greater number of retirement years than clients might be assuming at present.

The Baby Boomers are an awesome market for financial planning. Most of them know they need help and are willing to accept it. They want to become wealthy and are getting over their spending sprees. Reaching age 50, they are scared and are willing to change their average savings from between 4 and 6 percent to up to 20 percent. So, if the financial adviser provides the service Baby Boomers want and need, the adviser will be well rewarded with the satisfaction of a job well done and with remuneration sufficient to provide for the adviser's own retirement.

HOW DO YOU FIND BABY BOOMER CLIENTS?

Finding Baby Boomers is not difficult. After all, there are 76 million of them. Finding Baby Boomer clients, however, will take a little more effort. A significant majority of Baby Boomers are worried about their financial futures, and over two-thirds are willing to admit they have not spent enough time planning for retirement. So it seems this is a vast group of people eager for some professional advice from a financial adviser. A financial adviser's dream? Well, yes and no. As some wag aptly put it, "Baby Boomers are walking contradictions." The Boomers may not admit openly that they need professional help, but they definitely will appreciate it if and when they get it.

You won't find Baby Boomer clients by continuing to use the same old traditional methods. An applicable statement for the past was, "You can lead a horse to water, but you can't make it drink." Clients were not that difficult to interest because most knew nothing about investing, but they were difficult to convince that the recommended portfolio was indeed proper. A more applicable statement for most Baby Boomers today would be, "If you can lead a horse to water, then it will drink and say thank you." It is more difficult to get Baby Boomers interested in considering a financial adviser. A majority of Boomers believe that they are sufficiently competent to choose investments. They know about the wealth of information available to them on the Internet, including up-to-date stock ticker prices and the ability to execute trades while on-line. What the financial adviser must do today is convince these Boomers that personal research and professional advice are not incompatible. In fact, they make an unbeatable combination. However, before you can do this convincing, you have to get the subject's attention. So, how do you lead this horse to water?

Baby Boomers are always improving themselves. They join physical-fitness clubs, they listen to self-improvement tapes, and they attend seminars and workshops on topics that interest them. So, one way to attract potential Baby Boomer clients is to provide seminars and workshops on topics that interest them. Such events should definitely be educational in nature and contain no overt selling of any product except yourself. Also, seminars and workshops should be focused on the lifestyle and interests of the Baby Boomers. Attract them with clever titles, such as, "How To Be A Financial Role Model For Your Children," or "You, The Internet, and Your Financial Adviser, A Perfect Triangle," or "What Are You Missing When You Research and Trade on the Internet?" or "What To Do When You Become an Active Member of The Sandwich Generation."

You can come up with more clever titles than the ones just suggested. Always keep the potential client in mind. What does he really want to know? The last title, for example, is intended to attract those Baby Boomers who find themselves trying to support their children and one or both of their parents at the same time they are saving for their own retirement. In case you believe that this is a small group, then consider the following fact: a 50 year old Baby Boomer has an 80 percent chance that at least one parent is living, and a 27 percent chance of both parents living. Few, if any, Baby Boomers have planned financially to support their parents, their children, and save for their own retirement. However, the troublesome fact is that few to none of the Baby Boomers' parents planned on living as long as they did, and the retirement funds of many are beginning to look insufficient.

Whatever title is given to the seminar or workshop, the topic should be addressed as thoroughly as time permits and then concluded with a talk or activity that projects the message, "You need me!"

In these seminars or workshops, regardless of the topic, don't fail to stress the merits of having a complete financial plan, one that is designed to fit an individual client's financial needs, objectives, and risk tolerance. Those Baby Boomers who think they are adequately preparing for themselves and their families might be surprised to recognize the value of a financial plan custom designed to fit their needs, and their needs can differ tremendously from those of their neighbor or best friend. Comparing two hypothetical clients might be an interesting exercise: two clients that appear to be alike, but require entirely different financial plans.

It is the task of the financial adviser to convince potential clients that they need the adviser without seeming to denigrate what the potential clients have already done. Baby Boomers want to hear positive comments about the good things they are doing along with helpful suggestions on how to plan for retirement. Remember, the egos of Baby Boomers can be more fragile than the eggs of robins.

Another tip: Always project a youthful, positive image, whether working before a large group or one on one. This does not mean you must visit a plastic surgeon or buy a toupee if you are a wrinkled and bald seventy-year-old financial adviser. Just project youthful optimism. Fitness guru Jack LaLanne still packs them in at seminars all over the country, and he is in his 90s. This goes to show that an energetic and vivacious 90 something can outdraw a sullen and grouchy 32 anytime. Boomers will not tolerate a Dr. Gloom who reminds them of what they have not done and should have done. They want a Dr. Helpful Hal or Hanna who praises them for their efforts and encourages them to consider additional steps that might be appropriate. A good financial adviser listens to and addresses his clients' psychological and economic needs.

When considering ideas for workshops, give some thought to aiming at specific market groups. For example, the number of single, never-married women Baby Boomers is estimated to be 20 million. That's quite a niche to target. Word of mouth after a seminar for singles could double or triple attendance at the next workshop.

Another group to consider is divorced women. The number of women divorced in mid-life tripled between 1982 and 1992, which means there are millions of single women out there. Since all have been married and many are single parents with live-at-home children, these women have had many experiences different from those had by never-married women. Keep in mind, however, that both groups of women do have much in common. They budget more for savings than men do. They also have an innate ability to analyze and solve problems, but because many were raised to be nurturing caregivers, they are not comfortable giving top priority to their own needs. However, once-married women, particularly those with children, and never-married women have had significantly different life experiences, and many of these experiences can make it difficult for the two groups to relate to one another. Therefore, it might be more valuable to everybody if separate workshops were held.

One more suggestion for targeting a niche group is to give some thought to having a workshop for families. Baby Boomers believe it is important to teach their children about finances, although fewer than 1 in 10 ever spend much time doing it.

A word to the wise is sufficient: A financial adviser must be well prepared to conduct any of these suggested workshops. In fact, a financial adviser must be well versed in the field just to sit down and talk with one or two Baby Boomers, because Boomers can be quick to spot and reject someone who doesn't know as much as they do. So, this means that the adviser should be well educated in all areas of financial planning. Obtaining a Certified Financial Planner (CFP) license and then pursuing additional education to earn the designation Chartered Financial Consultant (ChFC) is a great beginning. Advanced degrees, such as a Master of Science in Financial Services as offered at The American College, will also help establish the adviser as a knowledgeable professional. Baby Boomers are impressed by letter designations after a professional's name as long as they are legitimate and indicate specialized training. Boomers want to work with experts in each field, and they look for competence and integrity. Education could be the most important ingredient desired by the Baby Boomer, and the adviser's success rate will be in direct proportion to his ability to combine education and simplicity. A financial adviser, properly educated and licensed, who serves as a consultant and performs every act as a trusted adviser will soon have Baby Boomer clients looking for the adviser rather than the other way around.

As financial advisers develop their marketing efforts, it is important for them to know the extent and movements of their target. In 2007, the youngest Baby Boomer will be 42 years old, and the oldest will be 60. Over the next 20 years, this mass of people will need a whole range of financial services.

Figure 1.7

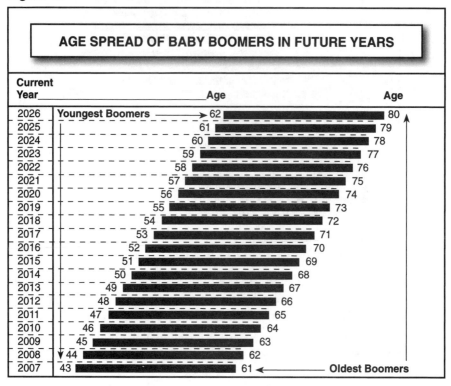

Don't forget the Echo Generation. They, too, are a target moving along right behind their parents. They also will be requiring the attention of a financial adviser, and if the Boomers are pleased with their advisers, then there is every reason to believe their children will choose the same wise people to advise them. In 2007, the youngest Echo will be 13 and the oldest 31.

Figure 1.8

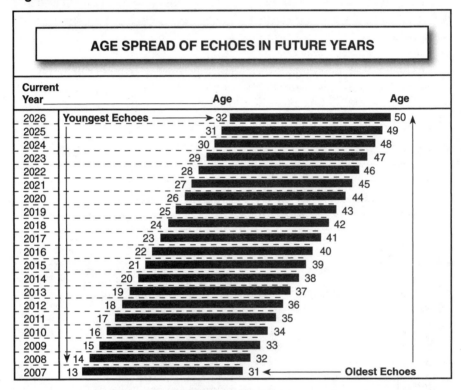

SOME FACTORS AFFECTING PERSONAL CHARACTERISTICS

The most important factor to keep in mind is that making generalizations about Baby Boomers as a group is extremely risky. The age-spread graph previously shown illustrates an age span of 35 through 53 for the year 1999. A span of 19 years is much too great a time period to even consider the Baby Boomers as a homogeneous group. However, some general observations should not be ignored.

In 1970, the oldest Baby Boomers started to marry. The average age of the married couple at that time was 23 for the male and 21 for the female. By 1998, the average ages for a newly married couple increased to 27 for the male and 24½ for the female. This delay of marriage seems to be a trend that is expanding to even older average ages. This means that the significant cost of a marriage ceremony is delayed, although inflation does increase the cost somewhat. It also means that first marriages at older ages bring fewer divorces and fewer financial pressures. Less financial pressure comes about because of greater savings and better job status of both partners.

It may be hard to think of Baby Boomers as grandparents, but this is about to happen, and by the year 2012, the peak of grandchild births could be greater than the peak year of Baby Boomer births – 4,268,000 in 1961. Grandchildren often lead to a desire for special accumulation funds, and the financial adviser should remain alert to opportunities to make such suggestions.

Much has been written about the triple-squeeze or the sandwich generation. Baby Boomers caught in this triple-squeeze face the increased cost of financial assistance for parents while educating their children and, at the same time, trying to prepare for their own retirement. As mentioned before, a 50-year old Baby Boomer has an 80 percent chance of having at least one parent still alive. Not all of these parents need assistance, so this heavy burden does not affect all Boomers the same. Nevertheless, the adviser should be asking for information in this regard.

The older Baby Boomers are approaching their peak earning years, and the trail of Boomers coming behind them can hardly wait their turn at these big bucks. So, right now and continuing for a few decades, Baby Boomers have the tools and the opportunity to save more. With proper help from their financial adviser, Baby Boomers have the opportunity to save much more.

Many Boomers will inherit a considerable amount of money. It has been predicted that in the coming years, trillions of dollars will be transferred from parents of the Baby Boomers to the Boomers or their children. Even so, most Baby Boomers do not believe that any money they might inherit will become a major source of retirement income. Of those who do expect to inherit money, the average amount is estimated to be $48,000. This average is the median, which means that of those expecting an inheritance, the number who receive $48,000 or less is equal to the number who receive $48,000 or more. However, regardless of the amount they receive, these fortunate Boomers can benefit greatly if they have a financial adviser to help them at the time.

Baby Boomers should want to be a part of their financial adviser's professional network. The advisor should be a strong and dependable referral source of other professionals who are specialists and who display a genuine desire to be of service to the client. As reported in the Scudder Kemper Baby Boom Generation Retirement Preparation Study, "Financial advisers should be prepared to assist with the financial ramifications of career transitions and the funding of secondary employment skills, as well as be prepared to assist Boomers in balancing short-term needs against long-term goals. Advisers may also want to consider providing non-financial related referrals to professionals who can handle marital, lifestyle, and social needs."

Baby Boomers want help in understanding the pros and cons of tax-deferred investing. Many Baby Boomers will be changing jobs, willingly or otherwise, late into their 40s and 50s. If and when they change jobs, they need directions on how and into what they should roll-over the assets in their 401(k) plans. They also will appreciate being alerted to the possibility of a career change and suggestions for including in their financial plan funds for starting up a new business or for obtaining the education necessary to take on a new career.

Baby Boomers have been – and many still are – big spenders. As they grow older, the big bucks become associated more with savings than spending. Boomers are sophisticated, adventurous, high-tech, and fun loving. They prefer quality items and luxury travel, and often will cash-in savings in order to enjoy a once-in-a-lifetime experience. In this regard, they seek experiences more often than the accumulation of goods. However, either of these two costly choices can be a challenge for the financial adviser of the Boomer.

Many Baby Boomers spend more on restaurant food and entertainment than on groceries, apparel, or household furnishings. They have a high esteem for financial advisers and believe their adviser to be a reliable source for investment advice. However, Boomers are unlikely to surrender complete control of their assets to a financial adviser. To the Boomer, the term adviser does not imply controller.

Look for opportunities to socialize with Baby Boomer clients and potential clients. Include them in your circle of acquaintances, friends, and other clients. Remember, once established, Boomers want a long-term relationship, and so does the wise financial adviser.

If the financial adviser is perceived as a figure of authority, then the development of any other kind of relationship will be difficult. John Green of the University of Akron's Ray C. Bliss Institute of Applied Politics says, "There are only two things that make the Boomers distinguishable from any other generation: one is their numbers, and the other is their mistrust of authority. It makes them very unpredictable. They don't trust very well. They're not good followers." Therefore, it is very important that financial professionals establish themselves as advisers, where the title adviser means someone who will assist and not someone who is the boss demanding action.

While 60 to 70 percent of the Baby Boomers worry about their financial future, only 25 percent use financial advisers. Any financial advisers worth their salt should recognize the opportunity evident in these statistics. Boomers need to learn that they can maintain control, can perform a great deal of personal research themselves, and can then benefit from professional advice. For example, Baby Boomers often develop a potpourri of investments that are completely out of sync with their risk tolerance or financial objectives.

Financial advisers have in the Baby Boomers a prospect-list of millions of people who have yet to learn the tremendous advantages of being served by a competent and qualified financial adviser.

Caution: Although statistics are included in some of the above statements, all statements should be considered generalizations. They should be used only as possible characteristic indicators, and not as an absolute that is applicable to all members of the group. If it is determined that a Baby Boomer does not have one or more of the characteristics mentioned above, it would benefit the adviser to probe further to understand this deviation from the majority. Please note the word *majority* as opposed to the word *norm*. With the Baby Boomer generation, there is no norm. However, the financial adviser will be able to serve each client much better as his knowledge of the client increases. These characteristics along with other information to be provided later will enhance tremendously the ability of the financial adviser to achieve optimum understanding of each and all Baby Boomer clients.

The youngest Baby Boomers will soon arrive at that time when they have purchased all baby toys and most adult toys. Older Baby Boomers already have arrived at this point and have shown a very strong desire to shift from consumerism to capital formation. Thus, it is reasonable to assume the youngest Boomers will also display the same desire to focus more on wealth accumulation.

According to B. Douglas Bernheim, Professor of Economics at Stanford University and a consultant for Merrill Lynch, this increased desire to accumulate wealth is strongly motivated by a desire for a comfortable retirement. He bases this on the assumption that Baby Boomers, like current retirees, want to maintain the same standard of living in retirement they have enjoyed during their working years. This is not an alarming assumption. No one wants to reduce his standard of living. However, the cost of a long retirement will be expensive, regardless of the starting age, and a primary goal of capital formation fits the bill.

In July 1997, the Society of Financial Service Professionals conducted a survey entitled Financial Planning for Baby Boomers. The respondents were 350 financial planners who stated the highest current financial concerns, needs, and desires of Baby Boomers at that time and as projected ten years into the future.

1997	**2007**
91% Capital Growth	93% Retirement Planning
88% College Funding	92% Estate Planning
81% Home Ownership	77% Home Ownership
78% Retirement Planning	72% Capital Preservation

Even though retirement planning was fourth on the list of most important concerns, needs, and desires in 1997, now (2007) it is number one. That projection has come true.

At a meeting of the Financial Planning Association in May 1998, Steven J. Devlin, Ph.D. and associate director of the University of Pennsylvania's Boettner Center of Financial Gerontology, informed the audience that nearly 50 percent of males born in the second half of the Boomer years (1956-1964) were confident they had enough money for retirement, and only 40 percent of those born in the first half of that era (1946-1955) were confident. Dr. Devlin also stated, "Two generations living in retirement [at the same time] is something our country has never seen before." Having to financially assist one's children and one's parents at the same time while trying to accumulate funds for one's own retirement is a new challenge never faced before the sandwiched Boomers.

In 1998, the findings of the eighth annual retirement survey sponsored by the Employee Benefit Research Institute and the American Savings Education Council and Matthew Greenwald & Associates, a market research company, were released to the public. Included in the survey was the fact that 45 percent of the respondents said they had tried to calculate how much they need to save for retirement. This was a 13 percent increase over the percent given two years earlier.

According to a poll conducted in 1998 for the American Association of Retired Persons (AARP) by Harry O'Neill, Vice President of Roper Starch Worldwide, 8 out of 10 Baby Boomers say they plan to work at least part time after they retire. Merrill Lynch did a similar study in 2003 and obtained almost the same results.

Financial advisers who want to be of service and value to Baby Boomers should be well educated and prepared to be conversant in all of the areas listed in the table shown below. How to apply this knowledge to the wants and needs of Baby Boomers will be discussed in this book. What all Baby Boomers really need is comprehensive financial planning. The chapters that follow provide step-by-step procedures to use in such financial planning. The structure of this financial planning guide will include the topics shown in Figure 1.9.

Figure 1.9

FINANCIAL PLAN	
	Page
Personal Data/Assumptions	1
Financial Objectives/Risk Tolerance	2
Net Worth Statement	3
Itemized Investments/Liabilities	3a
History Net Worth Statement	4
Income Tax Information	5
Income Sources	5a
Cash Management Statement	6
Property and Liability	7
Medical	7a
Disability Income/Long Term Care	7b
Life Insurance	7c
Life Insurance Cash Value	7d
Protection Recommendations	8
Emergency Fund	9
Investment Portfolio	10
Portfolio Pie Chart	10a
Investment Recommendations	11
Estate Analysis	12
Retirement Analysis	13+
Education Funding Analysis	14
Miscellaneous	14a
Action Items	15

The author in no way intends that any of the reader's financial plans will be exactly as described in this book. Each planner will have his preferred system. However, the following chapters will provide ideas each adviser might choose to incorporate into any personal system. The chapters will also offer suggested techniques for gathering and presenting information that should enhance the final plan.

Chapter 2

Obtaining the Needed Information

In order to ensure a successful relationship with clients, the financial adviser should get to know as much about them as possible. They will appreciate the interest, and the information obtained will help the adviser give them advice appropriate to their wants and needs. Fortunately, there are ways to obtain this information that are not difficult to implement and actually will enhance the affinity between the adviser and the clients.

HARD FACTS AND SOFT FACTS

It should be recognized at the outset that there are two kinds of facts to obtain from clients: hard facts and soft facts. Hard facts are those not subject to question because they can be verified. Facts such as names, addresses, annual incomes, etc., are hard facts. Soft facts are those that are subjective, those that are determined more by the client's mind or attitudes than by anything in the external world. Facts such as tolerance for risk, annual income sufficient for a comfortable retirement, etc., are soft facts.

THE PRE-FACT-FINDER KIT

To help learn more about the client, a Pre-Fact-Finder Kit is reproduced in Figures 2.1 through 2.5. Reproductions of these seven pages should be given to new clients to complete before the first financial-planning meeting. If these forms are used, it can be assured that many of the important hard facts needed will be obtained.

A preliminary meeting with the client is recommended before the first financial-planning meeting. This get-acquainted meeting gives the adviser an opportunity to explain what he can do for the client, what it will cost, and provides the prospective client with a chance to ask questions. This meeting helps the adviser and the prospective client determine compatibility and whether or not to proceed. If the

Figure 2.1

PRE - FACT FINDER KIT
FINANCIAL PLANNING DOCUMENTS NEEDED

BRING THE FOLLOWING TO OUR FIRST MEETING

ALL   INSURANCE POLICIES (LIFE - HEALTH - AUTO - HOME - LIABILITY)

PERSONAL/FAMILY DOCUMENTS	BUSINESS DOCUMENTS
TAX RETURNS (3 YEARS)	TAX RETURNS (3 YEARS)
WILLS (BOTH SPOUSES)	FINANCIAL STATEMENTS (3 YEARS)
TRUST INSTRUMENTS	DEFERRED COMPENSATION PLANS
ASSETS ITEMIZED	RETIREMENT PLANS
LIABILITIES ITEMIZED	STOCK OPTION/PURCHASE AGREEMENTS
CASH MANAGEMENT STATEMENT	BUY-SELL AGREEMENTS
SALE/PURCHASE CONTRACT	EMPLOYMENT AGREEMENT
LEASES	ARTICLES OF INCORPORATION
POWER OF ATTORNEY/APPOINTMENT	PARTNERSHIP AGREEMENT
SEPARATION/DIVORCE/PRE-NUPTIAL	EQUIPMENT LEASING AGREEMENT
EMPLOYEE BENEFITS BOOKLETS	OTHER
LATEST STATEMENTS OF BROKERAGE ACCOUNTS	
LATEST STATEMENTS OF MUTUAL FUNDS	
ANNUITY CONTRACTS & RECENT ANNUITY STATEMENT	
OTHER	

Figure 2.2

LIST OF IMPORTANT ADVISORS

PERSONAL ATTORNEY: _____
NAME OF FIRM: _____
ADDRESS: _____
TELEPHONE (BUS.) _____

BUSINESS ATTORNEY: _____
NAME OF FIRM: _____
ADDRESS: _____
TELEPHONE (BUS.) _____

PERSONAL ACCOUNTANT: _____
NAME OF FIRM: _____
ADDRESS: _____
TELEPHONE (BUS.) _____

PERSONAL BANKER: _____
NAME OF FIRM: _____
ADDRESS: _____
TELEPHONE (BUS.) _____

LIFE INSURANCE AGENT: _____
NAME OF FIRM: _____
ADDRESS: _____
TELEPHONE (BUS.) _____

AUTOMOBILE AGENT: _____
NAME OF FIRM: _____
ADDRESS: _____
TELEPHONE (BUS.) _____

HOMEOWNERS'
 INSURANCE AGENT: _____
NAME OF FIRM: _____
ADDRESS: _____
TELEPHONE (BUS.) _____

SECURITIES BROKER: _____
NAME OF FIRM: _____
ADDRESS: _____
TELEPHONE (BUS.) _____

Figure 2.3

CASH MANAGEMENT STATEMENT

ANNUAL EXPENDITURES: FIXED   _____

HOUSING (MORTGAGE/RENT) $_____
PROPERTY TAXES   _____
HOUSE UPKEEP/REPAIRS/MAINTENANCE   _____

UTILITIES & TELEPHONE   _____
FOOD/GROCERIES   _____
CLOTHING & CLEANING   _____

INCOME & SOCIAL SECURITY TAXES   _____
DEBT REPAYMENT   _____
TRANSPORTATION (AUTO/COMMUTING)   _____

AUTO, HOME AND LIABILITY INSURANCE   _____
MEDICAL/DENTAL/DRUGS/HEALTH INSURANCE   _____
DISABILITY INCOME INSURANCE   _____

LIFE INSURANCE   _____
EDUCATION EXPENSES   _____
                                                 _____

TOTAL FIXED EXPENDITURES $

ANNUAL EXPENDITURES: DISCRETIONARY

VACATION/TRAVEL $_____
RECREATION/ENTERTAINMENT   _____
CONTRIBUTIONS   _____
GIFTS   _____

HOUSEHOLD FURNISHINGS   _____
EDUCATION FUND   _____
PERSONAL CARE   _____
OTHER   _____
                                                 _____

TOTAL DISCRETIONARY EXPENDITURES $
                                                           _____

TOTAL ANNUAL EXPENDITURES $
SAVINGS $_____
INVESTMENTS   _____
                                                 _____

TOTAL ANNUAL EXPENDITURES & ACCUMULATIONS $

ESTIMATED INCOME $

Figure 2.4

ITEMIZED INVESTMENTS - PAGE 1

REAL ESTATE

TYPE	DATE OF PURCHASE		PURCHASE PRICE	CURRENT MARKET VALUE	OWNERSHIP
PRIMARY RESIDENCE			$	$	
SECONDARY RESIDENCE					
RENTAL PROPERTIES					
VACANT LOTS					

CASH ACCOUNTS (CD's, MONEY MARKET, SAVINGS, CHECKING, TREASURY BILLS)

TYPE/NAME	MATURITY DATE	CURRENT INTEREST RATE		CURRENT VALUE	OWNERSHIP
				$	
CORPORATE BONDS					
GOVERNMENT BONDS					
MORTGAGES OWNED					
LAND CONTRACTS					

STOCKS/WARRENTS/OPTIONS

NAME OF COMPANY	SHARES	DATE OF PURCHASE		PURCHASE PRICE	CURRENT MARKET VALUE	OWNERSHIP
				$	$	

Figure 2.4 (cont'd)

ITEMIZED INVESTMENTS - PAGE 2

MUTUAL FUNDS

NAME OF COMPANY	SHARES	DATE OF PURCHASE		PURCHASE PRICE	CURRENT MARKET VALUE	OWNERSHIP
				$	$	

ANNUITIES

NAME OF COMPANY	FIXED/ VARIABLE	CONTRACT DATE	CURRENT INTEREST RATE	PURCHASE PRICE	CURRENT SURRENDER VALUE	OWNER/ BENEFICIARY
				$	$	

MUNICIPAL BONDS

NAME OF COMPANY	UNITS	MATURITY DATE	CURRENT INTEREST RATE	PURCHASE PRICE	CURRENT MARKET VALUE	OWNERSHIP
				$	$	

Figure 2.4 (cont'd)

ITEMIZED INVESTMENTS - PAGE 3

LIMITED PARTNERSHIPS   (REAL ESTATE, OIL & GAS, EQUIPMENT LEASING, OTHERS)

NAME OF COMPANY	UNITS	DATE OF PURCHASE		PURCHASE PRICE	CURRENT MARKET VALUE	OWNERSHIP
				$	$	

RETIREMENT PLANS   (IRA, TSA, 401(k), PENSION, PROFIT SHARING, KEOGH, SEP)

TYPE/NAME	SHARES	MATURITY DATE	CURRENT INTEREST RATE		CURRENT MARKET VALUE	OWNERSHIP
					$	

MISCELLANEOUS ASSETS

NAME OF COMPANY	CURRENT VALUE	OWNERSHIP
PERSONAL PROPERTY	$	
LIFE INSURANCE CASH VALUE/DIV.		
PRECIOUS METALS		
COLLECTIBLES		
BUSINESS		

Figure 2.5

ITEMIZED LIABILITIES

	BALANCE OWED	CURRENT INTEREST RATE	DATE OF FINAL PAYMENT	MONTHLY PAYMENT
MORTGAGE	$			$
LIFE INSURANCE LOANS	$			$
INVESTMENT LOANS	$			$
BANK/PERSONAL LOANS	$			$
CREDIT CARDS/CHARGES	$			$
OTHER	$			$

decision is positive, then either at this meeting or later, the Pre-Fact-Finder Kit is explained to the client.

Ask the new client to collect all of the documents listed on the first page of the Pre-Fact-Finder Kit (Figure 2.1) and complete all of the other pages (Figures 2.2 through 2.5) with the data requested before the next meeting. This may be the first time a client ever was asked to get his financial data so organized. Recognize that some items may not be immediately available and such temporary omissions should not be a reason to postpone the fact-finder meeting. Although the process may begin without all of the data, the importance of the client completing the Pre-Fact-Finder Kit needs to be stressed.

Cash Management Statement

A very important part of the Pre-Fact-Finder Kit is the Cash Management Statement (Figure 2.3). When clients are given the Pre-Fact-Finder Kit to complete, some time may be needed to talk about this part of the kit.

Clients are told to list all of their personal expenditures on an annual basis in the categories listed and to round off all amounts to the nearest $100. Ask if they have ever done this type of thing before. If they say no, or laugh rather nervously before answering, more time should be spent on the instructions. This part of the Pre-Fact-Finder Kit is important because it will be used, revised, and used again for many years into the future. It is essential that planning start with the correct data.

Have clients note each expense category on the Cash-Management Statement. Tell them that there are only three places to look for this required information: their checking-account register, their credit-card and charge-account statements, and their recollection of cash expenditures.

First, have clients review their checking-account register. Each amount in the register should be transferred to its proper category in the Cash Management Statement.

Second, have clients review their credit-card and charge-account statements. Consider it fortunate if they have kept these statements. If they have not, then a lot of guessing will be required. However, this activity will fortify the need to retain these documents in the future. Each amount identified on the statements should be transferred to a category on the Cash Management Statement.

Third, have clients determine the amount of cash they spent the preceding year – any 12-month period – and allocate it to the proper expenditure categories. When they give that you've-got-to-be-kidding look, tell them to guess each amount as best they can. Today, it will be a pretty-good guess; next year, because they will keep a better accounting, it will be a fairly-accurate amount.

Tell clients the Cash Management Statement will be revised, at least annually, and it is their responsibility to keep track of how the money is expended. Those clients who are knowledgeable about computers and spreadsheets will find it easier to use these tools to keep their records. But whether they use Quicken or quill pens, this very important information needs to be recorded if a meaningful financial plan is to be developed and maintained.

If this is the client's first time for developing a list of expenditures, then it is likely that some of the items will be soft facts. However, after two or three years of annual reviews, most all items will be hard facts.

THE FACT-FINDING INTERVIEW

The next meeting after the get-acquainted meeting is a fact-finding interview with the client. If applicable, both spouses should be encouraged to attend. This interview usually will last for two hours or so. After the meeting, the client will walk out feeling great. Why? When was the last time you had a conversation with someone where the entire time was spent talking about you, and the other person was not feigning interest but was sincere with every question asked and every note taken? A very pleasant experience, is it not?

Most of the information requested is fairly straight-forward. Names, address, telephone numbers, and so on, are simple to supply. However, by the time page 3 of the Personal Data is reached, the client will find that he may not know as much about himself and his family as he thought. This gradual awareness will be just the first of many times that a client will recognize the value of the services of the financial adviser.

Personal Data

The interview should begin with simple questions to put the client at ease. When filling in the Personal-Data (Figure 2.6) pages from the Fact-Finder Kit, ask questions such as, "What is your middle initial? Would you verify your address? How long have you lived there?" Observe carefully how the client responds to the questions. Is it easy or difficult for the client to discuss personal items such as age, health, previous marriages, the current spouse, children, and parents? Also, when interviewing two individuals – spouses, parent and adult child, non-married domestic partners – try to determine which one is more verbal, more knowledgeable, and more interested in this undertaking. Make note of any differences of opinion, recollections, and preferences. Proper probing will lead to a better relationship between the adviser and the client. Keep in mind that, at this point in the relationship, proper could mean that the adviser back off from further probing on any subject where the client or partner displays more than casual discomfort.

Figure 2.6

```
                        FACT FINDER KIT

                                    ┌─────────────────────────┐
                                    │ DATE                    │
                                    └─────────────────────────┘

                        PERSONAL DATA

  Name
            Client 1        _____

            Client 2        _____

  Legal Home Address  _____  How Long  _____


  Business Address

            Client 1        _____  How Long  _____

            Client 2        _____  How Long  _____


  Phone
            Home            _____

            Work-Client 1   _____

            Work-Client 2   _____
            .
            E-mail Address  _____


  Referred By
```

*** **Copy of Driver's License(s)**

Figure 2.6 (cont'd)

	DATE OF BIRTH	PLACE OF BIRTH	AGE	SOCIAL SECURITY	OCCUPATION	HEALTH/SMOKER MISCELLANEOUS	AMOUNT OF SUPPORT
Client 1							
Client 2							
Children/ Grandchildren							
Client 1							
Father							
Mother							
Client 2							
Father							
Mother							

PERSONAL DATA - PAGE 2

ANNUAL INCOME

	Current Year	Next Year
Client 1	$	$
Client 2	$	$

Figure 2.6 (cont'd)

PERSONAL DATA - PAGE 3

Citizenship

	United States	Other (Specify)
Client 1		
Client 2		

Have you ever lived in a community property state? Yes No Which State?

Marital Status

Single   Married/Date   Divorced/Date   Widowed/Date

If any former marriages, to whom?   **Client 1**   **Client 2**

Alimony?	Yes	No	Amount $	Who
Child Support?	Yes	No	Amount $	Who

Legal Documents

Do you have a:	Client 1		Client 2	
Will	Yes	No	Yes	No
Trust	Yes	No	Yes	No
DURABLE Power of Attorney (Medical)	Yes	No	Yes	No
DURABLE Power of Attorney (Financial)	Yes	No	Yes	No
Are there prenuptial or postnuptial agreements?	Yes	No	Yes	No

Custodianships

Have either of you ever made a gift under the uniform gift to minors act?   Yes   No

Gifts Or Inheritances

Do either you or your children expect to receive gifts or inheritances?   Yes   No

Education

What is the level of your education?
   Client 1
   Client 2

Military Service

Did you serve in the military?

Male	Yes	No	When
Female	Yes	No	When

Indicate any service-connected benefits

Quite often the new client will be on good behavior during this first meeting and might be reluctant to share some information. The client might even be successful in preventing the adviser from obtaining some of the exact information and understanding that is really needed. Just remember, this is the beginning of the relationship. Keep all avenues of communication open. Avoid all criticism and evaluation, even implied. The values of the adviser cannot be allowed to creep into the conversation. Remain calm, patient, and nonjudgmental, and the information will continue to flow. On the other hand, if the mistake of criticizing is made, the client will shut down and everybody loses.

Both the adviser and the client need to understand the reason why these questions are being asked. For example, after a client indicates that his father has died, ask how old the father was when he died and what was the cause of death. The reason for asking is that parental longevity and state of health can be indicative of the genes carried by the client. Even though more and more evidence indicates that one's genes (heredity) are responsible for only a small percentage of quality of life and longevity, the answers to the questions do provide some information in this quest of learning all about a new client. After a client indicates a previous marriage, ask how long the marriage lasted. The reason involves the possibility that there might be some future Social Security retirement benefit based on the former spouse's account. Be patient when probing in such areas, particularly if the client has difficulty remembering. It sometimes can be difficult to remember pain.

Even though the adviser will review a client's income tax returns, ask about current income and projected income over the next few years. Some advisers might be hesitant to ask about income, but it is necessary. It is important to establish up front that the practitioner needs to know everything. Don't worry. The vast majority of clients will not hesitate to answer any question asked.

At some point, the adviser will review all of a client's legal documents. Even so, it is a good idea to ask about them at this meeting. This creates a chance to learn, for example, if the client even understands the difference between a living will and a living trust. By asking about a will, clients, especially younger Baby Boomers, will say, "Well, we just haven't gotten around to it yet." Also, by asking about a trust, clients may respond, "Yes, we have a trust, but it needs to be changed." Without asking, two important points would have slipped right into the world of eternal procrastination.

When the adviser comes to the section on gifts and inheritances, know that some studies project that Baby Boomers will inherit a sizable amount of money, estimated at between $10 and $12 trillion. However, even if this estimate is correct, people are living much longer these days, and it might take several decades before any actual payouts. Also, because parents of Baby Boomers are living longer, parents have more time to spend their money, leaving less for the heirs to spend. Nevertheless, ask about possible inheritances, if for no other reason than to learn the client's feelings. Later in the relationship with the client, the adviser may want to take the approach that the client build for the future assuming no or low inheritance, unless there is overwhelming evidence that the likelihood of actual receipt is just short of guaranteed.

Asking about educational background can provide helpful insight into the client's attitude on higher education for his children. However, be careful not to jump to premature conclusions.

Asking about military service can reveal whether future government medical benefits might be available. This also might affect a decision on the purchase of long term care insurance, because under certain circumstances, former military personnel are qualified to use a Veteran's Hospital for long term care. Keep in mind that rules change, so if there is a possibility of the benefit being available to a particular client, undertake some research to make sure it is.

FINANCIAL OBJECTIVES QUESTIONNAIRE

A change of pace at this point in the interview is appropriate, and asking the client to use a pencil to answer questions on the Financial Objectives Questionnaire (Figure 2.7) serves this purpose very nicely.

If interviewing more than one person, such as spouses or life partners, each should be given a separate questionnaire. Explain the procedure. They are to prioritize the list of financial objectives. For their top priority, they should write the number 1. For their next choice, they write 2, and continue in this manner until their last priority item receives the number 8.

Read the list to them before they see it. This sometimes helps them with an overview of the eight items. Also, tell them that if they have a financial objective that is not on the list, they should write it at the bottom of the page and assign whatever priority number to it they want. In this situation, the lowest priority item would receive the number 9.

Encourage clients to ask any questions they would like as they fill out the questionnaires. This will benefit the adviser as much as it does the clients since such questions often provide additional insight into their level of knowledge and understanding of these issues. For example, a younger Baby Boomer might ask, "What does it mean to develop an estate plan?" This question alerts the adviser to the possibility that he

Figure 2.7

FINANCIAL OBJECTIVES

Rank in Order From 1 (Highest) to 9 (Lowest)

Use Each Number ONLY Once!

Item	Priority Item
Maintain/Expand *Standard Of Living*	_____
Enjoy a *Comfortable Retirement*	_____
Take Care of Self and Family During a *Long Term Disability*	_____
Invest and *Accumulate Wealth*	_____
Reduce Tax Burden	_____
Provide *College Education* for All Children	_____
Take Care of Family in the Event of *Death*	_____
Develop an *Estate Plan*	_____
Any *Others* Important to You (Specify)	_____

---

does not come from a family of great wealth, or at least, the family never discussed its wealth in front of the children. It also could mean that the client is not as well informed about financial matters as others might be. Answers should be non-judgmental. Say, for example, "For our purposes now, it means where you want your assets to go upon your death, and how important this is in relation to all of the other items."

The evaluation of the answers provided on the Financial Objectives Questionnaire will be discussed later in the chapter.

FACTORS AFFECTING THE FINANCIAL PLAN

A question that usually elicits interesting responses is, "Do you try to live on any kind of a formal budget?" A typical answer ranges from a chuckle to a loud guffaw. Once in awhile the response is, "Well, kinda." These answers should lead to the suggestion, "Why don't you tell me how it works in your home?" The response can vary from, "We save my paycheck and live off his," to "Well, this will take some time because it's a little complicated." Just remember to remain laid back, make no judgments, and learn more about your clients. (Figure 2.8).

Another good question to ask is, "Did you save or invest any new money last year?" New money is not the reinvestment of profits from current investments. The answer to this question, particularly if it is no, should lead to inquiry about the avail-ability of 401(k) or 403(b) plans at the client's place of employment. Sometimes the client can forget about an automatic deduction he elected some time ago.

When asking about charitable giving, find out about the client's interest in areas such as a religious institution, an educational institution, a children's organization like Save-the-Children or UNICEF, an animal group like a local or national humane society, etc. Answers could lead to discussing later on the giving of appreciated assets to a non-profit organization which can have a strong tax-saving result. Charitable giving is often not a high priority for many Baby Boomers, who are facing their own future survival problems. But for those more-wealthy and higher-income boom-ers – and there are a lot of them in a number of areas – charitable giving can be of great significance.

As the adviser reviews the question, "Are you satisfied with your previous investment results?," the adviser should pay attention to which partner responds first and how strong he or she feels about positive and negative results. Take notes. Then ask, "Are there any investments to which you are committed?" If there is one or more investments that must be kept for whatever reason, it is best for the adviser to know up front.

Approach the area of retirement with the question, "When would you *like* to retire?" After the most-often-given answer by the younger Baby Boomers of age 55, ask, "When do you think you *will* retire?" The answer might be the same, but more likely it will be a smile, or even a laugh. Wait for the answer. Whatever is eventually expressed, write it down. And make no judgments!

When seeking information for the estate analysis, if interviewing two or more people, start directing questions to one at a time. Direct the question to the less

Figure 2.8

FACTORS AFFECTING YOUR FINANCIAL PLAN

Budget   Do you live on a formal budget?   Yes   No

Savings And Investments

How much did you save or invest last year?

Where?

How much do you plan to save or invest this year?

Where?

Giving

Have you ever given more than $1,000 to any one educational or charitable organization in any one year?

How much?

Where?

Investments

Are you satisfied with your previous investment results?

Do you feel committed to any investments?

Retirement

	Client 1	**Client 2**
When Would You Like To Retire?		
When Do You Expect To Retire?		

Estate Analysis

Where do you want you assets to go when you die?

Client 1

Client 2

Reasons For Financial Plan

What should be covered in this financial plan?

Client 1

Client 2

verbal person. Say something such as, "Pat, you get this question first." This gently tells the other person to wait his turn. Ask, "If you had died last night, how would you want your assets distributed." This is not a difficult question for most people, and by directing it to the less verbal of the two, it gets the quiet one more involved. Of course the more verbal of the two should have an opportunity to answer the same question.

For the next question say, "Jan, you get this question first." This puts Pat on notice to pay attention and prepare an answer because both partners are expected to answer in turn. The question, "What should be covered in this financial plan?," is one of the more important questions because it may help reveal areas not yet discussed. Start by informing the clients that everything that should be covered should be in their financial plan, but you want to make sure that you place the proper emphasis on the issues most important to them. Then ask the more verbal partner, "What is most important to you? What do you want to make sure is included in your plan?" Then be quiet and wait for a response. Write it down. Then ask, "What else?" Write down the next response. Keep repeating this procedure until the client runs dry. Then turn to the less verbal partner and do the same, beginning with, "What is most important to you?" Remember the non-verbal client is an escape artist. This person will try to avoid responding by giving an answer such as, "I feel the same way she does." Then the advisor should respond, "Fine, but what is really important to you?" Most of the time that approach will elicit at least a few comments. Also, remember to keep asking, "What else?"

Be sure to have ample note paper on hand so that the clients are not interrupted as they reveal what is important to them.

INCOME AND/OR CAPITAL NEEDS

Education funding is very important to Baby Boomers who have children. To find out how clients feel about this area, ask, "Have you accumulated any funds so far? How much? In whose name? How many years will it be before your first child attends college? How many years will the child attend?" The adviser might also discuss a possible investment growth rate and the education inflation rate. The latter rate is much higher than general inflation. Also talk about how much it would cost right now to send a child to college. (Figure 2.9).

A word of advice to the financial adviser. Clients are going to ask a lot of what-if questions throughout the relationship. For example, after preparing a plan for accumulating the money to send the first child to Harvard or Yale, the client may ask, "What if we send Kim to one of our state colleges?" Or the client may ask, "What if we just plan to fund the first year?" It's imperative to have a computer program to

Figure 2.9

INCOME AND/OR CAPITAL NEEDS

EDUCATION FUND

NAME OF CHILD	AGE	AMOUNT OF CURRENT ACCUMULATION

SUPPORT FOR FAMILY MEMBER(S)

NAME	RELATION	ESTIMATED COST

BIG TICKET ITEMS IN THE NEXT 5 YEARS

ITEM	TARGET DATE	ESTIMATED COST	AMOUNT OF CURRENT ACCUMULATION

make different projections quickly. Baby Boomers tend to be impatient, particularly with the technologically challenged. (More information on education funding can be found in Chapter 6.)

The next section has to do with the parents of the clients. "How old are your parents? How is their health? Do you supply any regular financial assistance to your parents? Which ones? How much? Do you expect to supply financial assistance sometime in the future?"

Some clients may be among those Baby Boomers in the sandwich generation who are being squeezed in a triple play: (1) trying to accumulate educational funds for their children, (2) trying to accumulate retirement funds for themselves, and (3) anticipating the need for providing financial assistance to their parents.

More and more people today are attending higher educational institutions than anytime in the past. According to the U.S. Census Bureau, in 1960, only 8 percent of the population were college graduates; by 1995, this had increased to 23 percent and in 2000, 26 percent had a bachelor's degree or higher. Future competition for better jobs could accelerate this trend, so Baby Boomers feel obligated to send their children to college. Now, as Baby Boomers move into their 50s, the pressure to develop adequate retirement funds increases the pressure on their allocation of income. And, the third source of pressure is the realization that people are living longer, and if their parents do not have proper retirement income sources or have invested too conservatively for their longer lives, then the Baby Boomers will have to supply some assistance. It is better that your clients know at the outset how this triple squeeze might influence their lives so they have time to plan intelligently.

Another of the more important questions for Baby Boomers of any age is, "Over the next five years, what big-ticket items might occur?" Ask the question, then be quiet and take notes. When the client begins to slow down, ask, "Anything else?" For the most part, just listen. Sometimes, for whatever reasons, the client might initially respond, "Nothing." Then the adviser will need to probe. "What about a change of residence, or a new car, or that special vacation you always wanted?" When clients are finished having a good time discussing their wish list, then it is time to get serious with a discussion of their risk-taking propensities.

The Financial Attitude Questionnaire

One might suspect that assessing a new client's tolerance for risk in dealing with money would require an interview with a psychologist combined with the administration of an elaborate questionnaire. Unfortunately, most financial planners have only a limited background in psychology, and neither the financial planner nor the client has the time or patience to wade through an extensive questionnaire. Fortunately, there is a much easier way.

Figure 2.10 contains a financial attitude questionnaire that will provide both the adviser and the client with a reasonable picture of the client's tolerance for taking risks with his money. This questionnaire was developed by Denis Raihall, Ph.D., CLU, for The American College. This questionnaire contains four simple questions and requires only five to twenty-five minutes to administer, depending upon how familiar the client is with the terms used. The financial planner, should administer this questionnaire personally and encourage the client to ask questions. When this is done, additional insight into the client's knowledge base on financial matters will be gained. So, even if it requires twenty-five minutes or more to complete the form because of multiple requests from the client for additional information, the time will be well spent.

It is best to be honest with the client by explaining that a full psychological profile cannot be obtained with this brief questionnaire, but it will provide a reasonable estimate of the client's current risk-taking propensities. The scoring is on a scale of 0 to 23 with a margin of error of plus or minus 3 points. Therefore, it does provide the practitioner with the vicinity of risk tolerance. For example, if a client scores 2, a very low risk tolerance, it is highly likely that the client is nowhere in the neighborhood of 22, an extremely high tolerance. Actually, in most cases the questionnaire will provide a much more refined picture with dependable reliability.

Administering the Questionnaire

It is important to keep in mind that, for some clients, many words and concepts will be new. This, in itself, is revealing, and so the adviser should be patient while answering all of the client's questions. Should the questionnaire be administered to more than one person, each should be given a form. Learning as much as possible about each person, as well as the family unit, is important for success.

The first section asks the client to rate ten vehicles used for saving and investing money. The client is to circle a 1, 2, or 3 for each of these ten items. Emphasize to the client that the response should not be based on previous or current use of the vehicle, but on the client's comfort level. For example, if a client is very comfortable placing money in a savings account, then the client would circle a 3. If the client is very uncomfortable placing money in a savings account, then the client would circle a 1. If the client doesn't feel strongly either way, then he would circle a 2. Make sure that the client has circled a response for each item.

Figure 2.10

FINANCIAL ATTITUDE QUESTIONNAIRE

1) Rate the following methods of savings and investing.

	Slight Preference		Most Preference
Savings Account	1	2	3
Cash Value of Life Insurance	1	2	3
Government Bonds	1	2	3
Corporate Bonds	1	2	3
Tax Exempt Bonds	1	2	3
Mutual Funds (Stock)	1	2	3
Variable Annuities (Stock)	1	2	3
Common Stocks	1	2	3
Real Estate (Personal)	1	2	3
Tax Shelters (oil, cattle, commerical real estate)	1	2	3

2) Would you be willing to invest in a three-year investment which

    a) had a 90 percent chance of a 100 percent gain   Yes _____   No _____
        and a 10 percent chance of a 50 percent loss.

    b) had a 90 percent chance of a 50 percent gain   Yes _____   No _____
        and a 10 percent chance of a 25 percent loss.

    c) had a 90 percent chance of a 25 percent gain   Yes _____   No _____
        and a 10 percent chance of a 10 percent loss.

3) In the handling of your finances, would you be willing to
take above average risks in order to seek greater growth
with some or all of your investable funds?   Yes _____   No _____

If yes, indicate what percent of your investable funds you
would be willing to place in investments of above average risk   _____ Percent

4) Rank the items in order of importance. Using **seven as most important and one as least important.**
(Place a 7 after the most important, then 6 after the next most important, then 5, 4, 3, 2, 1.)

         a. _____   Liquidity (availability)
         b. _____   Current Income from investments
         c. _____   Future Income
         d. _____   Inflation Protection (assuring purchasing power)
         e. _____   Income Tax Deferral/Relief
         f. _____   Capital Growth
         g. _____   Safety of Principal

The adviser should consider stopping after the client has completed each section on the questionnaire and explain what is required to answer the next section. This also provides the client an opportunity to make one or more comments about the section just completed. Again, take notes.

Explain section two by emphasizing that this is a hypothetical three-year investment where, in (a) for example, the client knows for sure there is a 90 percent chance of doubling his money *and* a 10 percent chance of losing half of the money. Would the client make such an investment? Repeat in the same way with (b) and (c), if necessary. Make sure the client responds "Yes" or "No" to all three parts.

A frequently asked question is, "How much money are we talking about?" A response should be, "It doesn't matter," or "Any amount, because we will quantify that aspect in the next section." If the client persists, then say, "You pick a number, and you don't have to tell me." The client's most honest uninfluenced response is needed.

Read section 3 to the client. While reading, stress these italicized words: "Would you be willing to take an *above* average risk in order to seek a *greater* growth with *some* or *all* of your investment money?" Then say, "If you answer yes, then tell what percent you would risk. For example, 1 percent or 99 percent or 50 percent or whatever." These percents are unlikely to be chosen by the client, but they are useful to clarify what is wanted. The client now will read the question and will better understand it as his memory causes him to put the same emphasis as the adviser on the words *above, greater, some,* and *all.*

Introduce section 4 by saying, "The challenge here is to prioritize this list of important items. Only you should do it somewhat backwards writing a 5 for the most important, a 4 for the next most important, and so on. This will cause you to prioritize only five of the seven items." Encourage the client to ask for more information on any or all of the items. If the client has difficulty prioritizing the list, say, "I know. They all are important. Just pick out one that is a little more important than all the others." This will get most reluctant clients started.

Most clients enjoy responding to this questionnaire, but whether they enjoy it or not, when they finish, they feel much better knowing that the adviser is finding out what they feel and believe in order to help them.

Scoring and Evaluating the Financial Attitude Questionnaire

The number scoring can be done by almost anyone. See Figure 2.11 for the scoring. However, study the responses keeping in mind the following objectives for the questions.

- Section 1 discloses the client's level of *awareness* of the investment vehicles mentioned and whether any of them are disliked.

- Section 2 indicates the degree of tolerance for *loss*.

- Section 3 indicates the *degree* of the client's willingness to place money at risk.

- Section 4 is very important in that it indicates how *conservative* the client may be. Answers (a), (b), and (g) show a very conservative position. If the client placed a 5 for most important on any one of these three items, it likely means the total score is a bit on the high side.

The adviser should make a weighted average on the prioritization of these items by both partners, where applicable, to get a family or unit profile as well as two individual profiles. Often each partner will influence the other in their investment decisions. If the adviser knows how they feel both individually and as a unit, he will be better prepared to allocate their assets in order to obtain their objectives. However, always keep in mind the risk-taking propensity of each partner and do not stretch too far beyond either one's limit.

There is a story told by one financial planner. He developed an investment portfolio for a couple based on a risk analysis. The husband's risk score was 15, a healthy tolerance, and the wife's risk score was 5, a low tolerance. The husband appeared to be the dominate partner on finances and, therefore, the financial planner anticipated no problem with the growth portfolio he recommended. Then came the correction of October, 1987. It was not long before the husband was on the phone to the financial planner begging him to get them out of the market. He said his wife was driving him crazy. It seems the one with a low tolerance was making the one with a higher tolerance quite miserable. The financial planner pointed out that selling immediately would create a rather large loss and advised the client to hold on to the stock a bit longer. The client survived the aggravation for a few more weeks and then insisted that he and his wife get out of the market. The client had managed to hold on long enough before selling so that the loss was much smaller than it might have been. However, not only did the financial planner lose a client, but the client missed out on one of the greatest growth periods in stock market history. This financial planner learned a lesson: understand a couple as a family unit, but never ignore or discount too much a spouse who is at one or the other extreme on the risk scale.

Figure 2.11

EVALUATION FORM

FINANCIAL ATTITUDE QUESTIONNAIRE

1)   Rate the following methods of savings and investing.

	Slight Preference		Most Preference
Savings Account	1	2	3
Cash Value of Life Insurance	1	2	3
Government Bonds	1	2	3
Corporate Bonds	1	2	3
Tax Exempt Bonds	1	2	3
Mutual Funds (Stock)	1	2	3
Variable Annuities (Stock)	1	2	3
Common Stocks	1	2	3
Real Estate (Personal)	1	2	3
Tax Shelters (oil, cattle, commerical real estate)	1	2	3

2)   Would be willing to invest in a three-year investment which

   a)   had a 90 percent chance of a 100 percent gain
        and a 10 percent chance of a 50 percent loss.   Yes __3__ No __0__

   b)   had a 90 percent chance of a 50 percent gain
        and a 10 percent chance of a 25 percent loss.   Yes __2__ No __0__

   c)   had a 90 percent chance of a 25 percent gain
        and a 10 percent chance of a 10 percent loss.   Yes __1__ No __0__

3)   In the handling of your finances, would you be willing
     to take above average risks in order to seek greater growth
     with some or all of your investable funds?   Yes __2__ No __0__

     If yes, indicate what percent of your investable funds you
     would be willing to place in investments of above average risk

                                                       11% and above = 2
                                                       _____Percent
                                                       10% and below = 0

4)   Rank the items in order of importance. Using **seven as most important and one as least important.**
     (Place a 7 after the most important, then 6 after the next most important, then 5, 4, 3, 2, 1.)

              a. _____   Liquidity (availability)
              b. _____   Current Income from investments | Three points if most
              c. _____   Future Income | important is c, d, e, or f
              d. _____   Inflation Protection (assuring purchasing power)
              e. _____   Income Tax Deferral/Relief | Zero points if most
              f. _____   Capital Growth | important is a, b, or g
              g. _____   Safety of Principal

Figure 2.11 (cont'd)

EVALUATION FORM - PAGE 2

FINANCIAL ATTITUDE QUESTIONNAIRE

Total Potential Score   23 points

EVALUATION:

SCORE	RISK TYPE
0 - 5	No risk taking ability
6 - 10	Minimizing risk is of maximum importance
11 - 15	Have ability to invest in all investments but high risk type must be kept to 10% to 15% of total investments
16 - 20	Any percentage in high risk
21 - 23	One way ticket to Las Vegas "Gambler"

Question 4

If a, b, or g is rated 5 or 4 (top priorities) then the overall rating might be on the high side.

We also develop a weighted average for couples on their "MAJOR" concerns.

EXAMPLE

Mary		Robert		Weighted Average
Current Income	5	Capital Growth	8	Inflation Protection
Inflation Protection	4	Inflation Protection		
Tax Control	3	Future Income	5	Current Income
Future Income	2	Tax Control		Capital Growth
Safety of Principal	1	Liquidity		Tax Control
				Future Income

Scoring and Evaluating Financial Objectives

Again, the adviser should make a weighted average score for a couple. However, if their priorities are different, discuss this with them so that they can come to an understanding of how best to proceed using their individual responses as well as their combined weighted average response.

Baby Boomers, especially the younger ones, usually choose as their two top objectives "Standard of Living" and "Comfortable Retirement". With 100 percent allocation of resources, these two choices are mutually exclusive. Demonstrate this to the clients. Stretch out your left arm and say, "If you spend all your income today on your standard of living, then you're going to have a lousy retirement." Then stretch out your right arm and say, "If you save all your money for retirement, then you'll have a lousy standard of living today." Pause for this to sink in and then say, "You can't do both with 100 percent of your income, and I cannot tell you what to choose. You must decide on the allocation appropriate for you."

Clients will understand this rather simple explanation and will agree that adjustments must be made. What this experience really does for younger Baby Boomers is bring wealth accumulation to the table. It also makes them aware that some tough choices are going to be required. Baby Boomers who have crossed over into their 50s usually do not need this lesson. They already are quite frightened about wealth accumulation for a comfortable retirement, and they are quite desirous of doing more in the way of accumulation than ever before.

Concluding the Fact-Finding Interview

Ask for the Pre-Fact-Finder Kit and review the client's List of Important Advisors. Ask how they feel about each adviser. "Are you satisfied with previous service? Are there any problems? When is the last time you saw or spoke to your broker, insurance agent, etc.? Who are you most comfortable with? Do you plan to make any replacements?"

Next, go over the Cash Management Statement to make sure all the information is understood as presented. Ask for any explanations that are needed. In the same way, review the Itemized Investments and Itemized Liabilities to see if any further clarification is needed.

Then refer to the list of Financial Planning Documents Needed. The adviser should ask the client to hand him each item, one at a time, as the list is read. This is the easiest and fastest and most dependable way to make sure that all of the items are delivered. When anything is missing, make a note on the list and have the client prepare a new list of items outstanding. Ask the client when he will be able to bring or send the needed document to you. Make a note to put in your tickler file to call the client if the item or items have not been received on the given date.

One Final Question

Tell clients that all the necessary questions have been asked except one final question. Then ask, "Is there anything you thought I would ask about and did not?" Be patiently quiet and wait for a response. If anything is said, probe until you completely understand. "Tell me more," or "Explain how that works" is usually sufficient to get the detailed information you need.

Most times the answer will be similar to, "No, I think you covered everything." Respond by saying, "Let me ask the same question differently. Is there anything we didn't talk about that I should know?" Again be quiet and be patient.

When the clients have nothing more to say, conclude the session by saying, "If either of you think of anything that I might need to know, just call and discuss it with me. And, if I find I have a question for either of you, I'll call." This is important, because it gives the adviser verbal or tacit approval to call either partner if further probing on any subject might be better discussed with just one of the partners. In most cases, talking to only one is not necessary, but it is important to have permission to do so for those rare occasions when it is necessary. Conclude any such conversation by telling the client to give his partner your regards. This makes the point that the adviser is not going behind anyone's back, but leaves it to the client what to tell the partner. Also each partner has been given permission to call the adviser if they have something they wish to discuss privately. Of course, all partners are the adviser's clients, and the advisor has a responsibility of confidentiality to each. It is very rare that private issues will arise or be of significance, but if this is a major issue, proper action must be taken, even if it means removing one's self from the relationship and voiding the engagement agreement with a refund of all fees.

Note to Reader: This chapter 2 and chapter 7 provide a great deal of information and techniques of delivery. This is only one approach, and it is inappropriate to memorize these statements word for word. The intent is to illustrate concepts. As the advisor, your best results will be obtained by the development of your own presentation method. Use the material in this book as a guide or thought provoker and prepare your own personalized fact finder techniques. Remember, practice makes perfect. And, as you learn from your own experiences, perfection will be yours.

Chapter 3

Information Analysis and Meaning

After gathering the hard and soft facts from clients, the next step is to organize and analyze this data. Information that is organized in a clear and simple manner makes it easier for the financial advisor to analyze and easier for the clients to understand when an analysis is presented to them.

FINANCIAL STATEMENTS

The information for developing a summary of a client's assets and liabilities can be found in the Pre-Fact Finder forms. (See Chapter 2.) This data will be used and revised and used over and over again, so it is important to organize the data in a way that makes this easy to do.

Assets

The itemized investments in the client's list of assets should be arranged under appropriate categories. This makes it easier to organize additional details specific to the kind of investment it is. For example, there are differences in the information desired for the category real estate – which can include the primary residence, a secondary residence, rental properties, vacant lots, etc. – and the category cash accounts – which can include checking, savings, CDs, money markets, treasury bills, etc. Shown in Figure 3.1 is a suggestion for the type of information desired and how it can be presented on a form.

It is recommended that only the categories of investments that are currently owned by the client be shown on all financial statements. The first consideration should be clarity and understanding by the client. By customizing these statements, the financial advisor makes it possible for the client to see only that which he currently possesses and not a standardized form of a potpourri of every investment

Figure 3.1

(DATE)

MARY AND ROBERT SAMPLE

ITEMIZED INVESTMENTS
REAL ESTATE

TYPE	Date of Purchase	Purchase Price	Current Market Value	Ownership
		$_____	$_____	
		$_____ 0	$_____ 0	

CASH ACCOUNTS

TYPE/NAME	Maturity Date	Current Interest Rate	Current Value	Ownership
			$_____	
			$_____ 0	

STOCK MARKET

NAME OF COMPANY	Shares	Date of Purchase	Purchase Price	Current Market Value	Ownership
			$_____	$_____	
			$_____ 0	$_____ 0	

ANNUITIES

NAME OF COMPANY	Type	Contract Date	Current Interest Rate	Purchase Price	Current Surrender Value	Owner/ Beneficiary
				$_____	$_____	
				$_____ 0	$_____ 0	

LIMITED PARTNERSHIPS

TYPE/NAME	Shares	Date of Purchase	Purchase Price	Current Market Value	Ownership
			$_____	$_____	
			$_____ 0	$_____ 0	

RETIREMENT PLANS

TYPE/NAME	Shares	Maturity Date	Current Interest Rate	Purchase Price	Current Market Value	Ownership
				$_____	$_____	
				$_____ 0	$_____ 0	

LIABILITIES

Balance Owed	Due Date	Current Interest Rate	Monthly Payment
$_____ 0			$_____ 0

imaginable. Many clients, particularly Baby Boomers in their early forties, have not had the time or opportunity to learn that so many different investment vehicles exist let alone what the purpose for each might be.

A second consideration should be to educate each client about financial planning, but at this time, it would be an inappropriate distraction to have to answer questions from the client about unfamiliar investment vehicles. There will be a more appropriate time later to do this. Right now, it is the financial advisor's obligation to inform and to provide all information that is needed for the client to be able to make decisions. However, it is most important that the financial advisor not provide information that the client cannot understand or does not yet need. The advisor should start at the client's current level of understanding and slowly expand this knowledge, keeping all presentations simple and short. One thing that many Baby Boomers are not known for is a long attention span.

As this information is assembled, the advisor will begin to see the substance of the client's assets. This overview will start the formation of the advisor's understanding of what is missing, what is excessive, or where there is a shortage. Also, large losses or profits in specific assets will lay the foundations for later detailed exploration of, for example, the use of highly appreciated assets for charitable giving or gifting specific assets to parents or children who could sell them while in a lower tax bracket.

Liabilities

Itemized liabilities should be organized under appropriate categories: e.g., mortgage, life insurance loans, bank loans, etc. The information on each loan can be presented under common headings, such as balance owed, current interest rate, monthly payment, etc.

By placing each liability along with all of the pertinent information on its own line, the financial advisor can focus the client's attention on one thing at a time. It also makes it easier to make comments or notes about each liability. For example, a home mortgage of $100,000 or more is an anticipated and acceptable liability, particularly for relatively young clients, whereas a hefty credit card balance for non-essentials is not desirable and should be marked a priority item for attention.

The extent of debt is vital information in understanding a client's mentality. How easy has it been for the client to accumulate numerous debts or a large amount of debt? Has a debt repayment plan incorporated consideration of the interest rate charge, i.e., paying off the debt with the highest rate first? Also, it is often quite revealing about the client's priorities when a study is undertaken as to the purpose of the debt. Is the debt incurred for big ticket items such as cars and boats or incurred by using credit

Figure 3.2

ITEMIZED LIABILITIES				
Type	**Balance Owed**	**Current Interest Rate**	**Date of Final Payment**	**Monthly Payment**
Mortgage				
Life Insurance Loans				

cards for the everyday living expenses of food, clothing, toys, etc. The advisor has a responsibility, especially to young Baby Boomers, to establish that credit card usage is proper *only* if the charged amount is *always* paid by the billing date and without incurring *any* interest expense. This way, it is the proper concept of the use of other people's money; that is, taking advantage of the time lag from the date of purchase to the date of payment to keep this money working for the client during this period.

Because much, if not all, of the information gathered about clients will be reviewed and revised often, appropriate computer software is a virtual necessity for a financial planner. Many commercial programs are available, but finding the one that fits any given practice might be difficult. Take time to evaluate the information provided about each offering. Some commercial developers will permit the financial advisor to try out a program at no cost for a limited time.

It is suggested that the type of program required will allow the entry of itemized assets and liabilities and then print on command the following data.

Type of Data	Computed and Displayed in
Itemized Assets & Liabilities	whole dollars
Net Worth Statement	rounded to hundreds of dollars
History Net Worth Statement	hundreds net of liabilities
Investment Portfolio (Chapter 5)	rounded to thousands, in categories
Estate Analysis (Chapter 6)	rounded to hundreds, by ownership
Retirement Asset Allocation (Chapter 6)	rounded to thousands, in categories

It should be necessary to enter each bit of data only once in order to produce all types of reports that depend upon this data. Also, when the program is compatible with a service that down loads current values of investments, then the financial advisor will have a most efficient software program that provides current, complete, accurate reports with the least amount of time commitment on the part of the advisor and client. Most important, the information on the reports will be understood by the client.

Net Worth Statement

As was true for the client's itemized assets and liabilities, the client's net worth statement should have a format that makes the information easy to understand. For example, stating each asset and its liabilities, if any, on the same horizontal line makes it easier to see the net worth of the asset.

	Asset Amount	Liability Amount	Ownership
Primary Residence	$300,000	$130,000	Ms. Client
Stock Market	$110,000	$20,000	Ms. Client

Looking at the entry for primary residence, it is obvious that the client does not have a $300,000 ownership, but a $170,000 net ownership because of a mortgage on the residence. (Asset of $300,000 minus liability of $130,000 equals $170,000 net worth.) The entry for the stock market ownership shows it to be a margin account, so the net value is $110,00 minus $20,000, or $90,000.

It is not uncommon for younger clients to overstate their net worth. Many young people, when they have completed their current formal education and have become independent, set out to acquire possessions: clothing, cars, furniture, entertainment equipment, and so forth. This is important to them and they will want to include this "stuff" under personal possessions in their net worth statement.

Item	Asset Amount	Liability Amount	Ownership
Cash Accounts	$ 400	$ 0	Mr. Independent
401(k)	100	0	Mr. Independent
Personal Property	71,000	48,000	Mr. Independent
Total	$71,500	$48,000	
Net Worth	$23,500		

For the sample net worth statement shown above, the client will probably say with pride, "I have already managed to acquire quite a lot of valuable assets. Worth over $70,000, in fact. I have a new car, a 33-inch screen entertainment center with surround sound, a VCR, cable and satellite, a computer, lots of great furniture, and clothes that reflect the latest in fashion." In response, the financial advisor will smile and think, but *not* say, "Mr. Independent's net worth may be $42,500, but he has only $500 that will show up on his investment page."

Of course, there is nothing really wrong with acquiring these "spoils for the victor" from the education battles. They are his own choice and may be well deserved, but they represent fleeting assets and will be "used up" before Mr. Independent gets his first worry wrinkle.

In this and similar situations, it is the financial advisor's obligation to congratulate and educate, saying something such as, "You have done quite well in acquiring these important possessions. Now, you seem to be interested in taking the next step of wealth accumulation: the gathering of financial assets. Is this right?" No criticism should be made about past allocation of income. The advisor will soon want to address the debt problem incurred in the acquisition of all these wonderful possessions, but for now, it is sufficient that the client indicates a desire to start to include the accumulation of financial assets as well as stuff.

The net worth statement just shown reveals the need on the part of the client to understand the difference between assets and stuff. The advisor may not be surprised to find this need in clients who are twenty-something years old, but the advisor also should not be surprised to find that this need does not disappear when the twenty-somethings become forty-somethings. Even some clients in the latter half of fifty-something will need a wake-up call.

At the opposite end of the Baby Boomer spectrum, it is not unusual to see a net worth statement such as the one shown below for a doctor and spouse.

Item	Asset Amount	Liability Amount	Ownership
Primary Residence	$ 450,000	$ 355,000	Joint
Secondary Residence	150,000	100,000	Joint
Cash Accounts	16,500		Joint
Life Insurance Cash Value	8,000		Doctor
Stock Market	28,900		Doctor
Mutual Funds	11,100		Joint
Retirement Plans	780,000		Doctor
IRA	29,000		Spouse
Limited Partnerships	31,000		Doctor
Collectibles	10,000		Joint
Personal Property	200,000	$ 100,000	Joint
Total	$1,714,500	$ 555,000	
Net Worth	$1,159,500		

The doctor and spouse are millionaires, but they have 70 percent of this wealth in their retirement plans. Actually, it is closer to 76 percent of all financial assets, if the personal property category is eliminated. There is much more discussion on this in Chapter 4. Suffice it to say for now that this net-worth statement shows that about three-fourths of their wealth is at the future whims of Congress. As is well known, the government giveth and the government taketh away. So, the good doctor and spouse may be in a precarious position. They need good financial advice following an in-depth analysis of their retirement plan asset allocation. (See Chapter 5.)

These two examples show how an advisor can better understand clients through a study of their net worth statements. There is much more than what has been shown in these two examples that can be extracted from the numbers in the net worth statements. For example:

- Even though there is no way of foreseeing future income taxation, it should be assumed that certain assets will be subject to a reduction in value (asset minus income tax) when sold for use or reinvestment. This is easily seen and understood by the client who frequently buys and sells in the stock market. However, the client will have a tendency to forget about a tax liability for long-term investments in annuities and all retirement plans, IRAs, 401(k)s, etc.

- The Net Worth Statement provides the numbers and ownership information to indicate the extent an Estate Analysis is going to be necessary. (See Chapter 5)

- The placement of liabilities indicates whether debt is being used to obtain financial assets, such as real estate, stocks, etc., or "stuff" assets, such as entertainment centers, trail bikes, designer clothes, etc. Of course, as has been stated before, the younger Baby Boomer, in all probability, will need to use extensive debt just to set up housekeeping, but if the older Baby Boomer is still using this procedure, then it's a sign he hasn't learned the vagaries of such activities.

- The amount of life insurance cash value usually, but not always, indicates the client's propensity to own this asset. As will be discussed in Chapter 4, many young Baby Boomers will need to have a high concentration of life insurance coverage in term insurance in order to obtain the proper amount of protection needed. However, a zero or low level of life insurance cash value with an older Baby Boomer could indicate a combination of many things. For example, the client may have no relationship with a competent life insurance agent, or possibly received ill advised replacement of previously owned cash value insurance, or simply is a procrastinator. Whatever the reason, this shortage should act as a red flag for future attention.

- The importance of one asset over another can be a strong indication of the lifestyle selected by the client and will act as yet one more source of information to assist the advisor in the goal of understanding the client. Consider Martin and Mary.

Martin and Mary meet with their financial advisor to discuss the dream house they had just found. Martin starts the conversation with the advisor by saying, "I know you advised that the proper price range of a residence for us is between $140,000 and $160,000, but we've found this simply wonderful house for $210,000. Now we want you to tell us how we can buy it."

The advisor's brain quickly computes the numbers and just as quickly determines that Martin and Mary would really be pushing their resources a great deal both to raise the proper down payment and to handle the monthly payments. (More on these calculations in Chapter 5.) Pat, the advisor, raises her hand to stop Martin and says, "First, tell me more about the house." This gives her a little more time to think before responding. Of course, both Martin and Mary comply with this request and eagerly tell Pat about the perfect size and number of rooms and the beautiful area and the proximity to quality schools, and on and on.

Pat waits her turn. Then she says, "It sounds to me as if you have already decided to buy this house." Martin and Mary nod their heads and say, "It's the greatest, but we do want your advice." Pat replies, "If you allocate the necessary amount of resources needed for this residence, then you will curtail most of your other optional items of standard of living." Mary answers, "But Pat, the home will be our standard of living. We don't need anything else." Martin is smiling and nodding in agreement.

Pat knows it's their life and their money, and even if she could dissuade them from this excessive allocation of assets, she would not only be an ogre, but she probably would have a very difficult or even impossible time bringing any reality back into the discussion. So, she decides not to use any stalling tactics and says, "I have some misgivings of you putting yourself out on a limb this far, but it is obviously an extremely important thing for each of you, so here is what we need to attempt to get." The three of them make a list of how to get the best mortgage rates, where to shop for the mortgage, a couple of negotiation techniques, and off go Martin and Mary to buy their dream house.

The numbers on all financial statements are filled with similar hidden stories which, when understood, reveal the real client. The financial advisor should not hesitate to explore. The time and effort of such activities are more rewarding than just gaining more information. This time and effort produce a relationship between client and advisor as almost nothing else could. The enjoyment of numerous such relationships during an advisor's professional career can be greater compensation than all the money in the world.

History Net Worth Statement

The History Net Worth Statement (Figure 3.3) will not appear in the initial financial plan that the financial advisor develops, because there is no history yet. Even if your client has come with history and numbers from another professional, do not use this data to develop the history net worth statement. A major purpose of the History Net Worth Statement is to illustrate what has happened since the client started working with you. Therefore, to serve this purpose, there is no history prior to your first meeting with the client.

Figure 3.3

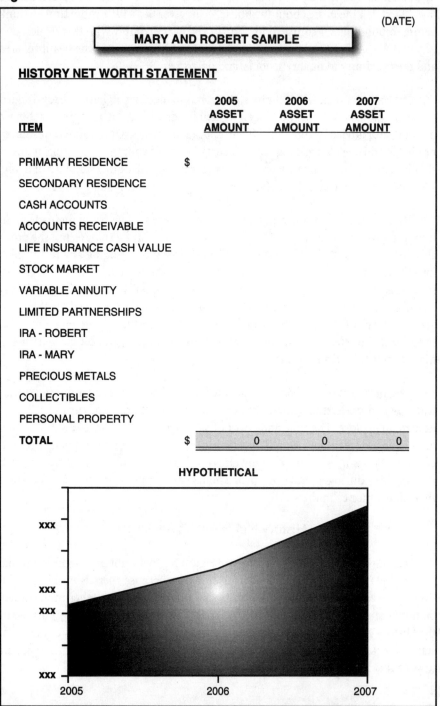

It is important that a complete history is shown on one sheet of paper for as long as possible. Start with the paper in the normal upright position. When the history generates more information than will fit on this page, turn the paper on its side, holding it horizontally. A third step would be to reduce the size of the information by using a smaller font (type size) or actually reducing on a photo copier to get more on one page. It has a positive effect on the client when the entire history can be seen all at once.

Keep in mind that all numbers should be net of liabilities. It may be possible to develop a computer program to generate this history without the need to re-enter any data. If not, the report should be generated and updated manually.

The most important value of the History Net Worth Statement is just that, the history. It does not matter whether a client's net worth is increasing or decreasing, but it is important for both the client and the advisor to be aware of the direction. For just about all Baby Boomers, the direction should be an increase, but if reversals occur, it is a red flag that something is needed. Sometimes, the reversal can be understood readily; e.g., a stock market correction, a loss in a court fight, or some uninsured loss of property. Other times, there may be deeper problems, such as an unbalanced budget causing a use of capital for living expenses. The important aspect is to know what's happening. Later in life, often in a person's middle eighties, capital can be used appropriately to balance the budget and to make lifetime gifts.

The second important benefit of a History Net Worth Statement is the trend line of each asset. For example, clients will go for many years without really knowing the correct market value of their home. This shows up on this statement usually when the home is listed at the same value for several years of history. This not only produces an incorrect net worth, but introduces inaccuracy in the asset allocation planning.

INCOME TAX INFORMATION

Income taxation has been an important part of money management since its inception in 1913, when the maximum income tax rate was 7 percent. The maximum rate has never been this low since the end of 1915. In 1916, the maximum rate more than doubled to 15 percent, and before the citizens taxed at the maximum rate could catch their breath, the rate more than quadrupled to 67 percent the following year. As the graph shows, the maximum rate has been 50 percent or higher for 62 out of the 97 years taxes have been imposed.

Figure 3.4

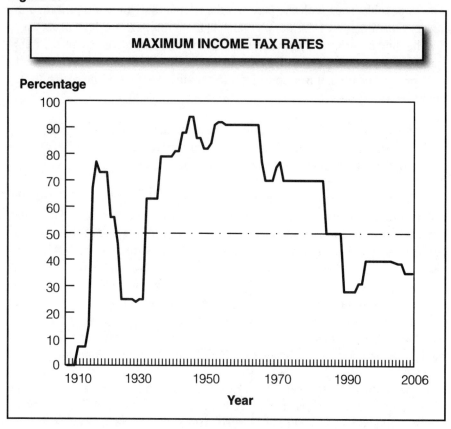

If a financial advisor is a specialist in income tax, there will be a tendency to place more emphasis on this aspect of the financial plan and to report more than would an advisor who is not a tax specialist. Whether this is of value to the client is moot. The important consideration is that each financial advisor be an individual with the right to place emphasis where he chooses, just as long as there is adequate and competent attention paid to all issues, including taxes.

The minimum that should be reported includes all sources of income (taxable or non-taxable), retirement plan contributions, net actual tax paid to the various governmental units, and itemized Social Security tax. All taxes should be totaled, the top marginal federal tax rate shown, and the amount of suspended loss carry-over stated. All of this information can be illustrated for at least the past three years on one financial plan page. This provides an excellent overview of where the client has been.

With a new client, a review of the income tax returns for the past three years will usually provide the financial advisor with enough information. Then, all future returns should be reviewed annually.

A client will assume that when a professional prepares the return, it will not contain any errors. However, errors can and do happen once in awhile, even with the most conscientious professional. One client often tells the story that when he surrendered a deferred annuity, duplicate 1099 forms were issued (for some unknown reason), and the accountant entered both on the client's tax return. Of course, this improperly doubled the tax on this distribution, and no one noticed. No one, that is, except the financial advisor who caught the error when reviewing the tax return. The financial advisor is this client's hero to this day.

A tax return reveals much more than just income sources and amounts. For example, excessive taxable income should tell the advisor to examine more closely the amount of cash assets in relation to other investments. If the amount of these fixed-dollar investments is excessive, then the client is paying more income tax than would be necessary and is missing out on the larger growth potential of other investments. It also might be an indication of more conservatism in the client than a risk-tolerance questionnaire indicated, or it could be that the client just doesn't know what to do with the money. The opposite end of the risk-tolerance scale might be emphasized by a stream of capital loss carryovers. None of this is indicated conclusively by the tax return, but such anomalies should raise a red flag and prompt further inquiry.

Another example of a red flag is when a client's tax return shows a large tax-exempt interest income and the client is in a 15 percent tax bracket. It is possible that such tax-exempt investments are not in the client's best interest. Inquire!

Each financial advisor should continue to develop improved techniques of discovery. For example, off season is a wonderful time to meet a client's accountant. Ask the accountant for help in better understanding the mutual client's tax return. This not only improves the advisor's skills and knowledge, it also has the potential of increasing the advisor's sphere of prospects. These benefits may cost a fee or perhaps only a breakfast or lunch, but the information gained and the new contact are valuable.

ANNUAL INCOME SOURCES

The development of a financial plan page on sources of income is a must for retired clients. Some Baby Boomer clients are in their sixties and may be retired. An Annual Income Sources (Figure 3.5) page should be prepared for such clients. The

Figure 3.5

```
                                                                    (DATE)

                 ┌─────────────────────────────────────┐
                 │        MARY AND ROBERT SAMPLE        │
                 └─────────────────────────────────────┘

INCOME SOURCES

                    YEAR          2007         2008         2009

PENSION                           $            $            $
     ROBERT
     MARY

SOCIAL SECURITY
     ROBERT
     MARY

ANNUITY

WAGES

          TOTAL BASIC INCOME      $     0      $     0      $     0


ADDITIONAL INCOME SOURCES

CASH                 $
STOCK MARKET
ANNUITIES
IRA/401(k)/403(b)
                     _____
     TOTAL           $              @ 6% =
```

preparation of this page is optional for other Baby Boomer clients, particularly the younger ones. The concept behind this is that a pre-retiree should not spend investment income; all living expenses and new investment funds should be covered by earned income. Income for these clients is easily reported at the bottom of the Cash Management Statement, discussed later in this chapter. However, a page on Annual Income Sources is very important for retirees. Even if a financial advisor does not yet have any retired Baby Boomers as clients, it won't be long before the advisor does have such clients. Just as they exploded on the scene as babies, the Boomers will explode on the scene as retirees.

Graduating into a retirement status requires many difficult adjustments. One very important question that comes up over and over again is, "Where will the money come from?" This question is answered with the information on an Annual Income Sources page. Not only does the information provide the answer, it also provides peace of mind if there is sufficient wealth to produce the desired standard of living in retirement. And if the information indicates a shortfall, it is best to know it as soon as possible. A shortfall might not be obvious from this page alone, but in concert with a Retirement Cash Flow Analysis (Chapter 5), it could provide specific information as to the amount of shortfall, when it will occur, and the adjustments that will be necessary.

Income of a regular nature, such as pension and Social Security benefits, is listed at the top of the Annual Income Sources page. Other sources of income might be annuity payments (including termination date, if any) or systematic withdrawals from both qualified and non-qualified investments. A total is found and compared with the estimated annual expenses found on the Cash Management Statement. Where it is possible with at least some degree of accuracy, several years could be projected. This adds peace of mind to clients, especially those who are very concerned.

At the bottom of the Annual Income Sources page, each investment category of assets that could be used to create additional income, if desired or needed, should be listed.

The total of the value of these additional assets is found and then multiplied by a percentage to obtain a potential amount of additional income. This percentage should be conservative, almost understating what return the client could earn on these assets. This understatement adds to the client's peace of mind. The example below uses a return rate of 6 percent.

Example:

Cash	$ 18,000
Stock Market	180,000
IRA/401(k)/403(b)	210,500
Deferred Annuity	99,800
	$ 508,300 @ 6% = $ 30,498

The example illustrates that up to an additional $30,000 could be created annually. If a larger or smaller rate of return is assumed, then the dollars available would change accordingly. The choice of 6 percent in the example was arbitrary. A return of 4 percent or even 8 percent could have been chosen. The percent chosen depends on what current rates are for different types of investments. The final choice is determined by the client, but the financial advisor should offer current information and advice. The advisor might suggest providing examples at two or three different return rates, if this is appropriate for the client.

CASH MANAGEMENT STATEMENT

A record that is of great importance in all financial plans is an itemized listing of all the client's expenditures. This is the Cash Management Statement, (Figure 3.6) and Chapter 2 tells how to collect the necessary information.

One reason this record is important is that it reveals a great deal of how the client thinks. A careful perusal of the numbers will divulge what is and is not of consequence to the client and, most important, whether the client has learned a fundamental of wealth accumulation: live within your income.

The first thing to look for is confirmation that the client's budget is balanced. If expenditures exceed income, then the financial advisor has an obligation to educate the client about what Charles Dickens wrote in *David Copperfield*, "Annual income twenty pounds, annual expenditure nineteen six, result happiness. Annual income twenty pounds, annual expenditure twenty pounds ought and six, result misery."

The financial advisor should probe to determine why the budget is not balanced and why it does not include provisions for wealth accumulation. Ask how long has this been going on and are there any plans for change in the near future? Depending upon the client's responses to such questions, some or most of the client's financial plan in the early stages will focus almost exclusively on debt removal. (See Chapter 5 for suggestions.)

On the other hand, if income exceeds expenditures, then the financial advisor should look to see if the budget includes provisions for new wealth accumulation. If not, why not? If so, at what percentage of income? Is this a proper percentage for this particular client?

The structure of the form ties together expenditures in major categories. The first major category covers the basic residence and general living expenses. This begins with "HOUSING" and goes down through "CLOTHING AND CLEANING." This category also provides the numbers necessary to determine the percent of income being allocated for shelter. By adding the items of mortgage payments, property tax, upkeep and maintenance, fees, utilities, property and liability insurance, and then dividing that sum by income, the answer sometimes indicates a condition that is often called "house poor." This is where a large percentage of income is being allocated to the residence. Earlier in this chapter, Pat, the financial advisor, had great concerns that Martin and Mary were going to find themselves house poor.

Figure 3.6

	(DATE)

MARY AND ROBERT SAMPLE

CASH MANAGEMENT STATEMENT

ANNUAL EXPENDITURES: FIXED	YEAR
HOUSING (MORTGAGE/RENT)	$_____
PROPERTY TAXES	_____
HOUSE UPKEEP/REPAIRS/MAINTENANCE	_____
UTILITIES & TELEPHONE	_____
FOOD/GROCERIES	_____
CLOTHING & CLEANING	_____
INCOME & SOCIAL SECURITY TAXES	_____
DEBT REPAYMENT	_____
TRANSPORTATION (AUTO/COMMUTING)	_____
AUTO, HOME AND LIABILITY INSURANCE	_____
MEDICAL/DENTAL/DRUGS/HEALTH INSURANCE	_____
DISABILITY INCOME INSURANCE	_____
LIFE INSURANCE	_____
EDUCATION EXPENSES	_____
TOTAL FIXED EXPENDITURES	$
ANNUAL EXPENDITURES: DISCRETIONARY	
VACATION/TRAVEL	$_____
RECREATION/ENTERTAINMENT	_____
CONTRIBUTIONS	_____
GIFTS	_____
HOUSEHOLD FURNISHINGS	_____
EDUCATION FUND	_____
PERSONAL CARE	_____
OTHER	_____
TOTAL DISCRETIONARY EXPENDITURES	$
TOTAL ANNUAL EXPENDITURES	$
SAVINGS	$_____
INVESTMENTS	_____
TOTAL ANNUAL EXPENDITURES & ACCUMULATIONS	$
ESTIMATED INCOME	$

How much one should allocate in this area is such a personal matter that definitive recommendations are difficult, if not impossible, to find. Even ongoing studies in this area have wide variations in results, but they seem to cluster around the 30 to 40 percent range for income to allocate to shelter. The bottom line is if a Baby Boomer client is spending 50 to 60 percent of income on shelter, then he has given up much of life's other pleasant experiences or, and unfortunately this is too often true, he has a deficit budget. If the Baby Boomer client continues to have a deficit budget, then he is on a one-way street to bankruptcy.

The next category starts with the revelation to the client of the significant portion of income never seen, or at least never really owned: income taxes and Social Security taxes. This is followed by total debt service requirements. This includes all debt other than a mortgage on the residence. The financial advisor should note what percentage of gross income is allocated to prior used or obtained items. A red flag should be raised if the repayment plan requires more than 10 percent of gross income. In fact, if the repayment plan requires more than 10 percent of net income (gross income minus income and Social Security taxes), this could reveal potential problems. The financial advisor should keep in mind that, for younger Baby Boomers, a maximum of 10 percent to service all consumer debt is often too stringent, if not impossible. However, by acknowledging this maximum safety level, the youngsters are setting a goal for themselves to achieve as soon as possible.

The final item in this category is transportation. This can be a major expense for those who have to drive or use public transportation to commute long distances. As Baby Boomers become parents and as children grow older, the family often looks to buy a larger house in an area where the pace is less frenetic and the schools are perceived to be good. This frequently requires a move farther away from the breadwinner's place of work. In such cases, there is little or no control over the expense of commuting, but it is important for all to recognize its effect on the family's standard of living.

In the next category, various insurance premiums as well as health expenses paid by the client are listed. These items can be expensive, but they also can be necessary for most Baby Boomers. The financial advisor can provide a real service helping a client evaluate his circumstances. A lack of or unusually small amount of premium for disability income and life insurance could indicate either reliance on group insurance coverage or insufficient benefits. The answers to this is found in the analysis of each insurance policy owned by the client. (More on this is found in Chapter 4.)

The rest of the Cash Management Statement involves expenditures over which the client has some discretion. Data in these areas help reveal attitudes of the client about what is important, even important enough to overcome a strong desire for other items. It is in these areas where potential reductions can be found, if such reductions are necessary or desirable. However, the financial advisor should keep in mind that when many Baby Boomers want something, they want it now. This can be true particularly for the younger ones, but it is not exclusively the province of younger Boomers to have this attitude.

To prepare the Cash Management Statement, the client spends a considerable amount of time collecting the data, and the financial advisor spends a considerable amount of time analyzing the data and presenting it in an organized format to the client. However, not enough can be said about how valuable all this spent-time is.

The Cash Management Statement can be full of problems as well as full of suggestions for solutions. The importance of this statement transcends the initial or even early years of an advisor-client relationship. It has unparalleled importance when getting started, but it also has far reaching meanings as Baby Boomer clients begin to think seriously about funding for their children's education and for their own retirement, often occurring at the same time. So the Cash Management Statement should be kept up to date and referred to on a regular basis.

Chapter 4

Developing the Three Core Areas of a Financial Plan

The three core areas of a financial plan are: (1) Protection, (2) Liquidity, and (3) Investment. There may be one or more other areas that are of immediate concern for a particular individual, but for the vast majority of clients, the core of a plan should be developed before exploring any of these other areas.

A professional financial planner will find it difficult if not impossible to be an expert in all areas of the financial plan, especially if the planner is just beginning his career as a professional. However, it is incumbent on every planner to learn at least the basics in all areas in which the planner's practice is involved. It also is very important that the planner be able to transmit this basic information in understandable language to a client and to highlight those areas most applicable to the client's needs. Even though the professional planner might think much of this information to be elementary, the client may not think it is. After all, in most cases, the client's expertise is not in the area of financial planning; otherwise the client would not be seeking the advice of a professional planner. So the professional should convey the necessary information clearly and completely, because the success of the planner as well as the client's success depends on the client understanding what is said.

The client usually does not want to become an expert, but he does need to have an understanding of each item in the plan. As the planner develops each area for a presentation, it is important to leave a lot of white space on every page so that the client's attention is properly focused on the point being imparted. Keep the language as non-technical as possible and stay on the point. In other words, make it clear and complete, but keep it simple.

PROTECTION

Many of the Baby Boomer client's needs in this area can be satisfied with one or more insurance programs. So this section will consider all insurance, personal and group, that the client may have or need. This includes also any employment benefits that the client may have. Note that it is not the purpose of this book to train anyone in the elements of any specific insurance product. A professional planner is expected to obtain such information as needed elsewhere. Having that out of the way, let's discuss the general kinds of insurance that clients should consider.

In general, the financial planner should encourage clients to self-insure those items or parts of items that can be managed easily within one's income and/or net worth without jeopardizing other financial goals. This self-insurance usually comes in the form of deductible and co-pay elections available in most insurance products. Explore each option with the client as dictated by the client's particular situation. Recommendations should be based on the largest amount of self-insurance that can be tolerated so that the maximum amount of personal resources can be allocated to other expenditures and wealth accumulation.

Liability

Liability insurance coverage can help prevent up to the complete loss of all of a client's wealth. Because we all have less and less privacy these days, it has become quite easy for the amount of a person's wealth to be exposed. The planner's objective is to help make sure that any transfer of the client's wealth is at the client's discretion, not that of a judge or jury. Therefore, the planner should give high priority to protecting each client's wealth, regardless of the amount, when discussing the acquisition of proper liability insurance coverage.

As a person's wealth accumulations increase, so should the amount of liability insurance, referred to as Umbrella or Excess Liability. When a client has a net worth of $250,000, the planner should recommend that a $1-million umbrella policy be purchased. As the client's net worth approaches $1 million, the liability insurance also should be increased.

A very important feature of this type of policy is called "Required Underlying Coverage." This states that the million-dollar benefit will not be available until the base policies – homeowner's insurance, auto insurance, boat insurance, etc. – have been used to pay their specified amounts of the required underlying coverage. Therefore, unless the client chooses to self-insure this amount, it is important that the client

Figure 4.1

(DATE)

MARY AND ROBERT SAMPLE

PROPERTY AND LIABILITY INSURANCE

HOMEOWNERS

COMPANY	POLICY NUMBER	EXPIRATION DATE
DWELLING		$
PERSONAL PROPERTY		
LIABILITY		
REPLACEMENT COST		
DEDUCTIBLE		

ANNUAL PREMIUM $ 0

AUTO

COMPANY	POLICY NUMBER	EXPIRATION DATE

	CAR 1	CAR 2
BODILY INJURY LIABILITY	$	$
PROPERTY DAMAGE LIABILITY		
COMPREHENSIVE DEDUCTIBLE		
COLLISION (BROAD) DEDUCTIBLE		
PERSONAL INJURY PROTECTION		
ANNUAL PREMIUM	$ 0	$ 0

TOTAL ANNUAL PREMIUM $ 0

EXCESS LIABILITY

COMPANY	POLICY NUMBER	EXPIRATION DATE
AMOUNT	$	

REQUIRED UNDERLYING COVERAGE

	BODILY INJURY	PROPERTY DAMAGE	SINGLE LIMIT
AUTO	$	$	$
HOME			
OTHER			

ANNUAL PREMIUM $_____0

TOTAL ANNUAL PREMIUM $_____0

obtains the required amounts of coverage in these base policies as itemized in the umbrella policy. For example:

REQUIRED UNDERLYING COVERAGE

	Bodily Injury	Property Damage	or	Single Limit
Auto	$100/300,000	$50,000		$300,000
Home				$100,000

Homeowners

The homeowner's insurance policy is an extremely complex contract and is seldom read by the client. Despite the policy's complexity, the planner should present the basics in an understandable manner to the client. Most clients really appreciate this simplified presentation. In addition to listing the amount of coverage for the dwelling, contents, liability, and deductibles, the planner also should discuss other important items such as replacement-cost coverage for both the dwelling and its contents. If the dwelling or its contents have increased in value since the client purchased the policy, then the coverage may be insufficient. The proper amount of coverage for the dwelling should be 100% of the current cost of rebuilding. Also, if expensive jewelry, furs, rare collectibles, or other such items are owned, the planner should discuss with the client appropriate insurance for these items, pointing out that in many cases, such unique items may not be covered in the basic homeowner's policy.

When reviewing a condo homeowner's policy, in addition to the items mentioned above, give attention to coverage for any additions or alterations that have added value to the unit. Also "loss assessment" coverage should be discussed. This coverage provides the condo unit owner with funds in case the condo association assesses a claim against each unit owner for a judgment won against the condo association which is in excess of its liability insurance coverage. Since the suit was against the condo association and not against the unit owner, the unit owner's regular liability coverage will not provide coverage. This loss-assessment coverage is usually very low in cost.

Auto

The two fundamental coverages for a client's vehicles are for liability and for damage to the vehicle. Liability coverage is often divided into two parts: bodily injury and property damage. The planner should make sure the liability insurance amounts are coordinated with the umbrella policy requirements, if applicable, or in large enough amounts that are commensurate with the wealth and social status of the owner or lessee of the vehicle.

An accident is one obvious way that damage can occur to a vehicle. This loss is covered either via a suit against the other party in the accident if they were at fault, or if not at fault or in a no-fault state, covered under the collision provision in the policy. Usually the amount of the deductible is optional. This is an opportunity for the client to save premium and for the planner to provide the client with a cost/benefit analysis. Non-accident damage to a vehicle is covered under the comprehensive provision. Clients understand this coverage best when the planner describes it as almost all bad things that can happen to a car other than a collision. Since this provision also has an optional deductible, the planner and the client should discuss the amount by determining the proper cost/benefit ratio.

Medical coverage is usually well-defined when someone is injured in an accident. However, in some states, responsibility for payment can become quite complicated for those who have Medicare.

Let's pause for a moment to review how Medicare changes a client's insurance status. Prior to the time when a person has Medicare, his individual or group medical insurance provides "primary" coverage. Clients readily understand this when they are told that primary coverage "pays first." Now, when a person changes to Medicare coverage, then it becomes the primary coverage. At this point, any other insurance is called supplemental or "secondary" coverage. Simple, so far.

The complication arises in some states that require mandatory medical and loss-of-wages coverage in the auto insurance policy. In these states that require the auto insurance policy to provide auto-accident-medical-expense coverage, this coverage can be either secondary or primary based on the insured's selection.

Normally, since the client has primary coverage from his employment medical coverage, the client should select the auto medical to be secondary. This saves premiums. The Medicare law is specific in that this type of state law causes Medicare to become secondary coverage for auto accidents. Without giving proper attention at this point to change the auto medical coverage to primary, a client can wind up with three sources of coverage – Medicare, supplemental health, and the auto insurance policy – all of which are secondary coverage, and no one will pay a claim. If the client resides in a state with this mandatory law, and has Medicare, review the auto-insurance policies to make sure that the accident-medical-expense coverage is specified or changed as the primary coverage. If the planner is not an expert in this area, then an expert should be consulted before advising clients.

Since Medicare is normally not available until a person is 65 years old, it seems an unnecessary inclusion in this book of financial planning for Baby Boomers. It has been included for two reasons. First, a Baby Boomer may become totally disabled and, after two years of disability, Medicare coverage is available regardless of age. Second, after a complete financial plan is in place, clients have a tendency to discuss parts with parents and others and feel quite good in being able to explain this complicated part of the Medicare law that might affect these others.

As the planner presents information for liability, homeowners, and auto, it should be illustrated all on one page. This provides the client with a good overview of all property and liability coverage and visually ties together required underlying coverage in the umbrella (excess liability) with the basic liability coverage in the homeowners and auto policies.

Medical

Most clients will have some combination of health coverage involving hospitalization, primary-care-doctor visits, major medical, visual and dental plans, and so on. Some clients may even have options to select from a variety of coverages to make use of a given amount of employer dollars. Under such circumstances, the planner and the client can discuss more, less, or no coverage in order to take the greatest advantage of the employer dollars. Some clients will be self-employed in any business from a mom-and-pop operation to the head of a corporation involving a number of employees. And some clients will be retired or semi-retired. Each will require individual attention.

When financial planners collect and present the data to clients, the planners should itemize the coverage on one page to visually enhance the client's understanding and to focus on any shortfalls, duplication, or improper coverage.

Disability

Many employers provide their employees with insurance in case of disability. However, there is often a limit to such coverage, such as a maximum length of time benefits will be paid or a maximum dollar amount that will be paid. In such cases, the planner should be prepared to suggest ways to "fill in the gaps."

Sometimes a client will want a better definition of disability in his coverage and should consider waiving or supplementing the group benefit with individual coverage. This is particularly appropriate when the employer contribution can be allocated elsewhere.

Clients not covered by employer-provided insurance should consider an individual disability income insurance policy. The presentation should include the

Figure 4.2

(DATE)

MARY AND ROBERT SAMPLE

MEDICAL INSURANCE

COMPANY	_____
POLICY NUMBER	_____
POLICY DATE	_____
TYPE	_____

HOSPITAL

ROOM AND BOARD _____

MISCELLANEOUS EXPENSE _____

SURGERY _____

SECOND SURGICAL OPINION _____

PRE-CERTIFICATION _____

PRESCRIPTION DRUGS _____

HOME HEALTH CARE _____

MAJOR MEDICAL

MAXIMUM $_____

DEDUCTIBLE _____

CO-INSURANCE % _____

$ OUT OF POCKET _____

TOTAL OUT OF POCKET _____

DENTAL/VISION

MAXIMUM $_____

DEDUCTIBLE _____

BENEFITS:

ANNUAL PREMIUM $_____ 0

Figure 4.3

(DATE)

MARY AND ROBERT SAMPLE

DISABILITY INCOME INSURANCE

COMPANY	_____
POLICY NUMBER	_____
POLICY DATE	_____
TYPE	_____

BENEFITS

MONTHLY $_____

SOCIAL SECURITY SUBSTITUTE   _____

COST OF LIVING RIDER   _____

PARTIAL DISABILITY (RESIDUAL)   _____

ELIMINATION PERIOD   _____

REHABILITATION EXPENSE   _____

TREATMENT OF INJURY   _____

BENEFIT PERIOD

ACCIDENT   _____

SICKNESS   _____

PREMIUMS

BASIC $_____

SOCIAL SECURITY SUBSTITUTE   _____

COST OF LIVING   _____
PARTIAL DISABILITY

TOTAL MONTHLY BENEFIT $_____0

TOTAL ANNUAL PREMIUM $_____0

various options open to the client, such as the type of contract, the amount, the elimination period, the length of coverage, and so on.

Again, as before, all benefits and costs should be summarized on one page.

Long Term Care Insurance

There is a continuing, almost endless stream of evidence in support of an ever-increasing life expectancy. Where their grandfathers may have lived to the ripe old age of 60, 70, or even 80, the Baby Boomers have an excellent chance of living to be 90, 100, or more. But as life expectancy increases, so too does the potential need for long-term care, professional care both at home and in a nursing facility. This can cost money, a lot of money.

In the field of insurance, long term care insurance is the new "kid on the block." Some financial planners may be tempted to recommend this protection to everyone. However, long term care insurance should come under the same discerning rule as all other types of insurance: only insure that which is not proper to self-insure.

The client's amount of wealth and desires for the allocation of this wealth play an important part in the decision to insure or not to insure for long term care. If the client decides to insure, then many more decisions need to be made, and the planner should be prepared to discuss all of them intelligently with the client.

If the client decides long term care insurance is desirable, then the next decision that must be made is the amount of coverage desired. This is a very individual matter, but an astute professional can be of great assistance to the decision maker. For example, where the client expects to be living at the time of need is significant because of the wide variance in cost from one area of the country to another. The difference in cost can be as much as three times or one-third as great when one moves from one major area to another. Also, the client's perception of the potential length of stay in a nursing home prior to recovery or death will have a major influence on the length of coverage selected. Such perceptions can vary over a wide range, and the professional should be prepared to play "what-if," as in, "Times are different now. What if you live another twenty years, even though your father did not?"

It has been observed that the inverse ratio of ability to pay the premium and the need for coverage is most exasperating. Those client's that can most easily afford the coverage may not need it at all, and the poorest who are least likely able to pay the premiums have the greatest need for coverage.

Figure 4.4

(DATE)

MARY AND ROBERT SAMPLE

LONG TERM CARE INSURANCE

COMPANY	_____
POLICY NUMBER	_____
POLICY DATE	_____
TYPE	_____

DAILY BENEFIT

NURSING HOME CARE $ _____

HOME CARE   _____

INFLATION ADJUSTMENT RIDER 5% - COMPOUNDED

ELIMINATION PERIOD

NURSING HOME CARE

HOME HEALTH CARE

PRE-EXISTING CONDITION   _____ (1)

CAN POLICY BE CANCELLED?   _____

PRIOR HOSPITAL STAY REQUIRED

SKILLED NURSING CARE   _____

INTERMEDIATE NURSING CARE   _____

CUSTODIAL NURSING CARE   _____

PRIOR SKILLED NURSING CARE REQUIRED

INTERMEDIATE NURSING CARE   _____

CUSTODIAL NURSING CARE   _____

PRIOR NURSING HOME CARE REQUIRED

HOME HEALTH CARE   _____

INFLATION ADJUSTED

ANNUALLY (5%)   SIMPLE   _____

                           COMPOUND   _____

ANNUAL PREMIUM $_____ 0

(1) IF REPORTED ON APPLICATION COVERED IMMEDIATELY

Consider these clients: A married couple in their 70s, who have good retirement cash flow. This couple has a net worth of three million dollars. They also have two residences – one summer, one winter – both debt free. It was recommended that long term care insurance was not necessary for them. Furthermore, it was recommended that the amount that they might have to pay for the premium for such insurance could be used for many other purposes, such as spending, gifting, or additional wealth accumulation. They agreed.

One month later, the husband called the planner from out of state. He had just attended a presentation of long term care insurance after which he had several long discussions with friends. He asked, "Are you sure I don't need this coverage?" The financial planner reaffirmed the original recommendation. "The coverage is not necessary."

One month later, he called again, and repeated the same scenario. And again he called, twice. During the last call the planner changed the dialog and said, "Listen, I give up! Just buy the policy from me. That way you will feel more comfortable, I'll receive a nice commission, and we'll both be happy!" There was silence on the other end of the line. Then he finally responded, "Well, if you really don't think I need the coverage … ."

The planner should note that this was not a guess nor an uninformed recommendation. The planner knew this couple. The planner had heard about their fathers and mothers, their grandfathers and grandmothers, their cousins, their aunts and their uncles, and most important, because the planner had listened, he knew how this couple lived, how they spent their money, and how they enjoyed rather than reluctantly faced life each new day. A guess on the planner's part? No, with what the planner knew, it seemed to be an absolutely proper recommendation.

When presenting the options to the client, as before, the planner should illustrate the benefits and costs on one page. Much more information and detail is available in *How To Sell Long-Term Care Insurance,* a publication of The National Underwriter Company.

Life Insurance

It is strongly recommended that, with all forms of insurance, the financial planner not rely solely on someone else's summary report. A client's memory, especially, should not be a substitute for the planner dissecting each and every insurance policy.

The above advice is especially true about life insurance. Changes after purchase can alter many outcomes, so the analysis of any policy and amendments should be made with the latest version in effect. Be sure to check the ownership/beneficiary of the policy, for example. A designation that is no longer appropriate could cause needless taxation or other hardships for the client unless there is a change more in keeping with the client's current circumstances.

If a planner does not have sufficient expertise, he should bring in a qualified consultant in the particular area in question. It's the absolutely rare professional who knows it all.

Life insurance is a highly specialized area, and the best education is obtained through studies that lead to a Chartered Life Underwriter (CLU) designation. After completing the several years it takes to accomplish the CLU designation, the designee will then know and retain the fundamentals of insurance. Without continuing education, however, the CLU will not be current and, in fact, even may begin to forget some of the details of the fundamentals. If the financial planner wants to be an expert in life insurance, first obtain a CLU designation and then keep current through continuing education.

When a client's current position in life insurance is summarized, the planner should use two pages. Show on the first page for each policy the name of the insurance company, the policy number, policy date, amount, type, cost, extra benefits, ownership, and beneficiary designations. Show on a separate page the policy cash values, dividends, and loans (living values). With this up-to-date summary, the professional has a very good understanding of the present coverage, types of coverage, ownership, and estate tax exposure of these benefits. However, this is just a beginning summary and provides only minimal data for a guessing game of whether the amount of coverage is proper.

There are many methods of determining the desired amount of coverage. A rule of thumb evolved over many years is that the amount of coverage should be a multiple of gross/net annual household income. The consensus is that a range from 3 to 8 times annual income should suffice. A centering phenomenon created an often used "5 times income." Therefore, a second-best answer to someone's question of how much life insurance he should own, when the planner must answer on the spot and with no opportunity to obtain any more information, is "5 times one's annual household income." The best answer is, "I don't know, but when I have the proper information on your particular situation, I can do an analysis that will produce the most accurate answer available based on complete information about you and the assumptions we select."

Since the Insurance Cash Flow Analysis is an off-shoot of the Retirement Cash Flow Analysis, an explanation of this form can be found in Chapter 5.

Figure 4.5

(DATE)

MARY AND ROBERT SAMPLE

LIFE INSURANCE

COMPANY/ NUMBER	DATE ISSUED	AGE AT ISSUE	DEATH BENEFIT	TYPE OF POLICY	ANNUAL PREMIUM	OWNER/ BENEF.	WAIVER PREM
ROBERT			$ _____		$ _____		
			$ _____ 0		$ _____ 0		
MARY			$ _____		$ _____		
			$ _____ 0		$ _____ 0		

NOTES: _____

_____

_____

A: OWNER:_____

   PRIMARY BENEFICIARY:_____

   CONTINGENT BENEFICIARY: _____

B: OWNER:_____

   PRIMARY BENEFICIARY:_____

   CONTINGENT BENEFICIARY: _____

Figure 4.5 (cont'd)

(DATE)

MARY AND ROBERT SAMPLE

LIFE INSURANCE

COMPANY/ NUMBER	BASE POLICY CASH VALUE	PAID UP INS. CASH VALUE	ACCUMULATED DIVIDENDS	LOAN	LOAN INTEREST RATE
ROBERT					
	$_____	$_____	$_____	$_____	
	$_____ 0	$_____ 0	$_____ 0	$_____ 0	
MARY	$_____	$_____	$_____	$_____	
	$_____ 0	$_____ 0	$_____ 0	$_____ 0	

A final page to use is titled, *Protection Recommendations.* (Figure 4.6) Put the category *Excess Liability* at the top of the page. This will help the client to get accustomed to large numbers, $1 million, $2 million, $5 million, etc. The client will accept these numbers easily because of the comparatively low premiums.

Then take the client through the homeowner, auto, medical, disability income, long term care, and life insurance recommendations. The planner should get all this on one page, so it is important to be brief, specific, but clear. Shown below is an example.

Excess Liability	Coverage is proper
Homeowners	Your Net Worth Statement states the value of your home is $300,000, yet you have the dwelling insured for $160,000. Is this the proper amount?*
Life Insurance	You both are grossly underinsured. You should obtain an additional $500,000 on each of you. See illustration.

Figure 4.6

(DATE)

MARY AND ROBERT SAMPLE

PROTECTION RECOMMENDATIONS

EXCESS LIABILITY

HOMEOWNERS

AUTO

MEDICAL

DISABILITY/LONG TERM CARE

LIFE INSURANCE

- There may be good reasons for only $160,000 of insurance on the dwelling, such as ocean or lake frontage, or an extremely valuable location, say 1600 Pennsylvania Avenue, Washington D.C.

LIQUIDITY

There are two categories under liquidity. They are: (1) Emergency Fund, and (2) Cash or Cash Equivalents in the investment portfolio.

Emergency Fund

An emergency fund should contain a certain amount of assets that can be used whenever needed and can be available with very little, if any, obstructions. For example, there should be no tax ramifications involved in obtaining and using the assets, and the assets should not be in investment vehicles that fluctuate in value. This means that these funds should be in cash-type accounts such as checking, savings, money markets, CDs, and so on, plus the loanable cash value in traditional (fixed dollar) life insurance policies.

The proper amount in the emergency fund depends on several factors.

- Income minus income tax *and* Social Security tax

- One or two family paychecks

- Amount of medical and disability income insurance

- Extent of debt service requirements

- Stability of job(s)

All of this should be illustrated on a single page. First, show the present liquid assets. Then, to find the proper amount for the emergency fund, show the gross family annual income *minus* income tax and Social Security tax, *multiplied by* a percentage from 25 percent up to 50 percent. The proper percentage to use is arrived at more by artistic talent than scientific formula. The more uncertainty in the client's circumstances, the greater the percentage used. The more the factors are positive, the smaller the percentage used. However, the minimum should never be less than 25 percent.

Whatever percent selected, it is imperative to convince the client to obtain this sum, if it is not already in place, before he starts or continues any other investing.

Figure 4.7

```
                                                          (DATE)

          ┌─────────────────────────────────────────┐
          │         MARY AND ROBERT SAMPLE          │
          └─────────────────────────────────────────┘

    EMERGENCY FUND

         PRESENT

              CASH ACCOUNTS                        $
              LIFE INSURANCE CASH VALUE

                                                   $_____



         PROPER
              CURRENT BUDGET - INCOME &
              SOCIAL SECURITY TAXES x .25 =        $_____


    ┌──────────────────────────────────────────────────────┐
    │ RECOMMENDATIONS                                       │
    ├──────────────────────────────────────────────────────┤
    │                                                       │
    │                                                       │
    │                                                       │
    │                                                       │
    └──────────────────────────────────────────────────────┘
```

The easiest way to destroy an investment program is for an emergency to occur immediately following a major drop in the market where the assets are invested, and there is no emergency fund.

Baby Boomers, especially younger Boomers, have had a strong tendency to spend as fast as it is earned and do not hesitate to create debt. For them to allow "idle" cash to lie around is a very difficult thing to do. There are all kinds of rationalizations to justify the spending of this money. However, they all are simply rationalizations. The challenge for a financial planner is to convince the Boomer client of how important it is to everyone in the family that proper cash reserves be obtained and maintained. And the planner must do this without implying that the client's rationalizations are just that, or worse, stupid.

As Baby Boomers age through their 40s and into their 50s, the other side of their rationalizing appears. Now, rather than expressing a strong argument for spending this cash, they begin to present arguments for reducing or eliminating idle cash. They say, "Why keep so much in cash when it produces such a low return. Let's invest it in higher-yielding, faster-growing investments."

Although their arguments have changed, the response must be the same. Proper liquidity is a fundamental not only in one's investment portfolio, but in all aspects of one's financial life. All professional advisors need to place proper importance on this issue and strongly encourage the Baby Boomers at all points along the age spectrum to build up and maintain the proper amount of liquidity for emergencies and to invest only the excess.

The second category of Liquidity, which is Cash and Cash Equivalents in the investment portfolio, will be covered in the third core area, Investments.

INVESTMENTS

The development of a portfolio of investments should be approached by first determining the categories to be included. There is no defacto standard number of categories or even a defacto list of categories. After the planner has given due consideration to the categories and asset allocations as presented in this chapter, he should develop his own. The planner might even consider starting with these six suggestions and then revise as reasons for alternatives are developed.

Note: Many years ago, when attending a workshop, I heard these six categories used for an asset allocation model. I have used this model all these years with very good communication results with clients, and for me, that's the bottom line.

Place each investment into one of the six categories. One category that may seem unusual is *Tax Favored*, especially when upon analysis, it can contain investments found in three of the other categories. However, the reasons for including this separate category will become more clear as all six categories are discussed in more detail. So, let's begin by explaining each category and then developing a model weighting for a generic allocation. Note that the specific weighting will change as the importance of each category fluctuates in our economy. Finally, a proper modification for different ages, risk tolerances, and financial objectives will be discussed.

Cash

The cash category includes all fixed dollar investments as listed previously in the liquidity section, plus other fixed dollar investments such as government and corporate bonds, accounts receivable, etc.

Stock Market

This category includes all individual or stock mutual funds. Of course, the development of this category should have extensive diversification within itself as will be discussed later.

Real Estate

Some financial advisors do not include real estate for the client's personal use in this category when developing an investment portfolio. However, there are several reasons for its inclusion that will be discussed later. For now, at least temporarily, accept the inclusion of the client's home, a secondary residence, and also vacant lots where future personal-use development is planned.

Precious Metals

This category includes gold, silver, platinum, etc.

Tax Favored

This category has four components – cash, stocks, real estate and retirement plans – that have some kind of tax advantage. Personal-use real estate is not included in this category even though one's primary residence does have tax advantages. Included in the "Cash" component are municipal bonds and fixed annuities. These have income-tax-free interest and tax-deferred accumulation respectively. Tax-favored investments included in the "Stock Market" component are equity investments in variable annuities and variable life insurance. Tax-favored investments in "Real Estate" are commercial as opposed to personal-use property held outright or in mutual funds, REITS, and limited partnerships.

All retirement plans where one has the best of all worlds with deductibility or excludability and deferral of income tax make up the fourth component in this category. This is such a powerful tax control part of financial planning that many advisors, especially those with accounting backgrounds tend to state, "Always maximize these contributions." However, as will be learned later, this is not always the best advice.

Collectibles

Included in this last category are tangibles such as rare coins, rare stamps, antiques, oriental rugs, paintings, artifacts, etc.

Remember that it is not the purpose of this book to explain the detailed aspect of each type of specific investment vehicle. Rather the purpose is to illustrate successful presentation techniques along with concepts of importance and how the planner can best utilize it all to communicate effectively with the client. Having once again stated the objective, let us proceed to develop and analyze an asset allocation model.

Asset Allocation Model

It is important that the planner help the clients to first visualize a generic allocation. This establishes a good range of holdings from which they can deviate with reasons appropriate to their own specific circumstances. It is to be expected, however, that any deviations will not stray too far from a well balanced portfolio.

ASSET ALLOCATION

CATEGORY	ALLOCATION
Cash	10-20%
Stock Market	15-25%
Real Estate	20-25%
Precious Metal	0-5%
Tax Favored	20-38%
Collectibles	0-5%

Cash (10-20%)

Cash and cash equivalents are fixed-dollar investments and, as such, have performed historically at a much lower level than equity investment vehicles. The cash category is very important to provide liquidity, an essential element for proper management of both general living expenses and emergencies or opportunities. For example, when an unusual but proper investment opportunity comes along, it is a terrible thing not to have the ability to participate because of lack of liquidity. Holding proper fixed dollar investments created the phrase, Cash is King.

There is another equally undesirable extreme: too much cash will destroy one's purchasing power. Life is best experienced with a proper balance in all things. A client's wealth accumulations likewise require a proper balance. If the planner messes around with this balance too much, the planner becomes the enemy.

Since cash sometimes produces only as little as one-half or less of the return as that produced by equity investments, the planner should recommend that only

Figure 4.8

(DATE)

MARY AND ROBERT SAMPLE

INVESTMENT PORTFOLIO

Investments	Thousands	Percent	Generic Range	Recommended Percent
CASH	$		10 - 20%	10%
STOCK MARKET			15 - 25%	25
REAL ESTATE			20 - 25%	25
PRECIOUS METALS			1 - 4%	1
TAX FAVORED			20 - 38%	38
COLLECTIBLES			0 - 5%	1
TOTAL	$ 0.0	0%	100%	100%

CASH

$_____

$ 0.0

STOCK MARKET

$_____

$ 0.0

REAL ESTATE

$_____

$ 0.0

PRECIOUS METALS

$_____

$ 0.0

TAX FAVORED

$_____

$ 0.0

COLLECTIBLES

$_____

$ 0.0

a small percentage of the portfolio be in cash. For virtually all Baby Boomers, this allocation should be very close to 10 percent of total investments. As already noted, too little in cash exposes a client to missed opportunities or a lack of funds required in emergencies. Too much in cash exposes the client to the ravages of inflation.

There is at least one time when the planner should recommend upsetting this delicate balance in liquidity. This time is when an analysis reveals a significant short-fall in liquid funds for emergency purposes. This occurs often with younger Baby Boomers, those who have not had time to accumulate much of anything, yet have a relatively high income that indicates the need of an emergency fund that is 30%, 40% or even 50% of total investments. See the following example.

Asset allocation			Emergency Fund Recommendation	
Cash	$ 6.5	13%	Increase liquidity from	
Stock Market	0.0	0%	$6,500 to $15,000.	
Real Estate	40.0	79%		
Precious Metals	0.0	0%	(Net Income of $60,000	
Tax Favored	4.0	8%	times 0.25 = $15,000)	
Collectibles	0.0	0%		
	$50.5	100%		

If this young couple accumulates an additional $8,500 in cash to meet the emergency fund recommendation, this would increase their asset allocation in cash to 25 percent.

Asset allocation		
Cash	$15.0	25%
Stock Market	0.0	0%
Real Estate	40.0	68%
Precious Metals	0.0	0%
Tax Favored	4.0	7%
Collectibles	0.0	0%
	$59.0	100%

This is 2½ times the "proper" amount, but the "real proper" amount is always the required higher of the two. If more cash is needed to create a proper amount in the emergency fund, then so be it. By the same token, if 10 percent of total invest-ments creates an excess based on the emergency needs, so be it also.

Stock Market (15-25%)

Regarding the 15-25% recommendation, remember that the Tax Favored category will also include investments in the stock market. If they were lumped all together, it would and should increase the generic allocation above the 15-25% range.

Another point regarding the 15-25% recommendation: a 15 percent allocation will not do the job of developing sufficient wealth. The only time a recommendation of 15 percent or less should be considered is when the client needs to bring his cash position to a safe level for emergency purposes or when the client has a very low risk tolerance. In the latter case, it should be a top priority to enlighten the client appropriately. Over time and with proper attention, the vast majority of hesitant clients can develop satisfactory levels of tolerance to the volatility of the stock market. However, if for whatever reason some clients cannot or will not increase their risk tolerance levels, do not push them. A reluctant client can destroy the plan which in turn will destroy the professional relationship. (See Chapter 2 for techniques to evaluate risk tolerance.)

Some clients will have few or no investments in the stock market outside of their qualified retirement plans, while others may have very high allocations in this stock market category. However, the closer a client can come to the 25 percent mark, tax-favored investments not counted, the better the client will be served by the plan. There will come a time, even for Baby Boomers, when they will have to begin withdrawing their retirement funds. Now is not too early to plan for preserving multiple options on the timing and use of totally taxable withdraws (qualified retirement plans) versus zero or only partial taxable withdrawals (non-qualified money in individual or mutual fund stock market holdings). This issue shall be explored further in Chapter 5 in the *Retirement Cash Flow Analysis* section. Suffice it to say that during the Baby Boomer clients' younger years, they should be encouraged to develop a stock market portfolio of 25 percent of total investments exclusive of those stocks in the tax-favored category.

Real Estate (20-25%)

Real estate has its ups and downs in the market, but it is not nearly as volatile as the stock market. Actually the stock market can have wide swings on a daily basis, but real estate does not.

As mentioned earlier, there is a school of thought that real estate for personal use should not be a component in an investment portfolio. Two statements to support this position are:

- One's home is not an income producing asset.

- One has to live someplace.

Regarding the first statement, it should be noted that a significant number of Baby Boomers are only able to buy their first home by buying a duplex or triplex or by renting out one or more rooms of a single-family dwelling. Regarding the second statement, buying is a major step up the wealth-accumulation ladder and renting is not. Often the equity in a house is the largest asset for many younger Baby Boomers, and it remains so for many years of their adult life. To ignore a personal home as an investment asset is improper.

There is another important reason for including personal-use real estate in the model portfolio. Giving it a slot on the asset allocation plan brings attention to the effect of real-estate ownership on the development of a proper balance in all aspects of the financial plan.

For example, a major consideration of first-time home buyers is how much of a residence can we afford, and what size mortgage should we have? These questions should be answered in the context of a total financial plan, not in isolation.

The size of the mortgage can be partially determined from the asset allocation page. Since the maximum recommended allocation for personal-use real estate is 25 percent, the home price minus 25 percent of total investments equals the amount of mortgage.

For example, suppose a client who has total investments of $60,000 is looking at a $100,000 house. $100,000 (price) minus $15,000 (25% of $60,000) equals $85,000 (mortgage).

This simple procedure might tell this client that $100,000 is more than he can afford to pay for a house at this time. The second step in this evaluation is to look at this client's Cash Management Statement (page 6 of the Financial Plan) to see if there is enough cash flow to maintain the mortgage payments.

It is recommended that a personal residence is an important first investment for young Baby Boomers. If planners use the general formula illustrated above, it will help prevent recommending an improper acquisition. Some who buy over their heads discover too late that they do not have enough resources to furnish the house or even maintain it properly.

A young Boomer lived in a city apartment with his parents. When he married, he and his wife moved into their own city apartment. Finally, circumstances were right, and they bought a house in the suburbs. One day at lunch, their financial planner asked how he and his wife liked their new home. "It's interesting," he said. "I learned for the first time that inanimate objects have needs." The planner looked puzzled. He continued, "Yes, when I get home at night, my wife tells me, 'Honey, the house needs this, the house needs that.' I'm glad you didn't let us overbuy."

Another point that can be made is that the first house does not necessarily have to be the last house. Many young Boomers can look forward to promotions or other increases in incomes. What with these increases and the new financial plan, a bigger house may be a possibility in the future when they have greater need for the additional room and/or a desire to upgrade the quality of personal residence.

A different situation arises for "older" Baby Boomers. When the children leave the nest, as they say, the old house which seemed just barely sufficient now seems sort of empty. This may be the time for them to consider selling and buying a smaller place. Not only will there be less maintenance, there will be more funds from the sale to supplement other asset categories. In this way, a so called non-income-producing asset (a house) has finally produced tangible income, even after all those years of it sheltering a loving family.

As Baby Boomers move into their 50s, they become very much more aware of where they stand with their desired wealth accumulation plan. It is at this time that they often find they have too much tied up in their personal-use real estate. This is when the planner might recommend that a mortgage or larger mortgage could possibly make more money available to put in *growing* investments while they still benefit in all future appreciation in their home.

When an asset category is included for personal-use real estate in a client's asset allocation plan, it not only provides recognition for this important asset, but also helps the client manage the allocation of resources to achieve the desired net worth and at the same time manage cash flow.

Precious Metals (0-5%)

For many years now, and perhaps for many years to come, this category has been and will be very low in importance. Historically, when a serious financial collapse occurs, precious metals become the only medium of exchange. Today we live in a world economy, and if there is to be a financial collapse, it will be virtually everywhere. Will there be a world-wide financial collapse any time in the foreseeable future? Definitely not! However, just in case, it might be prudent to own at least a small amount of precious metals, especially gold. One younger Baby Boomer client said when this point in the discussion was reached, "Oh, I see. It's like having an insurance policy in your investment program." The client was not at all off base.

When obtaining precious metals, the rule is to pay cash and take possession. There are some scams in this investment category, and more than once the story goes, "the vault was filled with wood ingots painted to look like gold." These real stories contain a valid warning about any dealer selected. A number of countries, including the United States, sell silver, gold, and platinum bullion coins at a slight premium over the current market price. This premium may be worth paying to have the guarantee of knowing one is buying the real thing.

Tax Favored (20-38%)

Until taxes are eliminated, prudent investors will properly attempt to pay as little as legally possible of their profits to the various taxing governments. The Supreme Court has ruled that people are legally required to pay taxes, but they are required to pay no more than what they owe. So, this should be the goal as an investor: stay legal, but pay only the required amount. Of course, this means that each person must be or must hire an expert who knows how to minimize taxes.

Since the maximum rate has been 50 percent or more in approximately two-thirds of the years since 1913, it makes sense for the prudent investor to seek some protection. Thus, the need for the tax-favored assets allocation category.

Many advisors simply combine tax-favored investments with those in other categories when ease of visualizing the big picture is the goal. However, having its own category in the initial financial plan places a proper emphasis on the importance of the category.

In 1986, after the top income tax bracket dropped to 28 percent, some planners advised clients with more than the recommended amount in the tax-favored category, and with an accompanying shortfall in another category, to stop making additions to the tax-favored category. In most cases this meant that, when possible, they stopped contributing to qualified retirement plans. This, of course, was fundamentally opposed by accountants.

It seems that many accountants have a bias toward always maximizing retirement plan contributions. In this case, the bias blinded them to an opportunity. Most of these accountants, when the total asset allocation picture was explained to them, agreed with the financial planners.

Many financial advisers felt that the very low maximum tax rate would not have a long life, but while it did exist, clients had a wonderful opportunity to improve the over-all balance of their asset allocation at minimum cost in taxes. Such opportunities have been rare, almost non-existent, since the inception of the income tax.

Warning! Reducing taxes is a hobby with some people and an obsession with others. If greed takes over in any area of investing, the client probably will suffer a significant loss. This is especially true in the tax-favored category. One must always keep in mind that what Congress giveth, Congress can taketh away. It is absolutely improper to subject too much of your wealth to the whims of the government. So, don't set the allocation in this category too high for clients or allow clients to increase a reasonable recommendation too much.

The investments in this category should be balanced as with the primary categories of cash, stock market, and real estate. Investments in IRAs, 401(k) plans, and 403(b) plans for almost all Baby Boomers should be in equity as opposed to fixed dollar vehicles. Because of the very long-term nature of these accumulations, an amount approaching 100 percent should be in equity. Only if there is a likely need for liquidity should money market or bond accounts be recommended. Keep in mind that it might be possible to obtain a loan from a 401(k) plan should there be a need for liquidity to meet an emergency.

Make sure clients are aware that, because these assets are not taxable until withdrawn, these funds probably will not be touched until age 59½ and more likely not withdrawn until age 70½. Even then, the withdrawal can be spread over the remainder of one's life, which could be another 30 years.

Collectibles (0-5%)

Over half of all clients have zero collectibles in their financial plans. This is true because of the extremely long holding period required for any possible profit. Also, such profits may not be significant and they are not guaranteed. The enjoyment of the beauty, or quality, or rarity of a collection is important, because significant appreciation could take 40, 50, 60 or more years.

If a client does want to collect rare coins, stamps, or works of art, recommend he always buy the highest quality he can afford and always deal with an expert in the field. It takes an expert in any area of collectibles to help select quality, and it takes the high integrity of such an individual to assist in buying at an appropriate price. Get such expert help, or don't start a collection as an investment.

Putting It All Together

It is important to keep all related numerical data similar in nature; that is, if one number in a column is expressed to the nearest tenth, then all numbers in that column should be expressed to the nearest tenth. Also, always use a "common size" financial statement approach.

It is rewarding to see a client readily understand what could have been an extremely complex subject. When both dollars and percentages are shown, the client can easily see the whole picture and how the parts are related to each other. It is not unusual to hear a client suddenly say, "Oh, I see. I have way too much of this, and not nearly enough of that."

EXAMPLE FOR A YOUNG BABY BOOMER

	Thousands	Percent	Generic Percent	Recommended Percent
Cash	$ 4.0	5%	10/20%	10%
Stock Market	25.9	31%	15/25%	25%
Real Estate	33.0	40%	20/25%	25%
Precious Metals	0.0	0%	0/5%	1%
Tax Favored	20.1	24%	20/38%	38%
Collectibles	0.0	0%	0/5%	1%
	$83.0	100%		100%

This presentation might prompt the client to say, "Oh, I see. I have only half enough cash, a little too much in the stock market, way too much tied up in my home, and not enough in tax favored." This is a typical and accurate statement that a client would make. However, without proper guidance from an advisor, the client might proceed improperly. For example, the advisor should say, "Yes, you should increase your cash reserves by $4,000 as soon as possible. This is a top priority. Any other immediate changes would not be advisable. This allocation picture is somewhat distorted because of the relatively small total amount of investments. This will change. Just be patient.

"What this asset allocation picture is telling us is the direction in which we should be headed. Keep what you have. Don't make any advance mortgage payments, don't add any more to your stock-market portfolio. Increase your 401(k), 403(b), IRA, if possible, and/or increase your premium in your variable universal life insurance policy or variable annuity or commercial real estate. First, however, develop more cash. The amount is the greater of the need for emergency funds, on page 9 of your financial plan, or 10 percent of your total investments, on page 10 of the plan."

EXAMPLE FOR A 50 YEAR OLD BABY BOOMER

	Thousands	Percent	Generic Percent	Recommended Percent
Cash	$ 37.5	6%	10/20%	10%
Stock Market	108.8	19%	15/25%	25%
Real Estate	95.2	16%	20/25%	25%
Precious Metals	5.0	1%	0/5%	1%
Tax Favored	330.0	57%	20/38%	38%
Collectibles	7.0	1%	0/5%	1%
	$583.5	100%		100%

Figure 4.9

INVESTMENT RECOMMENDATIONS

CASH — is 6 percent of total investments. This should be increased by $21,000 as soon as possible. This is top priority.

STOCK MARKET — is 19 percent of the total. This should be increased by $37,000 after you hold proper cash. Your present international mutual funds should be increased by $25,000. Consider XYZ Fund. Also, your small cap allocation is a little low. Discuss.

REAL ESTATE — is 16 percent of the total and should be increased. Consider developing additional cash for both advance payments and to pay off the entire balance. Discuss your interest in changing residence or the purchase of a secondary home.

PRECIOUS METALS — is 1 percent, and this is proper.

TAX FAVORED — is 57 percent of total investments and is improper. You should sell your municipal bonds. Also, temporarily stop all contributions to your 401(k) plan which are in excess of your employer matching amount. This will temporarily increase your income tax, but the benefit of a balanced investment portfolio is overriding. Discuss.

COLLECTIBLES — is 1 percent and is proper.

After the data on the investment portfolio page is discussed, the adviser should summarize the data and recommendations. An example is shown below.

Naturally each client has different goals, needs, desires, risk tolerance, and priorities, but this is the spice of life to a financial planning consultant.

Chapter 5

Developing the Other
Areas of a Financial Plan

The preceding chapter provided guidance on developing the three core areas of a financial plan (protection, liquidity, and investment) for presentation to Baby Boomer clients. This chapter provides guidance on developing a presentation of other important areas of a financial plan, including estate analysis, retirement planning, education funding analysis, becoming and remaining debt free, determining how much real estate can be afforded, and mortgage feasibility analysis.

ESTATE ANALYSIS

Notice that the topic of this section is *estate analysis*, not *estate planning*. A financial planner is qualified to do estate analysis, but unless the planner is also an attorney, he is not qualified to do estate planning. Estate analysis involves reviewing, calculating, and recommending in all areas of an estate, but it does not include the drafting of legal documents. Estate planning does involve the drafting of legal documents and, therefore, requires an attorney. When discussing this area of financial planning with a client, the planner should use the term *estate analysis* in conversation as well as in writing. Not only is this correct, but it also reminds the client that some recommendations may require an estate planner – a lawyer – to put the recommendations into effect.

Who Is the Owner Now?

When developing the list of a client's assets and liabilities during the fact-finding interview, the financial planner should always indicate ownership. Sometimes, ownership will be a trust if the client has received advice in the estate area. Sometimes, ownership will be joint ownership. In such cases, it is important to make sure that such registrations clearly indicate whether it is "with the right of survivorship" or "tenants in common." The former means that at the death of one of the joint owners, the property becomes solely owned by the surviving joint owner. The latter means that each party, or tenant, owns a specific amount of the whole and can pass this property interest to a beneficiary of his choice through a bequest or device in the will. The difference can be significant in many instances of estate analysis, and the financial planner should make sure clients whose documents contain such legal designations understand their meaning. So, the first thing to make perfectly clear is who owns what right now.

Death Distribution Planning

For a large majority of young Baby Boomers, the most important object in managing one's estate is to make sure that the surviving partner, domestic and/or business, can transfer assets easily to whomever the deceased chose and that there are enough assets to take care of the survivor's needs. Therefore, for most Baby Boomer clients, estate analysis leads to proper insurance planning and the establishment of wills, trusts, and durable power of attorney documents.

For those Baby Boomers who have acquired considerable wealth, it is important to make sure they know that sophisticated planning is the way to reduce taxation (federal estate and gift tax and, where applicable, state inheritance tax) upon the transfer of assets. If the estate involves large amounts of retirement-plan benefits, deferred annuities, U. S. Government EE and HH bonds, or any other asset that either does not have a stepped-up cost basis at the death of an owner or is not transferring directly to a spouse or a charity, then note the additional planning required in this area.

It would require large volumes of information to cover the whole area of estate analysis and, therefore, is beyond the scope of this book. Suffice it to say, clients will be well-served if the financial planner begins estate analysis with the clear identification of ownership and, especially in the case of young Baby Boomers, a complete review of proper insurance.

Federal Estate Taxation Calculations

Even the youngest of Baby Boomer clients should be exposed to what death taxation is all about. Where even modest wealth exists, the control of the taxation of this wealth is important and should be of great interest to these clients. The best way to communicate this information is with a simple one-page summary. (See Figure 5.1 for a sample form.)

Here is how to use the Estate Analysis form for clients Mary and Bob Sample. At the top of the form, complete a listing of the net assets (gross value minus debt) by type of asset and ownership. This information should be on the Net Worth Statement of the clients' financial plan.

Figure 5.1

(DATE)

MARY AND ROBERT SAMPLE

ESTATE ANALYSIS

1.) **ASSET**	**ROBERT**	**MARY**	**JOINT**	
PRIMARY RESIDENCE	$	$	$	
SECONDARY RESIDENCE				
CASH ACCOUNTS				
STOCK MARKET				
FIXED ANNUITY				
VARIABLE ANNUITY				
LIMITED PARTNERSHIPS				
IRA				
PRECIOUS METALS				
COLLECTIBLES				
PERSONAL PROPERTY				
LIFE INSURANCE				
TOTAL	$_____0	$_____0	$_____0	$_____0

2.) There would be zero death taxes at either death (one death)

3.) The following taxation would occur when both of you have died:

ESTATE TAXATION
   Assumes First to Die is:

	PRESENT	**PROPOSED**	**2009**
GROSS ESTATE	$	$	$
EXPENSES			
TAXABLE ESTATE	$_____	$_____	$_____
GROSS TAX	$	$	$
FEDERAL CREDIT	(780,800)	(780,800)	(1,455,800)
TOTAL TAX	$_____	$_____	$_____

Plus Income Tax on All Retirement Plans

RECOMMENDATIONS

At this point it is important for the clients to understand that, if all assets transfer to a surviving spouse, then there will be zero death taxes to pay at the first death. However, at the death of both spouses, there will be death tax obligations that must be considered.

First, show tax obligations assuming a deceased spouse left everything to the surviving spouse. Show this under Present Plan. Then show the full unified credit used to bypass the estate of the surviving spouse under Proposed Plan.

Use the bottom of the page for considerations and/or recommendations. It is almost always wise to recommend that your clients see their estate-planning attorney to discuss wills, trusts, and durable powers of attorney, both medical and financial. Also, request permission to send their attorney a complete copy of their financial plan. Understand that this creates business for the attorney – and you have already done some of the leg work and presented the information in a well-organized format. Few, if any, attorneys will resent the recommendation and accompanying analysis. In fact, this might encourage referrals from the attorney.

This one-page estate analysis is usually sufficient even for those Baby Boomers who have accumulated considerable wealth, and it puts the subject on the table for future consideration with those who have small estates at present.

Federal Estate Taxation is going through significant changes as it has in the past. Therefore, the importance of estate calculation continues to change. However, the importance of estate planning to accomplish an owner's desires for distributions of assets with or without tax considerations may be paramount.

Legal Documents

As has been stated already, unless the financial planner is an attorney, he should not draft legal documents. However, the financial planner has an obligation to review the client's legal documents. For many clients, most legal documents might just as well be written in the language of an alien nation. In fact the language used is a special language that is understood, for the most part, only by attorneys and judges, and its use is required in legal documents to avoid any misunderstandings among any legal minds who review such documents. The role of the financial planner is to help the client understand what is in a document and to make sure the document says what the client wants it to say.

In Figure 5.2 there are forms that can be used to outline a will and a trust. This kind of summary is very useful when the financial planner discusses the contents of the will or trust with the client. These forms should be kept on file for future reference and periodic review.

Figure 5.2

WILL

Date _____

Name:
Address:

Revoke Previous Wills: Yes/No

Execution Date:
Codicil Dates: Pay Debts: Yes/No

	Primary	Contingent

Personal Property:

Special Bequests:

Organ Donation:

Cremation:

Remainder:

Personal Representative/Executor:

Guardians/conservators of Children:

Common Disaster Sequence:

Special Clauses:

Generation Skipping Protective Language:

Drafting Attorney Name:

Figure 5.2 (cont'd)

TRUST

Date _____

Name Of Trust	Type:	Testamentary
Execution Date:		Revocable
Amendment Dates:		
		Irrevocable

Grantor: Address:

Current Trustee:

Successor Trustee:	Durable Power Of Attorney	Yes/No
	Living Will	Yes/No
Trustee Removal Power?	Assignment	Yes/No
	Affidavit	Yes/No
	Patient Advocate Designation	Yes/No

Marital Trust:	Yes/No
Beneficiary:	
Key Terms:	
Simultaneous Death Clause:	Yes/No
Six Month Equalization Clause:	Yes/No

Residuary Trust:	Yes/No
Beneficiary:	
Key Terms:	
Premium Payments To	
Irrevocable Trust:	

Beneficiary At Death
   Of Grantor And Spouse:

Special Gifts:

Other Distribution Requirements
   And Times:

Additional Key Terms:

Generation Skipping Provisions:	Yes/No

Who Is Beneficiary If All Prior
   Are Deceased:

Special Considerations:

Special Clauses:	Yes/No
Qualified Domestic Trust:	Yes/No
"S" Corporation Provisions:	Yes/No

Funding Complete:	Yes/No

Drafting Attorney Name:

The first primary function of a financial planner is to learn the desires of the client; that is, who gets what, when, under what circumstances, and so forth. Then, the financial planner should review the legal documents to make sure that the documents reflect the client's desires. Where there seems to be a difference, this should be discussed with the client to see if it is a misunderstanding on the part of the financial planner or a misunderstanding on the part of the client's attorney. In the latter case, or where the client has changed his mind since the document was executed, the financial planner should encourage the client to return to the attorney for appropriate changes.

Young Baby Boomers are great put-off artists, particularly when it comes to having wills drawn up. They are too busy making a living and trying to live on what they make. So, the greatest service a financial planner might render these people is to keep the discussion of wills on the table until they take care of this obligation.

Some Final Comments

The most important contribution a financial planner can render in the estate-analysis area is to get the clients to take whatever action is needed. There are many techniques to use to persuade the clients to take such action. Suppose, for example, a client is reluctant to pay attorney fees for any service. Show this client how revocable trusts can save tens if not hundreds of thousands of dollars in taxes with the proper use of the unified credit. Also show how an irrevocable trust can be the owner of life insurance and keep it out of the taxable estate entirely. These examples and others are familiar to most financial planners, but they are often new information to the client, and when the client sees the tax savings, attorney fees may look like a bargain.

The managing of estates is a very interesting specialty, and a financial planner who wanted to be a specialist in this area could render a needed service and produce a lucrative income as well.

RETIREMENT PLANNING

Everybody, not just the Baby Boomer, hopes to have a comfortable retirement. Baby Boomers, however, are more focused on the reality of what is required because they are rapidly approaching the point of retirement. The older the Boomer, the greater the interest and willingness to dedicate a substantial amount of resources to achieve this goal.

Retirement Plans Asset Allocation

The asset allocation area of a financial plan is generally broken into two parts: (1) retirement plans over which the client has little or no control, such as pension plans with commingled assets provided by the company where the client is employed, and (2) all other allocation of retirement assets. It is the latter category where the client needs special assistance, and it is this category where the financial planner can provide an important professional service.

In some cases there may only be a few thousand dollars in one or more IRAs. Then little attention is required in the area of retirement asset allocation, and most of the time can be spent helping clients accumulate more wealth. However, as Baby Boomers age and change jobs, funds in retirement plans from prior employers may become available. A client had little or no control over these funds, but now must make important financial decisions about how these funds can be rolled over into a self-directed IRA. A qualified financial planner can help.

In much the same way as the financial planner presents a proposal for the allocation of all assets, he should develop a separate proposal for the allocation of retirement funds. This separation enables the financial planner to demonstrate to the client how to take advantage of appropriate concepts of investing. For example, where possible, the client can utilize annuities outside the retirements plans to take advantage of tax deferral. Investments that have higher turnover can be placed in retirement plans to avoid the commensurate taxation if kept in non-retirement plans.

This part of the financial plan should be presented very simply on a single page. Show an itemized list of investments in categories, i.e. cash, bonds, mortgages, stock market, and real estate. Looked at this way, the client can easily recognize when the funds are out of kilter with the agreed-upon allocations. For example, a client might respond to the presentation shown below by saying, "I can see I have too much in cash and nothing in real estate." Then, the client and the financial planner, working together, can develop a more satisfactory proposal.

	Present		Proposed	
Cash	$ 70.6	19%	$ 2.9	1%
Bonds	19.9	5%	19.0	5%
Mortgages	0.0	0%	0.0	0%
Stock Market	282.3	76%	300.0	81%
Real Estate	0.0	0%	50.0	13%
	$372.8	100%	$372.8	100%

This is an excellent opportunity to give specific investment advice right on the page that includes all of the detailed information. Again, this makes it easier for the client to understand and to take action. (See illustration in Figure 5.3.)

Projecting Retirement Income Needs

It is interesting to note how few clients give any thought to how much money they will need when they retire. At best, they save as much as they think they can and then hope it will be enough. It is the responsibility of the financial planner to point out how much more wise it is to know what may be down the road in time to make plans for any contingency. There are enough unpleasant surprises in life without deliberately creating more.

Figure 5.3

		(DATE)
MARY AND ROBERT SAMPLE		

RETIREMENT PLAN ASSET ALLOCATION

CASH	$ _____	
		$ 0.0
BONDS	$ _____	
		$ 0.0
STOCK MARKET	$ _____	
		$ 0.0
REAL ESTATE	$ _____	
		$ 0.0
		$ 0.0

	PRESENT		PROPOSED	
CASH	$ 0.0	0%	$ 0.0	0%
BONDS	0.0	0	0.0	0
STOCK MARKET	0.0	0	0.0	0
REAL ESTATE	0.0	0	0.0	0
TOTAL	$ 0.0	0%	$ 0.0	0%

RECOMMENDATIONS

If retirement is more than five years down the road, as it is for most Baby Boomers, then the answer to how much will be needed is not much more than an educated guess. The world is changing so rapidly that it is almost impossible to factor in all the many variables. For example, everything has its cost, but technology causes a reduction in the price of some items so rapidly that there is no way to know future costs. By the same token, technology will result in new items on the market that all of us will think we must have. Having said all of this about how difficult it is to accurately project future costs, the financial planner can render an important service in projecting retirement cash flow based on the use of a replacement-ratio method. The reason these calculations should be made at all is that the amount needed for retirement, in all probability, will be much more than a young or old Baby Boomer would have imagined. Knowing this now, when something can be done about it, may be the greatest gift the financial planner can give a client.

The first step is for the clients to make some estimate of what amount of income they will need in retirement. This estimate should be a percent of their current income. Studies indicate that this estimate will range from 68 percent up to 90 percent of pre-retirement income. In most cases, the lower the income level prior to retirement, the greater the replacement percentage will be.

The replacement ratio method uses a percentage of net pre-retirement income as the amount required to continue a pre-retirement standard of living. For most clients with incomes of $60,000 or more, the most commonly used percentage is around 75 percent. So, here is an example of the calculations for a client earning $100,000 per year who chooses a replacement ratio of 75 percent:

Calculation Example

Gross pre-retirement income	$100,000
Income and Social Security taxes	- 25,000
Long-term savings	- 10,000
Net pre-retirement income	$ 65,000
Replacement ratio	x 0.75
Net retirement income	$ 48,750
Income tax	+ 5,750
Gross retirement income	$ 54,500

Note that the calculation includes the elimination of Social Security taxes and long-term savings. It also reduces the tax based on a larger pre-retirement income to the tax based on the smaller amount needed in retirement. However, as you know, everyone should keep in mind that nothing is more uncertain than tax rates.

All living expenses are such a personal matter that this example should only be used to help make estimates. The financial planner should monitor the client's actual expenses after the first year of retirement and use these figures for future projections, doing this each year thereafter. Many retirees spend more in their first year of retirement than they do in the following years, because it's an adjustment year from the old lifestyle to the new lifestyle. Thus, the financial planner should monitor expenses annually.

The client in the example may assume that $54,500 is not a difficult goal to achieve. This is where the financial planner begins to educate this client. The $54,500 must be increased by an estimated inflation rate for each year between now and the year of retirement. For purposes of illustration, assume an annual inflation rate of 3%.

> **Assumptions**
> Future inflation rate: 4%
> Years to retirement: 10 years
> $54,500 @ 4% for 10 years = $80,673

Now the goal is $80,673. Recognize that this is not good news to the client. So, point out that, over the next 10 years, the client's annual income should also be increasing. However, before the client begins to accept the figure of $80,673 as the annual amount required in retirement to maintain the desired standard of living, another dose of reality must be introduced. The $73,243 must be adjusted annually for inflation or deflation. The assumption of a 3 percent rate of inflation probably is, based on history, a reasonable rate to assume. If the client retires at age 65 with the target annual income of $80,673, then the above table shows how fast-moving this target becomes.

The reaction of some clients may be, "I'm not going to live that long, anyway. My dad retired when he was 68 and died when he was 74." Now here is another challenge for the financial planner: convincing clients that they are going to live longer than they think they are.

The subject of life expectancy could occupy an entire chapter if not a whole book. However, for the purposes at hand, consider the following.

- Baby Boomers will live longer than they anticipate.

- Baby Boomers want their money to last as long as they do.

- Baby Boomers do not want to reduce their standard of living at any time.

In order to address the last two facts, financial plans will have to accommodate the first fact. There is a popular weather forecaster, Willard Scott, on a network morn-

Figure 5.4

AGE	REQUIRED INCOME	AGE	REQUIRED INCOME
65	$73,243	83	$124,691
66	75,440	84	128,432
67	77,703	85	132,285
68	80,035	86	136,254
69	82,436	87	140,341
70	84,909	88	144,551
71	87,456	89	148,888
72	90,080	90	153,355
73	92,782	91	157,955
74	95,566	92	162,694
75	98,432	93	167,575
76	101,385	94	172,602
77	104,427	95	177,780
78	107,560	96	183,113
79	110,787	97	188,607
80	114,110	98	194,265
81	117,534	99	200,093
82	121,060	100	206,096

ing show who, when he gives the weather forecast, also wishes a happy birthday to someone who is celebrating a 100th birthday. While Scott retired from this show, he still substitutes from time to time, and when he does the weather, he still announces a 100th birthday. The network receives 500 requests a week for a relative to be so recognized. Imagine how many people do not bother to write to Willard. Add the number of people who don't watch the show to the 500 who write, and you get a glimmer of how many people each week are celebrating a 100th birthday. And this is today, not 5, 10, or 15 years from today. Most Baby Boomers really will live longer than they think they will.

Perhaps some clients are impressed with statistics. As of today, 8 percent of those individuals who are 65 years old will live to be 100 years old. The probability that at least one of a 65-year-old couple will live to be 100 is 16 percent. Now, if these statistics do not impress clients, then they should be told that when they and their spouse reach 65, the odds are fifty-fifty that one of them will live to be 92 years old. These statistics are current. Who knows what medical science will discover tomorrow to increase the probabilities.

Even if it is difficult to convince clients that they will live longer than they think they will, their financial plan should reflect the assumption that they will live a very long time. One hundred would not be out of the question.

Retirement Cash Flow Analysis

The following information is needed to develop a retirement cash-flow analysis for clients.

1. Year of birth for each client.

2. Year of retirement.

3. Estimated inflation rate.

4. After-tax rate of return on investments.

5. Estimated cost of living adjustments for Social Security and pension.

6. Estimated desired income in first year of retirement.

7. Annual residence mortgage payments and maturity date.

8. Social Security first year benefit for each client.

9. Pension first year benefit for each client.

10. Capital available for investing, excluding residence, personal property, and other assets that would not be potentially available to produce cash flow in retirement.

With the above information, the financial planner can develop a spread sheet to calculate an estimate of how long present assets, including future growth, will last and how much additional wealth needs to be accumulated. Also, with a few adjustments, other effects can be calculated, such as cash flow after the death of one of a married couple. There is software available to perform these calculations if the financial planner chooses not to develop the spreadsheet himself. (See Figure 5.5 for an example analysis for Mary and Bob Sample, each of whom was born in 1953.)

Figure 5.5

(DATE)

MARY AND ROBERT SAMPLE

RETIREMENT CASH FLOW ANALYSIS

ASSUMPTIONS

1. YEAR OF RETIREMENT   2020
2. YEAR BORN: *RETIREE 1*   *ROBERT*   1953
2A.   *RETIREE 2*   *MARY*   1953

3. ANNUAL INFLATION
   RATE FOR YEARS   *1-10*   3.5%   *11-20*   4.0%   *THEREAFTER*   4.0%
4. SOCIAL SECURITY INFLATION RATE   3.0%
5. AFTER-TAX RATE OF RETURN ON INVESTMENTS   8.0%
6. PENSION
   INFLATION AJD: *OPT 1 = COMPOUNDED INFL RATE*   0.0% *ROBERT*   0.0% *MARY*
6A.   *OPT 2 = FLAT FIXED DOLLAR AMT* $0 *ROBERT* $0 *MARY*

		1998 DOLLARS	RETIREMENT DOLLARS
7.	ANNUAL DESIRED INCOME (EXCLUDING MORTGAGE)	$55,000	$105,386
8.	ANNUAL MORTGAGE PMT (PRIN & INT ONLY) *ENDING* 0		0
9.	SOCIAL SECURITY *ROBERT* *STARTING* 2020		$19,000
9A.	*MARY* *STARTING* 2020		$9,500

10. CAPITAL AVAILABLE FOR INVESTING $324,000 $1,761,439
11. PENSION
    BENEFITS   *ROBERT*   *STARTING*   0 $0
11A.   *MARY*   *STARTING*   0 $0
12. ADDITIONAL ANNUAL INVESTMENTS NEEDED $0 $0

YEAR	AGE 1	AGE 2	REQUIRED INCOME	MORTGAGE PAYMENT	SOCIAL SECURITY	OTHER INC (EXPENSES)	PENSION ROBERT	PENSION MARY	AMT NEEDED FROM CAPITAL	REMAINING CAPITAL	SHORTFALL
2020	67	67	105,386	0	28,500	0	0	0	76,886	1,822,393	0
2021	68	68	109,074	0	29,355	0	0	0	79,719	1,885,277	0
2022	69	69	112,892	0	30,236	0	0	0	82,656	1,950,136	0
2023	70	70	116,843	0	31,143	0	0	0	85,700	2,017,019	0
2024	71	71	120,933	0	32,077	0	0	0	88,855	2,085,971	0
2025	72	72	125,165	0	33,039	0	0	0	92,126	2,157,038	0
2026	73	73	129,546	0	34,030	0	0	0	95,515	2,230,265	0
2027	74	74	134,080	0	35,051	0	0	0	99,029	2,305,696	0
2028	75	75	138,773	0	36,103	0	0	0	102,670	2,383,375	0
2029	76	76	143,630	0	37,186	0	0	0	106,444	2,463,343	0
2030	77	77	148,657	0	38,302	0	0	0	110,355	2,545,641	0
2031	78	78	154,603	0	39,451	0	0	0	115,153	2,629,534	0
2032	79	79	160,787	0	40,634	0	0	0	120,153	2,714,937	0
2033	80	80	167,219	0	41,853	0	0	0	125,366	2,801,752	0
2034	81	81	173,908	0	43,109	0	0	0	130,799	2,889,862	0
2035	82	82	180,864	0	44,402	0	0	0	136,462	2,979,130	0
2036	83	83	188,098	0	45,734	0	0	0	142,364	3,069,402	0
2037	84	84	195,622	0	47,106	0	0	0	148,516	3,160,497	0
2038	85	85	203,447	0	48,519	0	0	0	154,928	3,252,212	0
2039	86	86	211,585	0	49,975	0	0	0	161,610	3,344,314	0
2040	87	87	220,049	0	51,474	0	0	0	168,574	3,436,542	0

Figure 5.5 (cont'd)

(DATE)

MARY AND ROBERT SAMPLE

RETIREMENT CASH FLOW ANALYSIS (cont'd)

YEAR	AGE 1	AGE 2	REQUIRED INCOME	MORTGAGE PAYMENT	SOCIAL SECURITY	OTHER INC (EXPENSES)	PENSION ROBERT	PENSION MARY	AMT NEEDED FROM CAPITAL	REMAINING CAPITAL	SHORTFALL
2041	88	88	228,850	0	53,018	0	0	0	175,832	3,528,600	0
2042	89	89	238,005	0	54,609	0	0	0	183,396	3,620,157	0
2043	90	90	247,525	0	56,247	0	0	0	191,277	3,710,840	0
2044	91	91	257,426	0	57,935	0	0	0	199,491	3,800,237	0
2045	92	92	267,723	0	59,673	0	0	0	208,050	3,887,884	0
2046	93	93	278,432	0	61,463	0	0	0	216,969	3,973,267	0
2047	94	94	289,569	0	63,307	0	0	0	226,262	4,055,816	0
2048	95	95	301,152	0	65,206	0	0	0	235,946	4,134,898	0
2049	96	96	313,198	0	67,162	0	0	0	246,036	4,209,812	0
2050	97	97	325,726	0	69,177	0	0	0	256,549	4,279,787	0
2051	98	98	338,755	0	71,252	0	0	0	267,502	4,343,967	0
2052	99	99	352,305	0	73,390	0	0	0	278,915	4,401,413	0
2053	100	100	366,397	0	75,592	0	0	0	290,805	4,451,088	0

This analysis is based on the accuracy and consistency of the data and assumptions you have provided in items 1 through 11 and is not guaranteed. The figures shown are valid only as long as the data and assumptions remain unchanged. To maintain accuracy of this analysis, periodic updating is necessary to reflect changes as they occur.

EDUCATION FUNDING ANALYSIS

There is a continuing flow of research that illustrates the value of higher education, as the graph below illustrates.

So the message is Learn More, Earn More, Have More. But first comes the Pay More part.

Amount of Money Needed

Baby Boomers have caused or are simply part of a new phenomenon: the postponement of marriage and childbirth to older ages. The unintended consequence is the placement of college expenses for the children closer to retirement for the parents. The bunching of these requirements for accumulated money is further exacerbated when there is a need for the parents to assist the grandparents in their retirement. Young Baby Boomers should think through the timing of all this cash flow and, if possible, start early in accumulating wealth.

There is estimated to be $10 to $12 trillion that Baby Boomers may inherit. This might help some. There also is a propensity for grandparents to give to their grandchildren. If more of these gifts are in the form of money and start when the grandchildren are precious little babies, then this also might help some.

If the parents of adult clients are comfortably situated, then the financial planner might provide illustrations of how much one or more gifts could help in funding a grandchild's college education. Some assumptions are necessary for these projections. It is possible to show how many of these gifts will be necessary to sponsor four years of college with these assumptions: (1) an after-tax growth rate of 7 percent for investments, (2) a first year annual cost of $18,000 for college, and (3) an education inflation rate of 6 percent. (The education rate is greater than the general rate of inflation.) At this rate, a child born in 1998 will need $226,595 to pay for 4 years of college. A presentation can show what gifts will be needed.

Another presentation can show what would be required if the grandparents choose or are able to make annual gifts over a long period of time. Making the same assumptions as were made for the first presentation, it would take annual gifts of $4,937 to pay for the grandchild's education.

Investment Vehicles

Where the college education funds are invested is determined in part by time horizon and risk tolerance. It is the same as for any other wealth-accumulation evaluation. The closer one is to the time of need, the more conservative the investment vehicle should be. The same conservatism applies when lower risk-tolerance levels are involved. A proper approach would stay very close to the following recommendation, assuming adequate risk tolerance.

When Needed	Type of Investment
Within 2 years	Highly liquid without principal fluctuations
2 to 5 years	60% equity and 40% fixed dollar
Over 5 years	100% equity

Ownership

The answer to who should own the investments for the higher education of one's children or grandchildren is based on several criteria. As with most financial decisions, taxation should be considered. Taxation should not be the only criteria, but where favorable tax legislation doesn't have too many negative features, it should be part of the equation.

The Uniform Gifts to Minors Act (UGMA), or in some states the Uniform Transfers to Minors Act (UTMA), provides some tax savings.

Figure 5.6

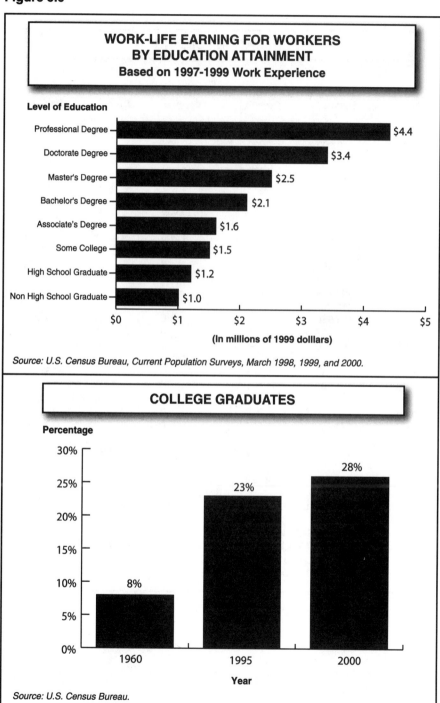

**WORK-LIFE EARNING FOR WORKERS
BY EDUCATION ATTAINMENT**
Based on 1997-1999 Work Experience

Level of Education

Professional Degree	$4.4
Doctorate Degree	$3.4
Master's Degree	$2.5
Bachelor's Degree	$2.1
Associate's Degree	$1.6
Some College	$1.5
High School Graduate	$1.2
Non High School Graduate	$1.0

(In millions of 1999 dollars)

Source: U.S. Census Bureau, Current Population Surveys, March 1998, 1999, and 2000.

COLLEGE GRADUATES

Percentage

Year	
1960	8%
1995	23%
2000	28%

Year

Source: U.S. Census Bureau.

Figure 5.7

EDUCATION FUNDING

Year	Starting Balance	Net Growth	Annual Deposit	With-Drawal	Fund(s) Ending Balance
2007	$ 0	$ 0	$10,000	$ 0	$ 10,000
2008	10,000	700	10,000	0	20,700
2009	20,700	1,449	10,000	0	32,149
2010	32,149	2,250	10,000	0	44,399
2011	44,399	3,108	10,000	0	57,507
2012	57,507	4,026	10,000	0	71,533
2013	71,533	5,007	10,000	0	86,540
2014	86,540	6,058	1,200	0	93,798
2015	93,798	6,566	0	0	100,364
2016	100,364	7,025	0	0	107,389
2017	107,389	7,517	0	0	114,907
2018	114,907	8,043	0	0	122,950
2019	122,950	8,607	0	0	131,557
2020	131,557	9,209	0	0	140,766
2021	140,766	9,854	0	0	150,619
2022	150,619	10,543	0	0	161,162
2023	161,162	11,281	0	0	172,444
2024	172,444	12,071	0	0	184,515
2025	184,515	12,916	0	25,689	171,742
2026	171,742	12,022	0	52,919	130,844
2027	130,844	9,159	0	56,095	83,909
2028	83,909	5,874	0	59,460	30,322
2029	30,322	2,123	0	32,432	13
TOTAL			**$71,200**	**$226,595**	

ASSUMPTIONS

2007 ANNUAL COST	$18,000
EDUCATION INFLATION RATE	6.00%
AFTER-TAX GROWTH RATE IS	7.00%

Figure 5.8

EDUCATION FUNDING

Year	Starting Balance	Net Growth	Annual Deposit	With-Drawal	Fund(s) Ending Balance
2007	$ 0	$ 0	$ 4,937	$ 0	$ 4,937
2008	4,937	346	4,937	0	10,220
2009	10,220	715	4,937	0	15,872
2010	15,872	1,111	4,937	0	21,920
2011	21,920	1,534	4,937	0	28,391
2012	28,391	1,987	4,937	0	35,316
2013	35,316	2,472	4,937	0	42,725
2014	42,725	2,991	4,937	0	50,653
2015	50,563	3,546	4,937	0	59,135
2016	59,135	4,139	4,937	0	68,212
2017	68,212	4,775	4,937	0	77,924
2018	77,924	5,455	4,937	0	88,315
2019	88,315	6,182	4,937	0	99,434
2020	99,434	6,960	4,937	0	111,332
2021	111,332	7,793	4,937	0	124,062
2022	124,062	8,684	4,937	0	137,683
2023	137,683	9,638	4,937	0	152,258
2024	152,258	10,658	4,937	0	167,853
2025	167,853	11,750	4,937	25,689	158,851
2026	158,851	11,120	4,937	52,919	121,988
2027	121,988	8,539	4,937	56,095	79,370
2028	79,370	5,556	4,937	59,460	30,402
2029	30,402	2,128	0	32,432	98
TOTAL			**$108,614**	**$226,595**	

ASSUMPTIONS

2007 ANNUAL COST	$18,000
EDUCATION INFLATION RATE	6.00%
AFTER-TAX GROWTH RATE IS	7.00%

A special trust, 2503(c) can be set up as the owner and provide a little more control. However, taxation can be a strong deterrent to this option.

Additional Sources

- Coverdell Education Savings Account
- Hope Credit
- Lifetime Learning Credit
- 529 Plans

Source	Address
College Board Online	www.collegeboard.org
Student Services	www.studentservices.com

MISCELLANEOUS

There are two more areas in which some clients will need professional help. Some will need help in getting and staying out of debt, and some will need advice about buying a home.

Helping Clients to Become Debt Free

The Baby Boomers have been described in a lot of different ways, but one of the best descriptions is *big spenders*. Unfortunately, too many Baby Boomers have spent a great deal more than their income and have become *big debtors*. It will be very unusual if a financial planner does not run into one of these big debtors among his Baby Boomer clients and should be prepared to provide the help they seek.

Easy credit and lack of proper and adequate education about how to handle money have created a debt millstone around the necks of many young people, and unless they take positive steps to change this, they never will achieve financial freedom. Many think that receiving a bail-out from their parents or winning the lottery would be ideal solutions, but they are wrong. People become debtors by spending more than their income, and it has been said, "If you keep doing what you've been doing, then you're going to get more of what you got." So, even if they receive a bail-out or win the lottery, most debtors will spend themselves right back into debt. They just cannot break their spending habits, and until debtors change their spending habits, they will continue to be debtors. If one or more clients fit this description, then the financial planner must help them break their bad habits.

The best cure for eliminating debt and staying debt free was described many years ago by George Clason in his book *The Richest Man in Babylon*. This book continues to be popular to this day and is still in print. Clason's recipe for eliminating debt is this: for every take-home dollar you earn (net income after taxes), you save 10¢, pay down current debt with 20¢, and pay all living expenses with the remaining 70¢. No new charges can be incurred unless they are paid out of the 70¢ and are paid monthly in full. Even those debtors who seem to be hopelessly in debt will become debt free if they apply this formula. It may take a year or more, but it can be done.

The formula is simple. It even sounds easy to follow until you realize that the people who must live on 70¢ of each net dollar earned have been habitually living on 110¢ or 120¢ per net dollar earned. Some of these people may not succeed the first time they try the formula, but they must keep trying again and again until they succeed. For those who have the resolve, the formula works.

One way to help clients who are in debt is to not fall for any clever ploys they may try. For example, many will propose that their investments be set up so that they can take all the profits, dividends, interest, etc., and apply them to reduce their debt. Clients who suggest this may be convinced that they must eliminate the debt, but they are not really resolved to do what it takes to become debt free. They are not yet ready to reduce their current and excessive standard of living. Do not let them get away with this ploy. Demonstrate to them the fallacies in their thinking.

First, wealth accumulation comes extensively from the compounding of profits, not from allowing the profits to be spent, even for reducing debt.

Second, most Baby Boomers who are in debt have accumulated very little that produces profits.

Third, even if clients managed somehow to accumulate some wealth, their plans simply will not work. Either one or both of these typical examples should be sufficient to convince them of the truth of this statement.

Example 1: Suppose the clients have $10,000 invested in growth mutual funds with a return (profits) of 12 percent. This would be $1,200 before taxes. Suppose they also have a credit-card debt of $7,000, which is what the average credit-card balance is in the United States today, and the annual interest rate is 16.9 percent, which is a typical rate. These clients would be paying $1,183 in interest from $1,200 in profits, leaving $17 a year to pay off the $7,000 balance plus taxes on the profits. Even if the clients had amassed $10,000 to invest, and they know of an investment that guarantees a 12 percent return, this plan only puts them further into debt.

Example 2: Suppose the clients have $20,000 invested in growth mutual funds with a return (profits) of 15 percent. This would be $3,000 before taxes. Suppose they also have a credit-card debt of $40,000, which is not all that unusual, and the annual interest rate is 12 percent. This is $4,800 in interest. Now, 15 percent profit is a high rate of return, and 12 percent is a low rate of interest in today's credit-card market. Even so, it doesn't take a high level of math ability to see that $3,000 income with $4,800 outflow is a recipe for disaster.

The best thing the financial planner can do for these clients is to gently but firmly tell them the facts of finance and encourage them to follow the 10-20-70 formula for becoming debt free.

Show clients the future. If they adopt and keep to the 10-20-70 formula, they will become consumer debt-free (all debt except mortgage), and they will have learned to live on less than they earn. They also will have developed an emergency fund with the 10¢ allocation to savings, and they will be able to spend the extra 20¢ of each take-home dollar earned on an increased standard of living.

What happens to many clients when they get to this point, especially if they are among the older Baby Boomers, is that they stay on their adopted standard of living based on the 70¢ figure and increase their wealth-accumulation rate from 10¢ to 30¢. More often, they will make a compromise, such as increasing their standard-of-living rate to 80¢ and their wealth-accumulation rate to 20¢. In any case, few if any of them return to their old self-destructive, in-debt days.

These clients, once in debt and now debt free, can have the same standard of living as before taking the cure, but without the debt, and they now can seriously begin the wealth accumulation that will make their future brighter. It's a great feeling to look down on past problems rather than looking up that non-ending hill of debt. Debt-free clients are happy clients, and they will be most grateful to the financial planner who helped by prescribing the formula for their cure, and who helped by being patient and encouraging them as they stumbled a few times before finally succeeding. You will reap the rewards of a job well done.

Determining How Much Personal Real Estate One Can Afford

The purchase of real estate for personal use often is the one investment most desired by Baby Boomer families. Almost all married Baby Boomers dream of owning their own homes someday. However, few Baby Boomers know whether they can afford to buy a home, and if they can afford it, they have no idea how much they can afford. This is another area where the financial advisor can provide much needed professional help.

To some extent, the purchase price of a home that the client can afford is a personal matter. One client may be willing to sacrifice some non-necessities in order to buy a desirable home. Another client may rather sacrifice in the size or amenities of a home rather than give up even a few other items. This makes it difficult to develop standardized formulas to predict how much house a client can afford.

Another factor that influences how much house a client can afford is the geographic area of the country. For example, houses in the New York City area and in many areas of California can be much more expensive than the same type houses in the Carolinas or the Dakotas. The old rule of thumb that the price of one's residence should be approximately twice the gross family income still makes sense for most parts of the United States. However, in certain areas, three or even four times the gross family income may be a necessary allocation to obtain a reasonable comfort level in a residence.

It is important to make sure clients understand that their income must maintain their total standard of living. If they spend more on a home, then obviously they have less to spend for other things. This may seem elementary, but not all clients will have thought this through. Those that haven't need to be reminded, "Live within your income. Allocate it as you will, but either stay within your present income or wait until you can increase your income."

It is not unusual for sales representatives in any field to encourage a young family to spend more than they can currently afford because they are young and will earn much more in the future than they are earning now. If you come from sales, you might have given the same advice to customers. However, you are a financial advisor now, and such advice may be misplaced with many of your clients. A financial advisor should assist clients to manage their financial affairs properly, which means they should base their decisions on their present circumstances, not on something that may or may not happen in the future. Of course, when clients are capable of improving their position, they should be encouraged to do so, but such encouragement must be based on current financial circumstances.

Preparing a Mortgage Feasibility Study

Although it is true that the personal nature of home ownership can make the development of a standardized analysis virtually impossible, it is possible to determine with considerable objectivity the proper amount of a mortgage for the client.

Quite a few Baby Boomers make decisions to purchase major items based on whether they can afford to make the monthly payments. No client should be allowed to think that, when buying a home, the mortgage size is solely determined by the amount of monthly payment that is affordable. Considerations that must be addressed include interest rates, number of years, the proper amount of down payment, and the ability to meet the monthly payment.

A very important consideration, often overlooked by many, is how the down payment (the amount of the client's wealth tied up in personal-use real estate) is related to the remainder of the client's wealth. To determine the proper amount of down payment, determine what is 25 percent of the client's total investments. (Total investments are discussed in Chapter 4.) In other words, total investments times 0.25 equals the target amount of a well-balanced investment portfolio to be invested in personal-use real estate. This product is not a magic number. It is simply a target amount. Young Baby Boomers, for example, can have a much higher percentage – even 90 percent – because it might be the only way to get started in home owner-ship. Nevertheless, it is better to have a good understanding of what the target is and what the target means when deviating from the rule.

What is proper, best, or desirous when determining the amount of the down payment has no relevance if the client cannot afford the monthly payments. The proper monthly payment is determined as shown below. These numbers represent the range of monthly payments that are considered "affordable."

Maximum:	Gross Annual Family Income x 0.25/12 = Monthly Payment
Ideal:	Gross Annual Family Income x 0.15/12 = Monthly Payment

Consider this analysis prepared for Mary and Bob Sample. The Samples have an investment portfolio, including the equity in their personal-use real estate, of $500,000. Their gross annual family income is $100,000. The current market value of their present home is $200,000. Their present mortgage balance is $100,000 with terms of 30 years at 8 percent (20 years remaining), and their monthly payment is $881. Their questions are:

1. If we stay in this home, should we refinance our mortgage?

2. If so, how much should our mortgage be?

3. Can we afford a more expensive home?

Interest rates are in a continual state of flux. From time to time, they decrease enough so that it is proper to consider refinancing. Some might have heard the old rule that it requires a 2 percent drop from present mortgage interest rates before you consider refinancing. Forget it. This rule is no longer appropriate, if it ever was. Here is how to respond to the Sample's first question.

Present monthly payment	$ 881
New monthly payment	- 776 [1]
Difference between two payments	$ 105
Cost to obtain new mortgage	$ 900
Cost divided by difference between payments	8.57+
Number of month to recover costs	About 8.6 months

[1] Terms: 20 years @ 7% for $100,000.

Therefore, the answer to the Sample's first question is, "If you plan to stay in your present home more than 9 months, then refinancing would be proper and in your best interest."

The Sample's second question was, "Since the answer is yes, then how much should we refinance?" The answer to this question depends upon their goals. Do they want to accelerate mortgage payoff? Do they want to take money out of their home for other use? Do they want to change the balance in their asset allocation?

Suppose the Samples want to improve the balance in their asset allocation from the present 20 percent in personal-use real estate to 25 percent. Assuming their home is worth $200,000 and they have a current mortgage of $100,000, then their equity is $100,000. (Property Value minus Mortgage equals Equity.) To find the percent, divide the equity by the total amount of their portfolio.

Present allocation: $100,000/$500,000 = 0.20, or 20 percent

Desired allocation: 25% of $500,000 = 0.25 x $500,000 = $125,000

The Samples' must come up with an extra $25,000 to reduce their present mortgage from $100,000 to $75,000, giving them $125,000 equity in their personal-use real estate category.

Another approach that accomplishes the same result over time is to refinance for a shorter period of years. This increases both the monthly payment and the portion of the payment allocated to principal.

The Sample's third question was whether they could afford a more expensive home. Based on their gross family income of $100,000 and using the rule of thumb that proper price should equal twice annual income, the Sample's should stay in their present home. However, if they want a $300,000 home, for whatever reason, then do the following calculations:

$300,000   Price of desired home
-125,000   Ideal amount to have in personal-use real estate
$175,000   Mortgage
Maximum monthly payment: $100,000 x 0.25/12 = $2,083
Ideal monthly payment: $100,000 x 0.15/12 = $1,250

Further investigation reveals that the Samples can get a 30-year mortgage at 7.5% with a monthly payment of $1,224, or a 15-year mortgage at 7.0% with a monthly payment of $1,573. Either of these monthly payments is close to the ideal payment and should represent no problem. Of course, this assumes Bob and Mary have an excess $25,000 to add to their net value from the sale of their present home, since the sale at $200,000 would only give them $100,000 after they pay off their current mortgage. Most Baby Boomers of all ages seldom have $25,000 lying around that is in excess of their current needs. So, a more usual scenario for these Baby Boomers is to have the maximum down payment on the new residence be whatever the sale of the old residence nets them. In the case of the Samples, this is $100,000, which would require a mortgage of $200,000 on the new home. This would obligate them to the following monthly payments:

$1,399   30-year mortgage at 7.5%
$1,798   15-year mortgage at 7.0%

Either of these monthly payments is within the proper range of $1,250 to $2,083, and would leave the investment allocation at 20 percent of total investments.

Obviously, there are many possible scenarios for your clients. However, the issue of personal use real estate should always begin with two fundamentals:

1.   Proper amount of monthly mortgage payments

       (Gross Annual Family Income) x 0.25/12 = Maximum Payment

       (Gross Annual Family Income) x 0.15/12 = Ideal Payment

2.   Proper amount tied up in personal-use real estate (equity or down payment)

       (Total Investments) x 0.25 = Target Amount

Chapter 6

Understanding Special Issues

There have always been special issues that can confront a financial advisor. This is what keeps the career from being boring. Three such issues involving Baby Boomers are discussed in this chapter. There is not necessarily any evidence of a causal relationship between Baby Boomers and these issues. It is just that the issues have become more prevalent with the appearance of the Boomers. A coincidence, so to speak. These three issues that can confront a financial planner are: (1) planning for non-traditional domestic partners, (2) the changing workplace, and (3) managing money for aging parents.

PLANNING FOR NON-TRADITIONAL DOMESTIC PARTNERS

Non-traditional domestic partners include same-sex couples and opposite-sex couples who are not married. Some financial planners may decide that personal moral or religious beliefs override their desire to properly perform the duties of an advisor to same-sex or opposite-sex-but-unmarried domestic partners. In such cases, the first part of this chapter may not be of value except possibly as general interest.

As has been stated throughout this book, it is essential that a financial advisor receive the hard and soft facts about clients without judgment or criticism. If an advisor is unable to act in this manner in any particular case, then the advisor should extract himself from the client relationship. This early termination of engagement should be executed regardless of the reason, not just in those situations involving non-traditional domestic partner relationships.

The problem for non-traditional domestic partner relationships centers mostly around the concept of uncharted waters. This is not to indicate that these relationships are new, but to emphasize the small percentage of the total population who make up such couples and the little data available about them.

Because non-traditional domestic partner relationships lack many benefits granted by law to married couples, problems arise. Not all of these problems are insurmountable, and it is incumbent on an advisor to at least be aware that the problem exists and take note of a few helpful sign posts along these otherwise un-charted trails.

Who Are Non-traditional Domestic Partners?

There is no definition, legal or historical, for non-traditional domestic partner relationships. There are some consistent qualifiers used by various companies who have found it in their best interests to offer assistance to these unmarried couples. Corporations can define dependents so that the definition includes non-traditional domestic partners and allows the partners to receive company benefits. However, this does not change the tax-law definition of dependent. Therefore, tax benefits cannot be claimed. Corporations allow non-traditional partners to receive company benefits because they believe there are other benefits derived from this policy. Examples of their thinking follows.

> "The bank recognizes that employees and their families have diverse needs, and that family concerns can impact work productivity and recruitment efforts. This policy is evidence of the respect and value we have for all of our employees."
>
> Union Bank 7/97

> "This (establishing of an expanded benefits program) reinforces the company's commitment to recruiting and retaining outstanding employees. We need a highly competitive benefits package."
>
> Wells Fargo Bank 7/97

The defining components of non-traditional domestic partner relationships are usually a matter of agreement as opposed to codified law. However, an ordinance in San Francisco states, "Domestic partner means anyone who has registered a domestic partnership with a governmental body pursuant to a state or local law."

Northwest Airlines includes in an application to its World Clubs a supplement entitled, "Affidavit of Marriage/Spousal Equivalency."

For Spousal Equivalent Domestic Partners Relationship:

I and _____ are spousal equivalents. Spousal equivalents means two adults who have chosen to share their lives in an intimate and committed relationship, reside together, and share a mutual obligation of support for the basic necessities of life.
Specifically, I declare and acknowledge that I and my spousal equivalent named above meet the following criteria:

1. We reside together and intend to do so indefinitely.
2. We are not related by blood to a degree of closeness that would prohibit legal marriage.
3. We are mutually responsible for basic living expenses.
4. We are both at least the age of consent in the state in which we reside.
5. Neither of us is married to anyone else.

Bob Blum, a consultant with William M. Mercer Inc., presented in October, 1997, a program entitled, "Domestic Partner Benefits Issues and Planning." Blum listed items that are common to many such employer plans under definitions of domestic partners:

- otherwise eligible to marry, but for restrictions due to same sex

- both of legal age

- competent to contract

- not of close blood relationship

- intention to remain so indefinitely

- same residence and intend to do so indefinitely

- each not married

- each jointly responsible for each other's welfare and financial obligations

- have registered the partnership, if available

All of the above seem to mirror the concept of legal marriage. The relationship is one of indefinite duration, and one where there is joint financial responsibility for each other.

What is of utmost concern to the financial planner, because it can be a trap for the unwary, is stereotyping. Traditional and non-traditional domestic partnerships encompass the entire gambit of personalities, attitudes, morals, religions, and ways people differentiate themselves. The financial advisor must keep in mind that he is dealing with human beings who have chosen to live together as homosexual, lesbian, or heterosexual couples. For any given set of circumstances, these couples have the same problems as traditional legally married couples. However, a major difference is that non-traditional domestic partners do not have the benefits that are available to legally married couples, and there are many such benefits. This is where a knowledgeable financial advisor can provide a real service.

The Internal Revenue Code produces many obstacles that the financial adviser needs to be aware of before he can develop proper strategies for the non-traditional couple. To quote a prominent estate planning attorney when advising his clients, an unmarried heterosexual couple, "Why don't you just get married. It sure would make your estate planning a lot easier."

Problems and Solutions: Estate Planning

The ability of married couples who are U.S. citizens to transfer to one or the other spouse any dollar amount of assets both while alive as well as after death with zero taxation is unparalleled. For many non-traditional domestic partners, however, this is a major problem. Of course, as the attorney said, they can "just get married," but too often this is not an option. Without question, many gay and lesbian partners, if allowed to legally marry, would do so and often improve their tax situation. Of course, where such marriages are not legal or otherwise possible, the use of the annual exclusion gift tax free might help if one partner has substantial wealth and the other doesn't. The unified tax-credit would also benefit most non-married partners. For such clients with substantial wealth, it is never too soon to see a quality estate planning specialist.

Problems and Solutions: Important Documents

All of the basic estate planning documents important for traditional married couples are equally important for non-traditional domestic partners where applicable – wills, trusts, and durable power of attorney (both medical and financial). Also, a separation agreement, contracts for ownership of residence and other jointly owned real estate, and any special circumstances agreements, such as a buy-sell agreement covering a first-offer-to-buy provision, can be very important documents. All must be executed by a competent and understanding attorney.

Wills and trusts should adhere to the same standard provisions used for traditional couples except for the marital trust section. If used at all, the term *marital* or *marital equivalent* should be clearly defined in the document. Since there are no marital tax provisions that are applicable, the use of different terms probably would add clarity.

The importance of a Durable Power of Attorney is especially true for non-traditional domestic partner relationships. Different terminology for these documents can be required by different states, but financial and medical matters must be spelled out clearly because there is no default mechanism or law to serve as a substitute.

The financial Durable Power of Attorney must state clearly the nature of the non-traditional domestic partner relationship. The definitiveness of the document will increase its effectiveness, particularly when the partners do not wish other parties, such as relatives, to be involved. The full description of the attorney-in-fact, the partner, should not rely exclusively on standard terminology, such as "a non-related party." These documents might require a larger attorney fee because of the non-standardized language involved and the time spent when drawing up the documents. However, this should not dissuade anyone from seeking anything but the best. As with all other situations dealing with money, make sure that not only are all the i's dotted and t's crossed, but that each issue is spelled out precisely.

As is emphasized throughout this book, if the financial advisor is not an attorney, then he should not draft any legal document. However, the financial advisor's attendance at the client-attorney meeting will provide an opportunity to assist in placing personal emphasis as needed.

The medical Durable Power of Attorney also needs to be specific right down to a clear statement that the "partner" has the authority to admit the ill partner into a hospital and to authorize treatment. If the client desires to authorize a partner to make the decision of life or death, within state requirements, then it needs to be made abundantly clear in writing. The use of not only state legislative language, but additional proper personal verbiage would be beneficial.

A contract stating under what circumstances jointly owned property may be sold also needs to be especially clear. Explain to the client that it is smart to prevent the other partner from putting out a for-sale sign without the client's permission. A buy/sell agreement will serve this purpose.

A contract detailing who gets what upon a dissolution of the domestic partnership can be legally enforced and, if created before the time of separation, can save a lot of anguish and money if it ever has to be utilized. Non-traditional domestic partners, like traditional domestic partners, can end their relationship by separation. It is usually not the initial intent of either, but contracts for this contingency can be beneficial.

Joint ownership of personal-use real estate is most often with the right of survivorship with married partners. However, a tenants-in-common form of joint ownership is somewhat more favored in non-traditional domestic partner relationships. This is because of the important difference in income tax laws. With traditionally married partners, as long as they are married, any amount can be transferred from one to the other tax free. With non-traditional domestic partners, there is a potential gift tax for all transfers above the annual exclusion. Therefore, great care should be taken in structuring the ownership in the first place.

It is not unusual for one partner to provide a larger portion of the down payment on a home at purchase time. Also, it is not unusual for one partner to pay all or a larger portion of the mortgage payment. Each of these seemingly innocent acts could trigger taxable gifts. A competent tax specialist should be consulted *before* the fact. Again, if this is not the financial advisor's specialty, he would be well advised to attend the meeting between the client and tax specialist. There is always something new or absolutely unique to each situation.

Problems and Solutions: Employment Benefits

The benefit-coverage most often sought from an employer by both traditional and non-traditional domestic partners is group medical insurance. Employer-paid premiums not being taxed to the employee, or the employee's dependents, and tax-free benefits are a wonderful dual combination.

With non-traditional domestic partner relationships, the employer must first have a formal plan allowing non-married domestic partners to qualify as dependents. However, even if the employer's plan defines dependent to include non-traditional domestic partners, this does *not* change the definition of dependent for tax laws. Stated simply, non-traditional domestic partners are not dependents for tax purposes. Therefore, when an employer plan does include non-traditional domestic partners as dependents, and the employer pays the extra premium for these dependents, the premium is taxable income to the employee. Fortunately, the second half of the usual situation is favorable: the benefits are *not* taxable income.

Other benefits may or may not be provided to non-traditional domestic partner relationships. For example:

- COBRA (an acronym for the Consolidated Omnibus Budget Reconciliation Act). The law doesn't apply to non-traditional domestic partner relationships; however a COBRA equivalent can be provided.

- The Family and Medical Leave Act of 1992 (FMLA) does not apply to non-traditional domestic partner relationships; however, a FMLA equivalent can be provided.

- Defined Benefit retirement plan survivor benefits to non-traditional domestic partners are unusual.

- Group Life Insurance premiums paid for by the employer on the life of a dependent non-traditional domestic partner are income taxable to the employee. These are not excludable as a de minimis fringe and are considered taxable income.

Financial planning for non-traditional domestic partners is just as important as it is for traditional domestic partners. All clients, traditional or not, have common areas of counseling need, and each has his own uniqueness. It is important for the financial advisor not to stereotype anyone, but to attempt to obtain an understanding of the individual, seek out each special situation, and find the solutions to all problems. The financial advisor has a responsibility to each client, irrespective of the diversity involved, to work in the client's best interest. Accept the responsibility, or don't accept the client.

THE CHANGING WORKPLACE

If there are any experiences that separate the Baby Boomers from previous generations, these two experiences are among them: (1) Baby Boomers are more likely to work for more than one employer, sometimes many more, and (2) Baby Boomers face a greater probability that they will have to work after retirement.

Opportunity or Disaster

Most Baby Boomers are quite likely to change or already have changed careers or employers more than once in their lifetimes. For many Baby Boomers, this change may occur many times. Downsizing, desiring to move, seeking new challenges, or whatever the cause, changes in occupations have become normal.

As Baby Boomers accumulate years of employment, age becomes a worrisome factor. Finding a new job or starting a new career after age 64 can be difficult. As shown in the graph on the next page, by the time they are 64, the chances of finding a new job may be less than one in five. The graph is based on 2004 data from the U.S. Bureau of Labor Statistics. Now, as Baby Boomers reach age 65 without sufficient assets on which to retire, or for the large number who choose to become re-employed, this becomes an extremely difficult task.

Figure 6.1

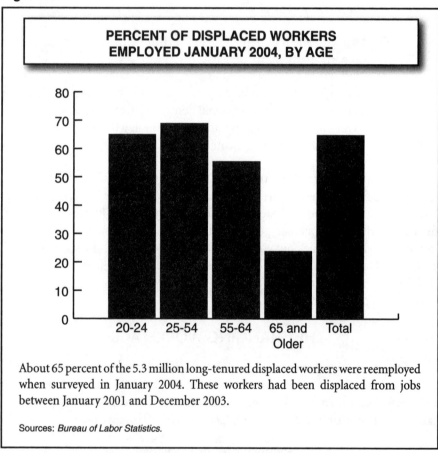

About 65 percent of the 5.3 million long-tenured displaced workers were reemployed when surveyed in January 2004. These workers had been displaced from jobs between January 2001 and December 2003.

Sources: *Bureau of Labor Statistics.*

A study conducted by DIG, Inc., for the entitled, *American Business and Older Workers: A Road Map to the 21st Century*, examines the attitudes of employers toward workers age 50 and older.

"Despite being highly rated for skills, experience, and work ethics by employers, older workers still face negative perceptions such as the lack of flexibility in the work place and adaptability to new technology," said Joseph S. Perkins, AARP Vice-president.

Suggested methods to help reverse these perceptions included:

- Cut back the length of the resume

- Learn about the company before an interview

- Approach the interview as someone eager to work

- Demonstrate flexibility

- Learn new skills

- Get coaching on interviewing skills

It is obvious that a disruption in employment or a permanent reduction in the level of income will cause major obstacles to wealth accumulation. Saving for a child's college education or for big ticket spending can be drastically altered. The positive side of a change in occupation or employer is sometimes an increase in income or a change to a happier and more compatible life style.

Of course, career changes have always been a possible consideration for many clients of a financial advisor, but today the likelihood of a Baby Boomer being involved in an employment disruption is much greater than it has ever been. The important point for the financial advisor to recognize is the potential of these disruptions when designing and implementing financial plans, and to suggest the creation of a specific contingency plan or fund. This may be as simple as setting a goal to amass savings of 6 months to 2 years income.

The second point for the financial advisor to recognize is that a change in the client's employment during normal working years has an effect on retirement income accumulations. Many if not most Baby Boomers desire to retire early, but most lack the savings to do so.

The Employee Benefits Research Institute notes that only one-third of pre-retirees have even tried to determine how much money they will need to save for a secure retirement. This is substantiated by the 0.5 percent savings rate in the United

States in 2005 – the lowest savings rate in over 60 years. The savings rate peaked at 9.5 percent in 1974.

Social Security is scheduled to gradually change the age of eligibility for full retirement benefits from age 65 to 67 which began in 2003. This change will also reduce the percentage of full benefits paid out for early retirement at age 62 from 80 percent to 70 percent. There is talk about advancing the full benefit age upward to age 70 or 72. There is also the possibility of speeding up the age change from age 65 to 67 for full retirement benefits by a number of years. Thus, Social Security may provide less and less support for Baby Boomers who must come up with adequate funds to retire.

Working in Retirement – Have To or Choose To

Assuming that this period of time called retirement is a part of the journey through life, and assuming that the projections of a much longer life expectancy are true, then how will anyone be able to find the money to finance 20, 30, or even 40 years of retirement? The only answer for many will be: work. Work longer. Go back to work. Whatever. If as several studies have shown, Baby Boomers are accumulating less than one-half, maybe only one-third, of what they will need in retirement, then work may be the best answer for survival.

Baby Boomers know they are not accumulating enough wealth and this provides many opportunities for financial advisors. It is terrible to have to stop working if one really wants to continue working, but it is just as terrible to have to go back to work only because one must in order to pay the bills.

Financial advisors must stress the benefits of keeping one's options open about the future. Financial advisors should propose reasonable plans to enable their clients to maintain a choice between working and not working after reaching retirement age.

MANAGING MONEY FOR AGING PARENTS

Hardly a week goes by without a report about a new or potential cure for some disease, or a report about better ways to live to improve one's health and to avoid illness. Life expectancy has increased at an amazing rate during this past century. When Social Security was initiated back in the 30s, it was not expected to cost anything because most workers would not live far beyond age 65. Now, most workers live well beyond 65, with quite a few living past 90 and 100 years of age. This longevity can be a blessing to many, but it can also be a curse to others. Many Baby Boomers are faced with – or will be faced with – the financial responsibility of caring for their aging parents.

The Potential Inheritance May Be Going, Going, Gone

It may not be common, but it is not unusual, for adult children to face a situation where they must manage the money of their aging parents. In such cases, there arises in the minds of the adult children, either consciously or subconsciously, a conflict of interest. Are they managing the money so that it provides a comfortable life for the parents as long as the parents live (and not necessarily any longer)? Or are they managing the money so that their own inheritance is not greatly reduced?

Some might gasp and say, "How could such questions even be considered when talking about our parents?" So, in just about all cases, important questions are not discussed, even after the actual management process begins. Then one parent dies and the surviving parent begins to develop dementia, the quality of life begins to slip away, and the parent becomes less and less conscious of the present time or surroundings. A new question begins to grow in the minds of the adult children: is this becoming a waste of money? When adult children are ready to admit they are harboring this question in their minds, they should be ready to share their concerns with their financial advisor.

A financial advisor can be an objective voice of reason at this very emotional point in the lives of these adult children. The financial advisor might find the situation easier if he has suffered through similar circumstances, but this is not essential. What is essential is for the financial advisor to recognize that the situation is filled with much emotion and little reason, and the advisor is being called upon to provide the latter.

The financial advisor must also not offer advice. Instead, the financial advisor should offer patience, a sympathetic ear, and a calm willingness to discuss alternatives. An effective way to do this is by asking questions rather than making statements. The advisor should help the client focus on the reality of the situation. For example, if the parent has been relocated to a nursing home, ask, "Is your mother physically comfortable where she is now? Is she cared for by a competent and attentive staff?" The advisor might also ask, "If you move your mother to Manybucks Nursing Home, will she know or appreciate the difference in her surroundings? What more do you think you *should* do for her? What more can you do for her? What more do you feel you should do for her?" The financial advisor can guide the conversation to the client's concern about money by asking questions such as, "How are you paying for your mother's care? How long do you think this money will last? Would you like to explore some options about making it possible for this money to last longer?"

Medicaid was designed to provide financial assistance, but only when there are insufficient assets and income for patients to pay their bills. Before your clients do anything about applying for Medicaid benefits, they should consult a specialist in this area of law. Unless the financial advisor is such a specialist, then it is in the best interests of everyone that no advice be offered on the subject of Medicaid except the recommendation to obtain such a specialist.

It is the fortunate financial advisor who can help clients avoid this situation. When a financial advisor collects hard and soft facts about a client, there should be a discussion about the client's parents. If at this time the financial advisor discusses long term care insurance, and the clients and parents see the wisdom of obtaining such insurance, then many financial problems that might have occurred will be solved in advance.

When The Potential Inheritance Still May Be There, But ...

It is a different situation when the parent is mentally capable of managing most of his affairs but, for whatever reason, never learned the financial fundamentals needed (or learned financial fundamentals that have been outdated for years). This situation usually occurs when the "financial spouse" dies and leaves an adequate or even large amount of life insurance or retirement accumulations to the surviving spouse. The adult children of the surviving parent should consider themselves fortunate if the surviving parent informs them of his financial accommodations. The adult children should consider themselves most fortunate if, in addition to informing them of the financial accommodations, the parent asks them for advice and assistance, particularly if the adult children have a financial advisor.

Consider as an example of this situation the Baby-Boomer couple Barb and Bob, both of whom are 50 years old. Sometime after Barb's father died, her mother asked her to help manage all the Certificates of Deposit (CDs) in which her mother had so diligently invested her sizable inheritance. She told Barb that she was not sure how to take money out of the CDs should she need it. She explained that her portfolio was diversified into several banks, with different monthly maturity dates, and in $1,000, $10,000, $25,000, and $50,000 units. She had a $100,000 CD for a while but decided it was too risky.

This investment portfolio, she told Barb, was worth about $485,000, and was probably never going to be needed. After all, her income from Social Security and her deceased spouse's pension was much more than she needed. Anyway, at age 75, how much longer would she live?

Barb and Bob discussed what they should do. They knew Barb's mother had about a thimbleful of money knowledge and were surprised that she had gone to all the trouble to obtain a "diversified" listing of CDs. Bob stated his extreme reluctance to get involved with Barb's mother's money. Bob and Barb decided the best thing to do was to convince Barb's mother to get a financial advisor, like they had.

With some reluctance, she agreed to see a financial advisor, but only if Barb would go along and be involved, and only if they went to Barb's advisor.

After a complete analysis, the financial advisor agreed that, at this time, Barb's mother was doing fine on Social Security and the Barb's father's pension, and the $485,000 of assets were not needed. However, if Barb's mother lived a long time, inflation would erode the purchasing power of her level pension benefit. Also, anytime in the future, if Social Security benefits are reduced – either by a reduction in the benefit amount or by less than full inflation annual adjustments – there could be a shortfall. Then Barb's mother would have to turn to the CDs for assistance. The financial advisor told Barb's mother, "Don't worry. All of my clients in retirement say the same thing to me, 'Make my money last as long as I do.'"

At this point, Barb asked, "How can you do that? How do you know how long the money must last?" The advisor replied, "Well, I really don't know. So I assume that at least one spouse will live to be 100. The latest actuarial figures state that for a couple living to age 65, one of them has a 16 percent chance to live to age 100."

Barb's mother interrupted by laughing. She said, "Me live to be 100. Oh, no, not me. No way." Barb said, "Mother, you are very healthy and active. Maybe these numbers really do apply to you." Barb's mother responded, "Well, maybe hypothetically. But even if I do live that long, how can it affect anything I do with my money right now?"

The financial advisor, having just been given tacit approval to continue, said, "Barb, your mother has a very low risk tolerance." Turning to the mother, the advisor explained the meaning of risk tolerance and then said, "Your risk tolerance will prevent you from investing properly in order to make your money last a very long time. You certainly are not alone in your present tolerance level, but you should think of this level as temporary and be willing to allow it to change over time. If change takes too long, then it could seriously hinder our efforts to make your money last as long as you do."

Barb interrupted. "Are you saying that Mother needs to invest aggressively but doesn't have the risk tolerance to do so?"

The financial advisor replied, "That is sort of what I'm saying. It's not that she needs to invest aggressively. It's just that she shouldn't be invested 100 percent in CDs. CDs alone won't get the job done. I would advise that a diversified investment portfolio includes bonds, stock, and real estate, in addition to CDs."

Barb's eyes lit up in recognition. "That's exactly how you set up our portfolio, with all those investment categories, and it has grown very well. Bob and I just wish we had more to invest." Barb's mother said, "So, what should I do?"

The financial advisor replied, "A strategy that has worked very well with other clients in similar situations is for you to borrow a bit of Barb's risk tolerance." Barb's mother tilted her head inquisitively. The advisor continued, "I feel that you have complete faith and trust in your daughter. Is this true?" Barb's mother nodded enthusiastically and said, "Of course. That's why I'm here. I'd trust her with my life." Barb's mother hesitated only for an instant and then continued, "I'd also trust her with my life savings. Is that what you mean?"

The advisor smiled and said, "That's exactly what I mean. What we need to do is develop an investment portfolio very much like your daughter's. Not exactly, but using the same investment categories with more conservative investments in each category." Both Barb and her mother nodded their approval to continue. So the financial advisor did." It appears that we will not need any cash flow from these assets for at least another five years. So we should lower considerably the percent of the investment portfolio that includes CDs, bonds, and other fixed-dollar investments." The advisor turned to Barb and said, "The percent of the fixed dollar investment won't be as low as yours, Barb, but because we desire growth rather than income at this time, the percentage will be on the low side in this category."

"I can live with that," Barb's mother said. "I just want to be sure that Barb stays very much involved with my investments. However, what if I don't live more than, say, 10 years. Why do I need to bother with all this?"

"A very good question," the financial advisor replied. "If we knew that you were going to live only 10 more years, and we were only concerned about your welfare, then we wouldn't have to do anything about your assets. However, this would totally ignore your daughter, in whom you say you place complete trust." The advisor looked at Barb's mother and again took her inquisitive look as permission to explain. "If we can earn an average annual return of 7 percent on all of your assets, then they will double in value in 10 years. Now you don't need this money if you die in 10 years, but wouldn't it be nice if Barb inherited more rather than less?" Barb's mother's face lit up with the knowledge she was accumulating. The advisor continued, "Actually, this plan addresses two possibilities. The first possibility, and the prime reason for all this planning, is the case where you live for a very long time. This plan will make sure the money will be there when you need it. The second possibility concerns Barb. If you die prematurely, then there is no longer any concern for your physical well-being, but your increased assets that were invested for growth will enhance Barb's well-being, and maybe the well-being of any grandchildren there may be. Now, does this dual-benefit plan make sense to you?"

Both Barb and her mother responded enthusiastically in the affirmative. Then Barb frowned and said, "Wait a minute. This is my mother's money. Why are you considering me at all?"

The financial advisor smiled, having anticipated this question, and replied, "You are absolutely right, Barb. It is your mother's money. So, of greatest importance is for the money to benefit your mother, for as long as she lives. As you both seem to agree, this requires a more diversified growth portfolio." The advisor paused and received the anticipated nod of approval. "Now, suppose your mother pulls a really dumb trick and dies on us too soon. Then, this plan will help to fulfill her second most important desire, to help make sure you have all the financial help you need or want. Your mother did say that more would be better than less."

Barb's mother looked at her daughter and said, "Barb, dear, please be quiet. This man knows what he's talking about." She turned to the advisor and said, "I like it. When and how do we start?"

"We start by setting our next appointment," said the financial advisor. "This will give you time to discuss my recommendation and develop a list of questions and any alternatives you would like to explore. As you are doing this, I will develop a tentative investment portfolio and a timetable for transferring CDs as they mature to avoid all penalties. Then, at our next meeting, we will discuss all of this, and if you are comfortable, we will begin implementing the plan." Both Barb and her mother had smiles on their faces, which naturally pleased the financial advisor very much.

The strategy of borrowing an adult child's risk tolerance does work, but not without lapses, especially when one or another investment under performs. At these times, it is essential to have a face-to-face meeting to review the reasons why the financial plan was put into effect and to shore up the client's sagging risk tolerance. For example, the advisor can point out that one of the reasons for diversification was that different investment categories grow and decline at different times. This is what adds stability to the total portfolio.

Money Talk: Starting Might Be The Hardest Part

Money and sex were once the hardest topics to discuss with parents. Today, however, parents and adult children seem to find it easier to discuss sexual topics, but when it comes to talking about money, it happens only when there is no other choice. Of course, each family is unique, but in general, the number of open discussions a family has had about sex have far out-distanced the number of open discussions they have had about money.

This closed mentality is not exclusive to either side, parents or adult children. Financial advisors are the obvious people to have extensive information about their client and the client's parents or adult children. The advisor needs to be keenly alert to a possible need for opening up this conversation. Sometimes a suggestion from the advisor that the client should ask his parent or adult child to meet the advisor will start the discussion.

The most common reason for instigating this kind of money talk is the adult child's perception that one or more parents are living way below their potential standard of living. This situation is often true because many people in retirement have a fear of running out of money. The Baby Boomer needs to understand that many parents have lived through some hard times. The parents might have been very frugal and probably denied themselves. Now in retirement, they continue these habits, even when it is no longer necessary to do so.

There are many true stories of people in their 70s, 80s, and 90s with sufficient wealth to maintain a higher standard of living, but they just can't get themselves to spend more money. A wonderful approach to this adjustment is for the financial advisor to "give permission" to spend. For example, "Yes, you can afford to buy that luxury car, or to take that cruise, or to take that trip around the world, or to continue living in your big house." It might sound silly, but it is a great relief for the parent to hear a professional financial advisor explaining how his money will last. Relating this kind of information to Baby Boomer clients might increase the likelihood that they will encourage their parents to come in to see the advisor. Sometimes a free get-acquainted meeting will be enough inducement.

The financial advisor usually can uncover situations that will improve the lives of both the clients and their parents or adult children. When this happens, a great service has been rendered. Even the advisor feels a wonderful rush of satisfaction for a job well done.

Chapter 7

Presenting, Implementing, and Monitoring the Plan

Here comes the good part. For the financial advisor who has done the homework completely and correctly, this part of working with clients will be the most personally rewarding. The homework involves beginning to know the client, studying all aspects of the client's particular circumstances, and analyzing the client's wants and needs. Now the financial advisor is ready to help the client start on the road to achieving goals.

When presenting the plan, the financial advisor's communication skills will be tested. The advisor first validates with the client the hard and soft facts and then makes recommendations offering adjustments that will assist in achieving the client's goals and objectives, at least from the advisor's point of view. Only after the client has given approval or discussed the desired modifications to the recommendations does the implementation begin.

It is appropriate at this point to involve specialists in the various areas of planning where necessary. Legal matters, accounting practices, insurance coverage, investment vehicles, and so forth, all require expert handling. The financial advisor usually will be an expert in one or more areas, but not in all. The important point is that whatever area needs to be addressed is addressed with proper dispatch and at the highest level of expertise available.

The next stage, monitoring, occurs after some agreed-upon time interval. The frequency of reviewing and monitoring a financial plan will vary depending upon each client's situation. Many advisors are comfortable with one a year as the norm. Others will feel the need for more frequent meetings. Most clients will need an annual meeting, at least, for the first few years. This provides an opportunity for them to hear and see reinforcement of the whys and wherefores of the recommendations and the results to date.

Then, of course, things change: income level, family members (both number and needs), losses (uninsured or underinsured), gains, gifts, and attitudes. When any significant change occurs, an accelerated review date is triggered. This process goes on and on.

PRESENTING THE PLAN

Up to this point, the financial advisor and client have met for a fact finding interview, the client has supplied the advisor with a great deal of material – legal documents, tax returns, insurance policies, etc. – and the advisor has organized, analyzed, evaluated, and prepared recommendations in a preliminary plan.

This preliminary financial plan needs to be communicated to the client in a manner that will produce immediate, precise, and understandable facts and directions. It is very important that the client's attention be focused on the topics one at a time. Yet it is even more important that the client have a clear overview of the whole.

The meeting site for the presentation is very important. This meeting site should be quiet, comfortable, and not subject to interruptions. All of these conditions can best be controlled in the advisor's office. The client's office or home is subject to all kinds of potential problems and is not recommended. The financial advisor should borrow or rent a proper place, if necessary.

An excellent technique that can be used to accomplish a successful meeting is to make the presentation by handing the clients one page at a time and discussing each item on the page. The clients are not being asked to evaluate anything. No agreement or disagreement is proper at this time. It works best when the advisor tells the client at the beginning of the meeting that no decisions will be made today. The knowledge that there will be zero pressure to make any decisions at this meeting will help relax the client sufficiently to be a good or at least better listener. Actually, encouraging active listening is very important. Ask the client to pay attention, to seek clarification, and to ask any and all questions that come to mind. Also suggest that they draw graphs, sketch pictures, write notes, or do anything else to ensure understanding. Knowledge and understanding are essential for making proper choices when decision time comes.

The Personal Data Page

The Personal Data page (See Appendix A page 216) of the plan is fairly elementary and allows the client to start participating in the process. Ask, "Is there anything on this page that is wrong? Are there any spelling errors? Are there any incorrect numbers?"

The financial advisor should watch the client for evidence of concern or other reactions. When the client seems to be down to the section on Assumptions, the advisor should re-assume the role of presenter by stating how these assumptions were developed (e.g., based on past history, actuarial tables, or whatever). It sometimes lightens up the atmosphere if the advisor says, "The numbers representing your remaining life expectancy are averages, and it is important to understand that average means only one-half the males/females your age will be dead in this number of years. So, if you choose the right half, you could live a lot longer."

The Financial Planning Page

The Financial Planning Page (See Appendix A page 217) provides a summary or listing of findings from oral responses to questions and written responses to the questionnaire the client completed in the fact-finding interview. It is strongly suggested that printed text on the page be kept to a minimum, since communication is enhanced by the amount of white space on the page.

Baby Boomers already have a pretty good understanding of what is important to them. At this point, all that is desired is a list or brief summary of the highest priority items. Also, when a couple is involved, a weighted average of both is essential information.

The important reasons for financial planning have been derived from the fact-finding questions answered by the client to indicate what, to him, is important to be included in this plan. Among other items, this might include college education needs, potential parental support, and big ticket items. Of course, a discussion of all items is indicated here.

The risk-taking-propensity questionnaire in the Fact-Finding Kit provides the level of the client's knowledge of investment and is reported and discussed. Question four of the questionnaire provides the information necessary to develop a weighted average of major concerns.

The Net Worth Statement and
Itemized Assets and Liabilities Pages

Now is the time to review the financials. These pages are presented to the client with the financial advisor asking him to eyeball the numbers. Ask, "Do any of these figures jump out as being wrong? Is there any obvious error? Is something missing?"

These pages provide a summary report. If all seems proper to the client, then the financial advisor should start validating this feeling with a review of the itemizations and details. Request that, before the next meeting, the client check with his records the accuracy of these numbers and call with any significant corrections.

The History Net Worth Statement Page

The History Net Worth page (See Appendix A page 220) will not appear in the initial plan. However, in the future, this page becomes a very important page to show progress, or the lack thereof, toward the desired goals. The assets are listed net of debt. For example, if the residence is worth $200,000, and the client has a mortgage of $75,000, then the net asset is $125,000. So, the amount of $125,000 is listed on this page, not $200,000.

Net assets can and should be listed thereafter for each regularly scheduled review meeting. It is important for the client to see what has happened, even when there is a reduction of total net worth. Actually, it can be more important for the client to see when his net worth has declined. This provides the basis of a discussion on what happened, why it happened, and what can be done about it.

With each presentation of the History Net Worth Statement, the financial advisor should try to include as many years as possible on one page. First, list the years with the page held upright; then, when more space is needed, turn the page on its side; finally, reduce the size of the type to fit more on the page. This last option should be a last option. The size of the type used to convey knowledge should be easy to read at, ideally, arms length. As one begins to diminish the size of the type, one begins to diminish the size of one's attentive audience.

The Income Tax Information Page

The income tax information page (See Appendix A page 221) simply begins with a listing of sources of income and allocation of retirement plan contributions (IRA, 401(k), etc.). This is followed by the various government taxes and the Social Security tax. Then total tax is computed and shown. The marginal federal tax bracket is indicated and its implications discussed. Finally, any suspended loss carry-overs are stated.

Three years of data are needed to illustrate a good trend-line, and all this information can provide points of discussion as needed. For example, excessive taxable or tax-exempt interest triggers the question of possible improper balance of fixed-dollar investments as compared to equity-type investments. Lack of or small amounts of retirement plan contributions begs the question, why?

The Annual Income Sources page (See Appendix A page 222) is used only with retired clients. Pre-retirement income for living expenses comes from wages and is reported at the bottom of the Cash Management Statement (see below). After retirement, income will often come from various sources such as Social Security, pensions, specific investment, annuities, etc.

Very often, clients in retirement – especially those who are early to retirement – are nervous about where the money is going to come from. This page can show the current-year sources and amounts of income as well as projected amounts, adjusted for inflation, for future years. An amazing amount of serenity permeates the atmosphere when, at least on paper, it can be demonstrated that enough money is available for future consumption. Note: listed at the bottom of this page are assets not being used currently that could create additional income as needed. This page is also helpful when selecting which assets to use currently to create income and which to postpone usage.

The Cash Management Statement Page

The Cash Management Statement (See Appendix A page 223) is presented to the client in a neat, clean, totaled, and printed format. The financial advisor and client, when reviewing this page, often notice certain numbers as being inappropriate. Keep in mind, however, that no decisions for any change should be made at this time. All that is being done at this meeting is a reporting of the facts. Sometimes at this initial stage of planning, what is being reported is inaccurate information provided by the client. Now this inaccurate information is being given back to the client in a very official-looking form. Nothing needs to be said. The client knows the information is wrong and knows it is his responsibility to correct it.

When total income exceeds total expenditures and accumulations, the obvious questions is, "Where is the balance of the money?" This can become a touchy subject, especially if one of the couple knows where at least some of the money unaccounted for has gone.

For example, Gordon and Greta had worked together to develop their Cash Management Statement. They felt comfortable that the numbers represented, more or less accurately, how they were spending their money. They had not totaled the listing before giving it to their financial advisor, Dave. At the presentation of their Cash Management Statement, Gordon and Greta were shocked to see their income was $140,000 and all expenses and accumulations were only $110,000. When Dave asked, "Where's the rest of the money?," both Gordon and Greta were seriously concerned. They knew they squandered some dollars here and there, but not $30,000! Later, discussions about their two rental properties revealed that there was a $27,000 negative cash flow from these investments. Gordon and Greta had no idea of this large annual expense. Actually, they just didn't understand the financial statement presented to them by their accountant. Or, it's possible they subconsciously didn't want to know that this investment required such large financial support.

The important point is that a common neglect in personal and family money management is the lack of good, solid information on "Where did the money go?"

The Cash Management Statement helps to correct this situation, but only if and when the financial advisor is successful in convincing the clients to keep good records.

Baby Boomers, especially younger ones, too often have total expenses exceeding total income. Again, at this point in the client's financial plan, the development of proper financial attitudes and knowledge is just starting. One way to get it jump-started is to introduce the subject into the discussion. The Cash Management Statement provides the opportunity to do this. Providing a little face-saving or just establishing a mutual understanding, the financial advisor can point out that, unless very good records have been kept, all of these numbers probably can be refined. Usually, the client knows this. If it seems appropriate, and it usually does, the financial advisor should suggest that the client review and change the amounts up or down and bring any changes to the next meeting. Do not get hung up on this page at this point. Remember, the purpose of the meeting is to provide detail that can be verified (or corrected later) and to give an overview of where the client is today, where the client would like to be some tomorrow in the future, and a possible way to get there using the advisor's recommendations.

The Property and Liability Insurance Page

The meeting needs a change of pace at this point. A good technique is to say something such as, "We're going to shift gears now and talk about insurance." Another way is to offer some refreshment or provide an opportunity to stretch. In other words, signal that the review of the financial statistics is over, and what follows now is a different subject. The next several pages deal with all areas of insurance.

Property and Liability Insurance (See Appendix A page 224) is very important coverage that just about all Baby Boomers need. They do not like paying the premiums, but they know it is important and, in some cases, required, such as when obtaining a mortgage on a house or, in some states, when obtaining a license plate for a car.

The client probably has never read an insurance policy and would be tempted to discharge any financial advisor who recommended that he do so now. However, a quick overview and a simple explanation of the coverage is very welcome. It can be amusing to see the client's face when, for the very first time, someone explains in an understandable manner that Bodily Injury Liability coverage of $25,000/$50,000 means that, if you have an automobile accident and a judgment is entered against you, the insurance company would pay up to $25,000 to any one individual or up to $50,000 to all people injured. This explanation should be followed quickly with the information that, today if anyone is injured seriously enough to sue, in all likelihood the suit would not be for $25,000, but for $2.5 million. And should the defendant be lucky and the judgment be for only $300,000, the insurance company would pay only $25,000, and the client would owe the balance of $275,000. This amount would put a hole in the pockets of most Baby Boomers.

An explanation of all of the items mentioned on this page will be greatly appreciated by the client. It does not take much time, and a wonderful service has been provided. Also, the financial advisor along with the planning process are enhanced in the eyes of the client.

Medical, Disability Income, Long Term Care, and Life Insurance are covered on separate pages (See Appendix A pages 225-229). These pages are handled in the same manner as the Property and Liability page, discussing each page to the detail that the particular client needs.

The Protection Recommendations Page

Up to this point, the financial advisor has been presenting the hard facts as provided by the client and understood by the advisor. Now, the advisor uses, the Protection Recommendations page (See Appendix A page 230) to make the first of many recommendations.

It is a good idea to begin with recommendations for excess liability insurance, particularly if the client has none or an inadequate amount. Even if the financial advisor is discussing large amounts ($1,000,000 or more) and the annual premium is relatively small ($100/$200), this prepares the client for acceptance of proper amounts of other types of insurance coverage, which often require a smaller amount. Allow lots of white space on the recommendations page. It is also important that the combination of all recommendations be limited to one page.

Insurance is a love/hate relationship for many people, especially younger Baby Boomers. Clients know there is a need for various kinds of coverage, but they hate to part with the money for premiums. Nevertheless, they love their foresight when a claim payment is received.

Keep the presentation simple, make it understandable, and use as few words as possible to do the job. An example is shown below.

MARY AND ROBERT SAMPLE

PROTECTION RECOMMENDATIONS

EXCESS LIABILITY   Purchase a $1,000,000 excess liability policy.

HOMEOWNERS   Coverage is proper.

AUTO   Change liability coverage as follows:

	Present	Proposed
Bodily Injury	$25/50,000	$250/500,000
Property Damage	$25,000	$100,000

MEDICAL   Coverage is proper.

DISABILITY/
  LONG TERM CARE   Coverage is proper.

LIFE INSURANCE   Bob: Change beneficiary to your
                            trust on all policies.
                            Increase total death benefit
                            to $500,000.
                            Add permanent insurance.
                            See illustration.

                    Mary: You have no coverage.
                            Is this appropriate?

The Emergency Fund Reserves

All training programs for financial advisors recommend that clients maintain proper liquid assets in case of an emergency. The recommended amount is also quite consistent: three to six months take-home pay. This information is so well known, though not necessarily accomplished by the Baby Boomer client, that to keep repeating it in the same way may sound so boring that it fails to get the message across. Therefore, an alternate approach is suggested on the Emergency Fund Reserves page. (See Appendix A page 231).

First, under PRESENT, determine what is currently available for emergency purposes. Second, under PROPER, illustrate a calculation of the proper amount using the formula:

$(Gross Annual Income) - $(Income and Social Security Taxes) x 0.50 = $(Proper Amount)

Sometimes when an advisor makes a point a little differently, a client might have one of those wonderful experiences of, "Oh, I see. I need 50 percent of my annual, after-tax, take-home pay." Actually, the amount could be more than 50 percent, depending upon proper insurance, such as disability income and medical insurance, and whether the household has more than one income earner. Since the recommended amount on the Emergency Fund Reserves page, as derived from the formula, can differ from the recommended amount for the cash-type investment category in proper asset allocation on the Investment Portfolio page (see below), the financial advisor needs to point out that the larger of the two numbers is the appropriate amount.

The Investment Portfolio Page

For most Baby Boomers, this is the page they have been waiting for. They want to talk about accumulation. They want to know whether they have been doing it right or want to know how to get started. The Investment Portfolio page (See Appendix A page 232) begins the process.

The financial advisor does not have to create any fancy preambles to this subject. The client's mutual feeling is, "Let's get at it." However, the advisor must be prepared to defend whatever position is taken. If the client has accumulated some amount of wealth, there will be pride of accomplishment involved, and the advisor should take care not to stifle this new and fragile relationship being developed between client and advisor.

Discuss the recommended percentages. Explain how diversification among the categories and within each category is important. Discuss how proper asset allocation produces more profitable portfolios and long-term safety. Remember, this is the presentation of the initial plan, not necessarily the final plan to be implemented. The financial advisor should structure the planning process to allow for both the advisor and the client to grow together, developing a relationship where both can benefit from a deeper understanding of their inclinations, limitations, and personalities.

Both the financial advisor and the client should begin this relationship with openness, maintaining an open attitude where all matters can be explored. However, the financial advisor must always keep in mind that it is the client's money and life style, and the client will do whatever he wants. The advisor should go along with the client by assisting in all ways possible the accomplishments of his desires. However, the advisor should be persistent when he believes the client is headed down the wrong path and should explain to the client what the anticipated results could or would likely be. The advisor should not give up on the client – of course, there can be a few exceptions – but should encourage the client to continue discussing his point of view with the advisor, and then, over time, what is really best for the client will prevail.

Life is a growing process for both the client and the advisor. Knowledge and wisdom will be gained from the process by all involved in time, one hopes, to make proper adjustments whenever needed.

The Investment Chart page (See Appendix A page 233) presents two graphs. The top graph shows where the client is today, and the bottom graph shows the recommended asset allocation by categories. It is very effective to illustrate the category with the most excessive percentage in red. Telling the clients that red means stop might make them laugh as well as make them aware of the importance of reducing this excess.

The objective is to get the two graphs to look alike. The closer the top graph comes to looking like the bottom graph, the more profitable and safer the total portfolio will be.

The Investment Recommendations Page

The Investment Recommendations page (See Appendix A page 234) is a repeat in writing of the information found on the Investment Portfolio page (See Appendix A page 232). Repetition is an excellent communication technique, and this very important aspect of investing warrants such repetition. It is a good idea for the financial advisor to place both pages in front of himself so that all important points which are stated on the recommendation page are covered.

Again, being consistent and keeping words and sentences to a minimum helps in the comprehension of the information. Here is an example.

CASH	is 47 percent of total investments. This is an extreme position and not in your best interest. Up to $111,000 should be invested in other categories.
STOCK MARKET	is 14 percent of the total and should be increased by $33,000. Continue investing in your present portfolio of mutual funds and add international funds. Consider XYZ and ABE international funds with approximately $11,000 in each.
REAL ESTATE	is 20 percent of the total. This could be increased by $15,000. Consider making a 13th monthly payment on your mortgage each year.
PRECIOUS METALS	is zero. You could have up to $3,000 in gold bullion coins; however, at this time, this category is of low priority.
TAX FAVORED	is 10 percent, which is very low. Increase your 401(k) contribution to the maximum. Also, consider investing in a deferred variable annuity ($25,000) and establishing a Profit Sharing plan for your side business. See separate page for this analysis.
COLLECTIBLES	is zero and is of very low priority.

The above example provides very concise yet quite specific recommendations based on repositioning the excess cash holdings leading to a much better allocation of assets. Often, much discussion will be generated by these recommendations and will almost always help the clients in making a change of the status quo.

The Estate Analysis Page

When showing the Estate Analysis page (See Appendix A page 235), the financial advisor should say, "We are going to shift gears again." This jars the client into paying more attention and provides him with an opportunity to make a fresh start. The financial advisor has already unloaded a great deal of information on the client. Regardless of the probably high, keen interest of the client, all of this can become somewhat overwhelming. Remember, one of the objectives of this presentation is to provide an overview of the entire picture; so keep driving on.

The estate analysis for the vast majority of Baby Boomers is mostly survivorship planning with a slight concentration of death taxation. As the Baby Boomer client grows older and becomes more successful in wealth accumulation, the taxation aspect becomes more pertinent. However, even at an introductory level of estate taxation, the Baby Boomer will have keen interest in how it works, and the inclusion of this subject is appropriate.

Listed at the top of the Estate Analysis page are assets by ownership followed by a simple format of how the tax is calculated. Usually, it is applicable to state that, at the death of the first spouse to die, there will be zero taxation. However, when both spouses have died, the calculation produces the amount of tax that is required to be paid within 9 months of death.

It is also very helpful in getting clients to their attorney when it is illustrated how the use of revocable trusts reduces taxation.

	2007	
	Present	**Proposed**
Gross Estate	$5,000,000	$3,000,000[1]
Expenses	(50,000)	(50,000)
Taxable Estate	$4,950,000	$2,950,000
Gross Tax	$ 2,108,300	$976,140
Federal Credit	(780,800)	(780,800)
Total Tax	$ 1,327,500	$ 195,340

[1] A simple explanation showing that when the first spouse died in 2007, $2,000,000 went into a credit shelter trust. This planning prevented this amount of money from ever being subject to death tax and, hence, a dramatic reduction in tax.

The client can quickly see how relatively easy it is for estate planning to save a great deal of taxes and, therefore, will recognize that the attorney's fee can be a real bargain. The primary objective of the Estate Analysis is to determine what legal documents the client should have, to review the present documents to determine appropriateness, and to get the client, if necessary, to set up an appointment with an attorney. This is a win-win-win situation for all. The attorney has an opportunity to see the client, the financial planner (assuming he is not an attorney) is highly regarded by both the client and the attorney, and, of course, the client has been properly served.

The Retirement Plan Asset Allocation Page

Where the client has an IRA, 401(k), 403(b), etc., it is wise to develop an asset allocation illustration to assist in understanding how to select and balance this investment portfolio of retirement plan assets. The procedure used for the Retirement Plan Asset Allocation page (See Appendix A page 236) is similar to that used for pthe Investment Portfolio page, except the Retirement Investment Portfolio will not include a Tax Favored category. Everything on this page is tax favored. Also, Precious Metals and Collectibles are usually not included. This leaves the three basic categories of Cash, Stock Market, and Real Estate. Some advisors may wish to subdivide the Cash category to also list Bonds and/or Mortgages.

The format is simple, clean, and provides an opportunity to illustrate this aspect of the entire plan on one page with ample white space.

If the client has no retirement plans where they select the investment allocation, then the Retirement Plan Asset Allocation page is used along with the Retirement Cash Flow Analysis. (See Appendix A pages 237-240.)

The Retirement Cash Flow Analysis page illustrates all income and outgo projected over the years of retirement. Since that can be a very long period – 20, 30, 40, or more years – it is extremely important for the client to understand that, when dealing with multiple assumptions over many years, the projection is probably wrong, but not so wrong that it is a waste of time. Your client should also be aware that the results must be continually updated as the assumptions and circumstances change. There is no way that anyone can know what the average inflation or investment growth rates will be over many years in the future. There is no way that anyone can know what Social Security benefits will be or how they will be taxed. Each client will experience many changes, good and bad, over 20 to 50 years of retirement.

The vast majority of Baby Boomers are not yet retired, and many have 10 to 30 years *before* the beginning of retirement. These years added to the potential number of retirement years actually precludes all projections from having much more than a modicum of accuracy.

So, why even bother? The answer is two-fold. First, the Baby Boomer client wants to know how much money will be needed for retirement and how long it will last. So, even a guess – particularly an educated guess using reasonable assumptions – is an appropriate service. What the customer wants, the customer should get. After all, even the Baby Boomers are learning that a comfortable retirement is and will be even more so in the future the responsibility of each individual rather than the employer or the government. Hence, Baby Boomers want the answers to important questions such as, "When will I be able to retire? Will I be able to maintain my pre-retirement standard of living? Will my money last as long as I do? Can I afford to assist my grandchildren? How much? When?"

The second part of the answer is that big brothers (the employer and the government) are not willing to carry the heavy burden of retirement on their shoulders. The lyrics to the song, "He ain't heavy, he's my brother," are changing to, "It's been nice knowing you, but now get off my back." So, it is the responsibility of the financial advisor to attempt to determine for the Baby Boomer client whether present assets will do the retirement job, or does the client need to place greater emphasis on these accumulations. The Baby Boomer client wants to know and is willing to pay for this information, and the financial advisor is capable of making these calculations and is in the business of doing so.

The Retirement Cash Flow Analysis pages are overwhelming at first. A full page of numbers, when strange looking, can be overwhelming, even for professionals. The financial advisor should tell the clients on their initial screening of the page that, within five minutes, they will understand everything on the page, money-back guaranteed.

Review all the assumptions at the top of the page. The items are easy to understand when taken one at a time: years of retirement and birth, general inflation rate, pension inflation adjustments, Social Security inflation adjustments, and the projected after-tax investment growth rate.

Line 7, annual desired income which includes estimated income tax, is the equivalent of pre-retirement take-home pay. See Chapter 5 for calculation methods.

Line 8 adds the needed extra annual income for mortgage payments, if any. These payments are usually for only a portion of the retirement years and usually are level payments. Therefore, the payments do not need to include inflation adjustments as in annual income on line 7.

Line 10 is the total value of all assets that could be used to create retirement income. Therefore, assets such as a non-income-producing residence, personal property, collectibles, precious metals, and so forth, are not included.

Line 12 is left at zero on the initial calculation in order to find out what will happen just as things stand now. If there is a shortfall – if the remaining capital becomes zero before an agreed-upon age of death, e.g., 100 – then a little trial and error procedure will render the amount that is necessary in annual accumulations to provide sufficient capital to make the whole thing work.

The financial advisor may wish to run several hypotheticals for the client, especially as the retirement date approaches. For example, if a shortfall occurs, the advisor can make one or more of the following changes:

- Reduce line 7

- Alter assumptions (rates of inflation or investment return)

- Change year/age of retirement

- Include income from part-time work after retirement

- Replace residence(s) with a less expensive home that would release money to be added to remaining capital

Also, a separate analysis is often desirable where it is assumed one spouse dies in a given year which then can alter Social Security and pension benefits and/or reduce income needed for the surviving spouse.

Younger Baby Boomers simply want to know whether they are on the right track. The answer in most cases is that more accumulation is needed. Older Baby Boomers are much more serious and will want and benefit from a more in-depth analysis. Both younger and older Baby Boomers will appreciate this presentation of how retirement planning works and will be happy that their financial advisor has the wherewithal to assist them in this very important area.

The Miscellaneous Page

The Miscellaneous page (See Appendix A page 241) will be omitted in some cases and could expand to several pages in others. As a pure miscellaneous page, a likely inclusion would be information on improper budget allocations, such as a listing of all expenses dealing with an excessive allocation of income to support a residence. An example is shown below.

Mortgage Payment (P & I)	$16,700
Property Tax	5,000
Maintenance/Upkeep	3,100
Insurance	900
	$25,700

This represents 59 percent of your income and is excessive. Options to consider include a lower-priced home, refinancing to lower mortgage payments, renting out part of the house, etc.

Other items could include consideration for a parent, sibling, or adult child assistance, special concerns over risk tolerance, resolving conflicting objectives, and so on.

Additional pages (See Appendix A pages 242-243) could include any special items particular to the clients, such as Mortgage Refinancing, Education Funding, or any request for more information.

The Action Items Page

The Action Items page (See Appendix A page 244) is set up as a checklist of items that the advisor and/or client should be working toward completing. These will include references to the pages on Protection Recommendations, Investment Recommendations, Estate Analysis, Retirement Asset Allocation, Education Funding, and so forth.

Often this page is the proper place to make specific investment recommendations if they were not specified in the Investment Recommendations. This could take the form of a listing of specific stocks or mutual funds to buy or sell, a specific annuity to invest in, and often a reference for the client to see his attorney to consider Wills, Trusts, and Power of Attorney.

It is important that the advisor state that, despite the title of this page, no action is expected at the presentation meeting; however, this page will serve as a checklist during the implementation stage.

Again, get all the information on one page, and keep the list to only a few action items, not more than 8 or 9. In some cases, secondary items of importance will need to be postponed. If the clients are given too much to do, often little or nothing gets done.

There are some clients who really want to do a particular project, even if it is of secondary importance. It should go on the list! It should go on because this sometimes provides the clients with a jump-start to accomplish other, more important items.

Financial planning involves a strong element of creativity, and the more an advisor knows about the client, the more this creativity will be stimulated. So, the extensive time allocated to really getting to know each client will pay off at this point in the planning process.

At the next meeting, the financial advisor and client will review any and all areas the client wishes to discuss, to ask for more clarification, or to suggest alternative approaches that should be explored. At some point, the plan is approved as presented or as modified, and implementation begins.

IMPLEMENTING THE PLAN

Many financial advisors have a sales background and are amazed by the similarities *and* differences between sales and counseling. One example of this is the amount of time spent on each of the three aspects of serving a customer. The aspects are the same, but the time spent on each differs.

SALES TIME LINES

FACT FINDING

PRESENTATION

CLOSE

COUNSELING TIME LINES

FACT FINDING

PRESENTATION

CLOSE

For someone making the transition from sales to counseling, it can be a real shocker to find how easy the product-placement becomes. It is a pleasant surprise, but really it is a natural extension of the process.

Just think about it. The financial advisor has allocated a great deal of time and effort to finding, analyzing, understanding, and solving problems regarding the client's situation. It is quite possible financial advisors understand their clients and situations better than their clients understand themselves and their situations. The advisor is the specialist in financial matters, at least when compared to the client, and if the advisor is not a specialist in some other areas, then he probably knows more than the client in these areas because of experience and because he has consulted with specialists in these areas. Hence, the financial advisor is in a position of having or quickly obtaining knowledge superior to that of the clients. In virtually every case, this position of superiority is readily accepted and appreciated and paid for by the clients. So, after the plan is presented and the clients have indicated it is an acceptable representation of their situation, the implementation is almost a walk in the park.

Financial advisors who have made the transition from sales to consultant know the truth of the following statements. When in sales, the customer will say to the salesperson, "I can't afford it." When in counseling, the client will say to the advisor, "Pat, can I afford it?"

Counseling is a different world. It requires a much higher level of representing the clients' best interests, a much higher level of competence, a much higher level of personal integrity, and the nice part, a much higher level of compensation. Therefore, as important as the implementation phase of financial planning is, it is a slam dunk when compared to all that preceded it. The advisor advises, and the client implements. The easier the advisor makes the implementation process, the happier the client will be, and happy clients stay for more.

Implementation involves putting the financial plan into action. Without implementation, there are only words and numbers. With implementation, there is a living, dynamic operation, and a much greater potential for a much better life and an improved chance of accomplishing all that the client desires.

Implementation should start with Action Items (See Appendix A page 244). The top of the list is all of the Protection (insurance) Items as recommended on the Protection Recommendation page of the financial plan (See Appendix A page 230). When the advisor is properly licensed for each type of insurance, he is a natural to make the changes, additions, or deletions. Otherwise, either the advisor or the client should contact the proper agent to make the adjustments agreed upon.

Each item in the list on the Action page should be discussed with an agreement on who is to do what. There usually is no specific order of necessity. Each case is unique, so the particular circumstances will usually dictate what comes first, then second, then third, and so on.

If the financial advisor is not the client's attorney, then the advisor should encourage the client to set up an appointment with an attorney to review all aspects of estate planning and all legal documents. Also, the advisor should suggest that the client or the advisor supply a copy of the complete financial plan to the attorney. Explaining this will save some time and maybe expense for the attorney. This also is an opportunity to get the advisor's name and quality of work in front of the attorney. As somebody once said, "It pays to advertise."

Usually clients are very interested in "getting things done" and, therefore, items should be handled with business-like dispatch. Other times, clients will need a more extended period to adjust to the newness. Once in awhile, clients will just not want to do this or that despite their knowing it is what they should do. In these cases, the advisor should keep going back to square one, being a good counselor, even teacher, by rephrasing the major points which led to the recommendations. Also, getting clients to talk about the issue or their concerns can be an effective technique to make them more comfortable and win them over. Rarely, but it does happen, the advisor will simply have to say, "You're just not comfortable in doing this, so let's just drop it." The client is relieved, and the advisor is respected for not pushing too hard and is in a proper position to re-initiate the issue at some appropriate time in the future.

For example, George, a financial advisor, recommended once again at the third annual review that the client purchase $100,000 of life insurance. The client said, "I've rejected that recommendation more than once in the past. Are you going to keep recommending it forever?" George replied, "No, I'm only going to recommend it for as long as you need it and can buy it." The client looked at the advisor for a long moment and then said, "Well, in that case, I guess I might just as well buy the damn policy." He did, the issue was closed, the advisor had done his job, and the client was properly served.

Implementation of a financial plan is the capstone of the process. In most cases, implementation is simply a function of the advisor or the client just doing it – sign here, ask the accountant, call a mutual fund representative, you do this, I'll do that – but until it is done, it ain't done!

MONITORING THE PLAN

A routine physical examination, a periodic dental check-up, and a financial review are all examples of monitoring the plan. It is a process of reviewing the current status of the body or the wealth, and it is an opportunity to introduce new concepts or products.

Putting things in order is the beginning, and monitoring the status of the plan is the ongoing process. This monitoring process should be customized to fit each client's needs and desires. For some clients, it might be a quarterly, semi-annual, or annual update. Some may wish a daily update on their stock portfolio or on some other aspect of their financial matters. Whatever is appropriate for a specific client is what the financial advisor should do. Offer the service or the client will find someone else who will.

For the vast majority of Baby Boomer clients, an annual review after the initial planning sessions will be proper. During the interval between the initial planning sessions and the first annual review, the financial advisor should call clients periodically. Suitable reasons for such calls can always be found, but the real reason is to reinforce in the client's mind the fact that his future is in competent and trustworthy hands.

After a few years of annual reviews, it may be appropriate to extend the interval between the periodic reviews to two years, but this should not be done until the client has a very good understanding of what he is doing and has a high comfort level.

When a client starts calling somewhat frequently, it often is an indication that concerns are developing, and this should trigger the next review. The other side of the coin is represented by the client not calling at all. The financial advisor should set up a system for reminding such clients that it is time for a review, similar to what many dentists do.

Scheduling the Review Meeting

A post card with a simple message is an excellent reminder.

> Financial Planning is an ongoing activity which requires periodic updating. Many factors are constantly changing that affect your personal considerations. Now, it's your move! Just call 555-1234 to schedule an appointment. We'll do the rest!

If there is no response to the postcard, and an improper amount of time has elapsed since the preceding review, then the next step should be a phone call. The message can be soft and should express personal and professional concern. For example, "It's been x months/years since our last meeting, and many circumstances have changed that affect you and your financial plan. Some of these changes may be personal to you. Other outside influences such as taxes, inflation, investment rates of returns, insurance, and so forth, may have had a significant effect on your plan. I really think we should schedule a meeting." The message needs to be one of concern for the client's financial well-being. The advisor will be seen as someone who cares and is going the extra mile to offer service.

Most of the review meeting will be a revisiting of the entire plan. This would include a summary review of the statistical aspects and a detailed discussion on alterations that are appropriate. So, an adequate amount of time should be allotted for the session.

Many young Baby Boomers will struggle for years just getting up to operating under a balanced budget. In these cases, the review meeting provides the financial advisor with the opportunity to discuss the basics of cash management, particularly those that are proving difficult for the clients to master. An emphasis needs to be placed on the importance of good money management, and a discussion on what the clients have been doing right, what they have been doing wrong, and what they can do to correct the wrong actions.

Older Baby Boomers' reviews often have an increasing emphasis on retirement planning. This, of course, includes wealth accumulation, which often includes a reduction in spending and the reallocation of those dollars into investments.

Preparing for the Review Meeting

The review procedure for all clients starts by the financial advisor contacting the clients and gaining their acceptance that this is the proper time for a review. Then comes the more difficult task of getting updated information from the clients, including both soft and hard facts. Some of this needed information can be obtained using the Financial Plan Update form (See Appendix A pages 245-246). This form establishes the importance of the advisor receiving updated information *before* setting an appointment. It states the fee that will be incurred, and if more than one advisor is available, it provides the clients the opportunity to select with whom they would like this review.

The financial advisor should review the pages of itemized assets and liabilities from the previous plan and then tailor them to make the process as painless for the clients as possible. Remember, Baby Boomers and patience are mutually exclusive. By deleting all items that the financial advisor already has in the files, the advisor has made the task less demanding for the clients. This also acts as a reminder to the clients that obtaining products from the advisor transfers some of the updating work from the clients to the advisor.

The clients are asked to update the number of shares in investments still maintained in their portfolios, and delete or add investments, insurance, and/or annuities as appropriate since the last review meeting. It is also important for clients to provide an update on present mortgage(s).

Items such as income tax returns not yet seen by the advisor and current insurance policies are often bulky to mail. Also, tax returns are important and confidential papers that many clients hate to allow out of their sight, so the clients are instructed to bring these items to the review meeting. Usually the financial advisor, or a staff person, can extract the required information in a short amount of time, and the advisor can evaluate and make recommendations on the spot.

The Financial Planning Update form (See Appendix A pages 245-246) is two pages back-to-back and addresses the most important concerns at this time. It provides current information on financial objectives and risk tolerance. The Financial Objectives are evaluated for currentness and appropriateness. Then they are compared with those originally provided by the client for any significant differences that should be explored.

The next two parts, Investment Objectives and Current Attitude, are studied to determine any changes in risk tolerance. The scoring is on a scale of 0 to 10, and the score is compared to that determined by the original financial attitude questionnaire, which had a scale of 0 to 23. The comparison is done by dividing the score obtained on the original questionnaire in half. This is not an absolutely accurate calibration, but neither is any other single evaluation of risk tolerance. A weighted average for two partners (spouses) is developed in a way similar to that used at the beginning of the client relationship.

If the client's highest priority (#1) in Investment Objectives is any one of the bottom three items – Appreciation, Inflation, Taxation – then 1 point is allocated toward the calculations to achieve their risk propensity score. No points are allocated if the highest priority is any of the top three – Liquidity, Safety, Current Income. Thus, the client's score in Investment Objectives is either 1 or 0.

The Current Attitude game requests that the client allocate 8 points among four investment objectives. Half points can be used. Tax Benefits and Appreciation are more aggressive determinants, whereas Cash Flow and Safety lean toward the conservative side. The financial advisor uses the following Evaluation Grid to find the total score for the Current Attitude game.

EVALUATION GRID				
Score	Tax Benefits	Current Cash Flow	Appreciation	Safety
1	0.0	4.0	0.0	4.0
2	0.5	3.5	0.5	3.5
3	1.0	3.0	1.0	3.0
4	1.5	2.5	1.5	2.5
5	2.0	2.0	2.0	2.0
6	2.5	1.5	2.5	1.5
7	3.0	1.0	3.0	1.0
8	3.5	0.5	3.5	0.5
9	4.0	0.0	4.0	0.0

The total score for the Current Attitude game is divided by 4 and the result-ing quotient plus the Investment Objectives score (either 1 or 0) equals the client's current risk-tolerance position on a scale of 0 to 10, with 0 representing almost no risk tolerance and 10 representing considerable risk tolerance. Of course, this pro-cedure is not highly scientific, but for the non-psychologist advisor, it does provide a ball-park/objective range for an investment portfolio that the client is not likely to destroy, say, after a severe stock market correction. The risk-tolerance position helps the advisor in designing an investment portfolio that matches the client's need for a proper rate of return with his comfort level.

Figure 7.1 shows one client's choices and how the client's risk-tolerance position is obtained from these choices.

Figure 7.1

INVESTMENT OBJECTIVES

RANK IN ORDER FROM 1 (HIGHEST) TO 6 (LOWEST)

_4_	Liquidity
_3_	Safety of Principal
_6_	Current Income from Investments
_1_	Appreciation
_2_	Protection from Inflation
_5_	Tax Reduction or Deferral

How to score: The client's top priority, number 1, is one of the bottom three items. Therefore, the score for this part is 1.

CURRENT ATTITUDE

Tax Benefits	Current Cash Flow	Appreciation	Safety
2.0	0.5	4.0	1.5

How to score: Use the Evaluation Grid.
The score for 2.0 under Tax Benefits is 5
The score for 0.5 under Current Cash Flow is 8.
The score for 4.0 under Appreciation is 9.
The score for 1.5 under Safety is 6.
The total score is 5 + 8 + 9 + 6, or 28.

How to find the risk-tolerance position:
Divide the Current Attitude Score by 4
(28 ÷ 4 = 7) and add the Investment Objective Score (7 + 1 = 8).
The risk-tolerance position is 8.

A risk-tolerance score of 8 represents an aggressive risk taker, similar to a 16 or 17 on the original financial-attitude questionnaire. When a client has been working with a financial advisor for several years, the client's actions will indicate more correctly the client's level of comfort with different asset allocation mixes than does a risk-tolerance position. However, these risk-tolerance positions have proven to have a strong correlation with reality and are quite valuable in the early stages of a client-advisor relationship. Furthermore, most clients have a better feeling about their relationships with a financial advisor who takes the necessary time to better understand as much as possible about them. So, not only do financial advisors who use the procedure just discussed have a better understanding of their clients, the vast majority of their clients approve of the procedure and appreciate their advisors even more.

The reverse side, or second page, of the Financial Planning Update form gives clients an opportunity to tell the advisor of planned expenditures or desires and to list important issues they would like to discuss. These items are very revealing to the financial advisor of what is going on in the client's mind. This could include some otherwise hidden dissatisfaction with previous advice or recommendations. Sometimes products or concepts that need to be re-sold are exposed. And, of course, the desire for a change of financial direction can often be relayed to the advisor more easily with a few written words than with words that must be spoken face to face.

Monitoring the financial plan is one of the most important tasks of financial planning. It provides an opportunity to continue to fortify long relationships with clients and to give even more individualized services to them. This often leads to increased compensation for the advisor as the clients seek more advice. Also, the conscientiousness exhibited by the monitoring process is often referred to by clients when talking with their friends and business colleagues, with the result that such direct and indirect referrals expand the financial advisor's practice. What is really nice about this last point is that the referrals are unsolicited.

John Todd, a recognized giant in the insurance deferred compensation arena, once said in a speech before a Million Dollar Round Table audience, "When you've been around as long as I have, you have to hide to keep from writing a million dollars worth of life insurance." Now just think about this for a moment. Todd is not saying that you have to hang around for a long time before you begin to reap rewards. Hidden behind his comments is the mathematical principle of geometric progression. If you so impress your first client that he tells two friends or colleagues who come to you for advice, and they tell two of their friends or colleagues who come to you for advice, and they tell…. How long do you think it would take to have more clients than you can handle and more money than you can spend?

To paraphrase John Todd, "When you have been in the financial planning business for a long time, you have to hide to keep from receiving more referrals than you can handle."

Chapter 8

Three Baby-Boomer Case Studies

The following case studies will highlight some typical problems and concerns, and will suggest methods for dealing with such problems and concerns.

The first case study concerns Jack and Jill, who are young Baby Boomers, ages 46 and 44 respectively, with a seven-year-old child. They are dedicated to building a strong family relationship and successfully developing two careers.

The second case study is about Bob and Bev, who are each 52 years old and have two adult children, ages 21 and 25. The younger child has one year of college remaining and probably will be on her own after graduation much like her older brother is now.

The final case study concerns John and Jim, ages 51 and 44 respectively, who are purchasing a home together, are sharing expenses commensurate with their different levels of income, and have been living together for about a dozen years.

Every attempt has been made to limit the demographic information of these three couples to a need-to-know basis. The author hopes that this will allow the reader to dive directly into the substance of the situations without the necessity of remembering excessive details.

JACK AND JILL – YOUNG BOOMERS

Young Baby Boomers like Jack and Jill have a tough row to hoe. Neither comes from wealthy parents, but both have the advantage of college educations. They married somewhat on schedule, which for Baby Boomers is in their late twenties and early thirties. Each brought to the marriage a small accumulation of financial assets, lots of possessions of furniture and clothes, a car, and, oh yes, a sizable debt.

Jack and Jill are very much in love with each other and have a strong determination to develop a wonderful life together. Early in their marriage they decided wisely to hire a financial planner. They agreed that the large millstone of debt they carried around their necks could possibly lead to major problems down the road, and so they decided the best course of action would be to remove this weight as soon as possible.

After making the wise decision to hire a financial advisor, Jack and Jill unwisely failed to pay attention to everything she advised. After meeting with their advisor for a couple of years, they finally realized what she meant by the question she kept repeating, "Why do you spend so much money on [whatever] when you both say it is not an important item? Why not change the way you allocate your income to first stop spending more than you earn, and then apply more to reduce current debt?" At this point, Jack and Jill finally realized that they and they alone would have to decide to change. Their financial planner could not do it for them. So, once again they asked their advisor to spell out how they can get out of debt.

The financial advisor thought, "Here we go again," but she sensed that this time she might actually get through to them. So, patiently, she repeated once more the proven system for getting out of debt. From each dollar of take-home pay, allocate 10› to savings, 20› to debt repayment, and live on the remainder.

Jack and Jill said, "We'll do it!" Although it was not so simple in the beginning, they did do it, and in a few years, they had only a mortgage on their home and a small balance on the loans for their cars. They were surprised that the 10› per dollar had accumulated to a proper emergency fund, and the deductions from their incomes for each of their 401(k) plans at work were starting to really amount to something. All this encouraged them during the dark days.

It wasn't easy, and there were some hard times, especially with the day-care expenses for their son, Jason. However, this expenditure was greatly reduced when, on the advice of their financial planner, they investigated and then started to participate in their employer's salary reduction (pre-tax) plan for child care expense reimbursement.

Further investigation led them to participate in the employer medical reimbursement salary reduction plan which reduced their income taxes even more. These tax savings have allowed them to start a special accumulation fund to pay cash, they hope, for their next car. Jack is not sure that this will be possible, but with the combination of driving each car longer (10 years), having lower car debt to repay, and maintaining a special sinking fund for a car purchase, he feels that soon this financial-planning scheme of saving interest expense and adding interest income will produce loan-free transportation for the remainder of their lives.

It took much counseling and some distasteful cash-flow decisions, but Jack and Jill were able to get out of their deep hole of debt in about a half-dozen years. It was after the fact when they realized that this could have been accomplished much sooner had their improper spending habits not been so deeply ingrained.

Now, Jack and Jill are celebrating their ninth wedding anniversary. They also are planning to upgrade to a more expensive home in a better school district and with a generally nicer environment for themselves and for their very intelligent son. The current financial decision they are pondering is what price home they can afford. Their financial planner recommended they consider this question from three angles. First, determine a ball-park figure for the proper price of a residence; second, determine the proper amount – the down payment – that should be tied up in their personal use real estate; and third, determine the proper amount of monthly mortgage payment they can handle. The advisor gave to Jack and Jill the formulas for these three determinations.

Proper Price Range of Residence

Lower	$82,000 (Annual Income) x 2	=	$164,000
Upper	$82,000 (Annual Income) x 2.5	=	$205,000

The proper price range is between $164,000 and $205,000.

Proper Amount of Down Payment

Lower	$164,000 (Price of Home) x 0.20	=	$32,000
Upper	$205,000 (Price of Home) x 0.20	=	$41,000
Goal	$49,000 (Total Investment) x 0.25	=	$12,250

The range for a down payment is from $32,000 to $41,000, but this is much greater than what should be invested in personal use real estate.

Proper Amount of Monthly Payment

Maximum	$82,000 (Annual Income) x 0.25/12	=	$1,708
Ideal	$82,000 (Annual Income) x 0.15/12	=	$1,025

The financial planner explained to Jack and Jill that these numbers should be considered approximations. However, they show a dilemma. Jack and Jill have sufficient income to afford a home in the $164,000 to $205,000 range with a mortgage payment (principal plus interest) ideally in the neighborhood of $1,000 per month. However, with their low amount of total investments, $49,000, only $12,250 should be tied up in personal use real estate. If the best interest rates are available only with a 20 percent or greater down payment, then $12,250 goal would indicate that the residence price should be no more than $61,250. Even if a residence could be found at this price, it would be unacceptable to Jack and Jill, because it would not fulfill their reasons for buying a new home.

Because Jack and Jill are relatively young, a financial plan should accommodate some deviation from the rules. The goals should be clear – in this case, no more than 25 percent of total investments tied up in personal use real estate – but something could be altered, at least temporarily. For example, Jack and Jill could buy a home for $165,000 with a 20 percent down payment ($33,000) and with a low mortgage payment ($879 @ 7% for 30 years). This would allow more funds to be invested to build up their total investments which would bring the amount of their money tied up in their home more in line with the goal of 25 percent of all investments. Alternatively, they could go with a 10 percent down payment with a higher mortgage payment ($1,090 @ 8% for 30 years). This would produce an amount tied up in personal use real estate of $16,500, which is not that distant from the proper amount of $12,250. Even this would require some attention to building up their total investments.

In this situation, their financial advisor probably should recommend they elect the higher down payment, if sufficient cash is available. Even though this exacerbates the imbalance in their investment portfolio, the lower debt service will allow for faster accumulations in other investment categories, and the psychological boost this would give to Jack and Jill could encourage them to achieve even greater accumulations. Furthermore, a lower mortgage payment will add flexibility to their cash flow in case any one of many possible problems arise in the future.

The point to recognize is that the financial advisor should present alternatives for Jack and Jill to ponder along with emphasis on two important concepts. The advisor should establish in the minds of the clients the considerable importance of achieving and maintaining a goal, even if it is not attainable at this point in their lives. Then, the advisor should help the clients understand the extent their choice may cause their plan to deviate from the goal and what the ramifications of this are. Of course, the advisor should discourage any action that results in an excessive deviation from what is in the clients' best interests and from what could sail them into troubled waters.

Jack and Jill have another area of concern and that is funding a college education for their young son, Jason. Their financial planner prepared an analysis of potential costs using what they agreed were reasonable assumptions.

Current Annual Cost of College	$15,000
Inflation rate for Education	6%
After-tax Rate of Growth for Investment	8%

Figure 8.1

JASON

EDUCATIONAL FUNDING

YEAR	STARTING BALANCE	NET GROWTH	ANNUAL DEPOSIT	WITH-DRAWAL	FUND(S) ENDING BALANCE
2007	$ 0	$ 0	$ 6,402	$ 0	$6,402
2008	6,402	448	6,402	0	13,252
2009	13,252	928	6,402	0	20,582
2010	20,582	1,441	6,402	0	28,425
2011	28,425	1,990	6,402	0	36,816
2012	36,816	2,577	6,402	0	45,795
2013	45,795	3,206	6,402	0	55,403
2014	55,403	3,878	6,402	0	65,683
2015	65,683	4,598	6,402	0	76,683
2016	76,683	5,368	6,402	0	88,453
2017	88,453	6,192	6,402	0	101,047
2018	101,047	7,073	6,402	17,085	97,437
2019	97,437	6,821	6,402	35,194	75,465
2020	75,465	5,283	6,402	37,306	49,844
2021	49,844	3,489	6,402	39,544	20,190
2022	20,190	1,413	0	21,569	35
TOTAL				**$96,030**	**$150,699**

ASSUMPTIONS

2007 ANNUAL COST	$18,000
EDUCATION INFLATION RATE	6.00%
AFTER-TAX GROWTH RATE IS	7.00%

The analysis based on these assumptions shows a need for an annual accumulation of $6,402, or about $533 per month. If Jack and Jill started now and continued making this allocation through the four years of college under the above assumptions, they will have the funds to pay the total costs of $150,699.

Jill asked, "Where are we going to get $533 a month?" This question is typical, and the answer often is, "It's not possible at this point in time." However, even if all the money cannot be found right now, the analysis puts the problem on the table. Quite often a smaller amount can be found and the accumulation program begun. More can be added to this category as favorable changes occur in the parents' financial situation. The important thing is to start the accumulation program, regardless of the initial amount.

Another suggestion is for Jack and Jill to show the analysis to their parents and grandparents who might be able to provide some assistance.

Other questions always arise. For example, where should Jack and Jill put the money, and who should own such accounts? When there are a few years or more in which to accumulate these funds, an equity investment should absolutely be the top priority. Probably, a growth mutual fund is the easiest and best place to start. Depending upon the amount accumulated, other investment vehicles should be added for diversification.

Next, a Uniform Gifts to Minors Account (UGMA) or Uniform Transfers to Minors Account (UTMA) are other important forms of ownership.

There is good and bad in each form of ownership, and proper analysis of the effects on each client should be made. For example, the aspect of how these accumulated funds will affect the availability of scholarships must be evaluated. Scholarship rules are in a constant state of flux and are difficult to anticipate many years into the future. However, each aspect of the clients' individual circumstances should be considered.

Jack and Jill have other needs, wants, and desires. However, the most important ones are getting out of debt, obtaining a proper residence, and starting an education fund for their son. Not far behind these is retirement funding, especially now for Jack. Ever since he turned forty, the thought of being able to retire early, maybe at 55, is very appealing. But how in the world will he ever be able to find the money necessary to do this? Oh well, that problem can be left for another day. This day, it's time to go house hunting.

Note: Jack and Jill had a heavy debt load, which is typical for Baby Boomers. They were set in their ways when it came to their spending habits, and this made it quite difficult for them to correct this detrimental practice.

It is often frustrating for a planner to render good advice only to have it ignored. Jack and Jill's financial planner was in a very precarious position. If she pressed too hard, the clients wouldn't come back. In other words, they would fire their financial planner, and everybody would be a loser.

A planner-client relationship can be delicate when the clients' old habits should be changed – even old habits firmly in place at young ages. The planner must remember it is the client's life and the client's money. Clients will only do what they want to do. So, when clients do not heed a recommendation immediately, the planner must be very patient, must use all of his teaching ability, and must remain gentle but tenacious. Then, hopefully, the client will keep coming back and everybody wins.

Setting high standards in each area of financial planning is the task of a financial planner. However, it may take time to get a client to achieve these standards, and the financial advisor must have the patience of a saint.

BOB AND BEV – OLDER BOOMERS

Bob and Bev are about to enter into a somewhat different life style: empty nesters with college expenditures behind them. Their daughter does have one more year of school, but money for that expense has already been accumulated and has been set aside. An accounting firm in a large city only 60 miles away has already committed her to a three-year contract after graduation. Bob and Bev's son lives and works in the same city their daughter will be working in, and he is doing very well. There are no current indications of any wedding plans for either child, but Bob and Bev recently agreed, "Weddings will probably be our next big expense."

Another consideration is their concern for Bev's mother. She seems to manage quite well since Bev's father died a few years ago, but Bob and Bev worry whether her mother's assets are sufficient for a potentially long remaining life. All attempts to discuss her mother's financial matters have drawn almost no response except, "Everything is just fine. Don't worry about me."

The real "biggie" for Bob is retirement. His original goal of retirement at age 55 went out the window a few years ago with the almost back-to-back costs of college educations. Furthermore, Bob decided to change employers a couple of years ago and accepted a very nice increase in income. However, he had to make a commitment to work to age 65. Bob feels he is in a count-down situation and has a little over a dozen years to really concentrate on wealth accumulation for retirement. The large rollovers from his former employer's pension plan and 401(k) plan will require proper attention. Both Bob and Bev know the importance of this self-directed IRA, and their financial planner, Ben, has convinced them they have invested much too conservatively and without proper diversification.

At a recent meeting with Ben, Bob and Bev discussed a proposal on how their IRA investment portfolio should be adjusted.

Ben explained that the proposal first presents their current position under "PRESENT" and the recommended allocation under "PROPOSED". Then comes an itemized listing of all investments. The issues of concern are spelled out under "CONSIDERATIONS". Then the "RECOMMENDATIONS" provide a step-by-step procedure for action. "RESULT" illustrates the portfolio allocation as it would be if the plan is activated. Ben assures them that, of course, all of these changes are subject to discussion and input from Bob and Bev. After a final allocation is agreed upon, the implementation is a matter of signing forms and other administrative procedures.

Caution: If the implementation of products involves a sales charge, the financial advisor needs to be especially prepared to defend each charge. Also, the recommended allocation, including real estate and a high stock market percentage, could be challenged by some advisors. However, each of these recommendations can be justified as being in the clients best interest. For example:

- There is minimal need for cash.

- Bob has a long-term investment horizon. At age 52, his use of these monies is at least a dozen years away and probably usage will be extended over the remainder of Bob and Bev's lifetime.

- Real estate adds desirable asset allocation diversification.

- Different families of funds also add diversification of management and corporate philosophy.

At the next meeting with their financial advisor, Bob expressed his real desire of being able to retire at 65. He said, "We will be able to start a major accumulation effort now and, well, it's just got to be done." Bev agreed, adding, "Now it's our turn. There are a few trips in our plans, but no other big ticket items are on the agenda." Bob reminded her, "Don't forget the weddings, whenever they may be." When they finished talking, they both looked at Ben, expectantly. "Would you prepare one of those Retirement Cash Flow Analyses for us so that we can see just how big the task really is?"

Ben smiled, because he had anticipated this request and had already put the retirement subject on their agenda. He handed the printout to them.

As Bob and Bev reviewed the analysis, they realized that not only did Bob have justification for his concerns about being able to retire at 65, but things were even more serious than they had anticipated.

Ben calmly discussed the important issues such as Bob's small pension due to his relatively short tenure with his current employer, and the fact they had accumulated only a relatively small amount of assets. (See $400,000 on line 10.) Ben pointed out

Figure 8.2

BOB AND BEV

IRA ASSET ALLOCATION

	PRESENT			PROPOSED		
CASH	$ 17.5	5	%	$ 1.0	0	%
BONDS	192.5	55		28.0	8	
STOCK MARKET	140.0	40		261.0	75	
REAL ESTATE	0.0	0		60.0	17	
TOTAL	**$350.0**	**100**	**%**	**$350.0**	**100**	**%**

CASH

ABC MONEY MARKET	$ 17.5	
		$ 17.5

BONDS

BOND FUND FOR SAFETY	$ 85.2	
GOVT BOND TOTAL SAFETY	77.3	
G.B. CORPORATION	15.0	
E.T. CORPORATION	15.0	
		$192.5

STOCK MARKET

AB INCOME & GROWTH	$ 41.00	
AB CONSERVATIVE GROWTH	28.9	
AB GROWTH	48.0	
AB FOUNDERS GROWTH	22.1	
		$140.0
		$350.0

CONSIDERATIONS

1. YOUR NEED FOR CASH IS LIMITED TO SMALL OPERATIONAL EXPENSES AND SHOULD BE REDUCED ACCORDINGLY.

2. YOU WILL NOT USE ANY OF THESE FUNDS UNTIL AT LEAST RETIREMENT (13 YEARS), AND PROBABLY NOT UNTIL WELL INTO RETIREMENT. THEREFORE, YOU HAVE AN EXCESSIVE ALLOCATION OF FIXED-DOLLAR ASSETS (BONDS).

3. YOUR STOCK MARKET PORTFOLIO IS ALL IN ONE FAMILY OF FUNDS AND SHOULD BE DIVERSIFIED INTO SEVERAL FAMILIES OF FUNDS. FURTHER, YOU HAVE ZERO INTERNATIONAL HOLDINGS AND THAT IS IMPROPER.

4. ZERO REAL ESTATE IS IMPROPER.

Figure 8.2 (cont'd)

RECOMMENDATIONS					
SELL			**INVEST**		
1. SELL BONDS			**4. INVEST IN TWO REITs**		
ALL G.B.			**(REAL ESTATE INVESTMENT**		
CORPORATION	$ 15.0		**TRUSTS)**		
ALL E.T.			CBC REIT	$ 30.0	
CORPORATION	15.0		BCC REIT MUTUAL FUND	30.0	
ALL BOND FUND					
FOR SAFETY	85.2				
PART GOVT BOND					
TOTAL SAFETY	49.3			———	
		$164.5			$ 60.0
2. SELL STOCK MUTUAL FUNDS			**5. INVEST IN THE FOLLOWING**		
			MUTUAL FUNDS		
AB CONSERVATIVE	$ 28.5		BC GROWTH	$ 50.0	
GROWTH			CD GROWTH	50.0	
AB GROWTH	48.0		DE AGGRESSIVE		
AB FOUNDERS			GROWTH	50.0	
GROWTH	22.1		EE INTERNATIONAL	35.0	
			FG INTERNATIONAL	34.6	
		$ 98.6			$219.6
3. INVEST FROM MONEY					
MARKET	$ 16.5				
		16.5			
TOTAL		**$279.6**	**TOTAL**		**$279.6**

RESULT				
CASH				**PERCENT**
ABC MONEY MARKET		$ 1.0		
		$ 1.0		0%
BONDS				
GOVT BOND TOTAL SAFETY		$ 28.0		
		$ 28.0		8
STOCK MARKET				
AB INCOME & GROWTH		$ 41.0		
BC GROWTH & INCOME		50.0		
CD GROWTH & INCOME		50.0		
DE AGGRESSIVE GROWTH		50.0		
EF INTERNATIONAL		35.0		
FG INTERNATIONAL		35.0		
		$261.0		75
REAL ESTATE				
CBC REIT		$ 30.0		
BCC REIT MUTUAL FUND		30.0		
		$ 60.0		17
TOTAL		**$350.0**	**TOTAL**	**100%**

Figure 8.3

BEV AND BOB
RETIREMENT CASH FLOW ANALYSIS #1

SIGNIFICANT ASSUMPTIONS

1.	YEAR OF RETIREMENT				2020
2.	YEAR BORN:	*RETIREE 1*	BOB		1955
2A.		*RETIREE 2*	BEV		1955

3.	ANNUAL INFLATION					
	RATE FOR YEARS	1-10 3.0%	11-20 3.5%	THEREAFTER		3.5%
4.	SOCIAL SECURITY INFLATION RATE					3.0%
5.	AFTER-TAX RATE OF RETURN ON INVESTMENTS					7.0%
6.	PENSION INFLATION AJD:	*OPT 1 = COMPOUNDED INFL RATE*		0.0%	BOB	0.0% BEV
6A.		*OPT 2 = FLAT FIXED DOLLAR AMT*		$0	BOB	$0 BEV

				2007 DOLLARS	**RETIREMENT DOLLARS**
7.	ANNUAL DESIRED INCOME (EXCLUDING MORTGAGE)			$80,000	$117,483
8.	ANNUAL MORTGAGE PMT (PRIN & INT ONLY)	*ENDING*	2024		$12,000
9.	SOCIAL SECURITY	BOB *STARTING*	2020		$22,000
9A.		BEV *STARTING*	2020		$11,000
10.	CAPITAL AVAILABLE FOR INVESTING			$400,000	$963,938
11.	PENSION BENEFITS	BOB *STARTING*	2020		$9,000
11A.		BEV *STARTING*	0		$0
12.	ADDITIONAL ANNUAL INVESTMENTS NEEDED			$0	$0

YEAR	AGE 1	2	REQUIRED INCOME	MORTGAGE PAYMENT	SOCIAL SECURITY	OTHER INC (EXPENSES)	PENSION BOB	PENSION BEV	AMT NEEDED FROM CAPITAL	REMAINING CAPITAL	SHORTFALL
2020	65	65	117,483	12,000	33,000	0	9,000	0	87,483	940,869	0
2021	66	66	121,007	12,000	33,990	0	9,000	0	90,017	913,562	0
2022	67	67	124,637	12,000	35,010	0	9,000	0	92,628	881,642	0
2023	68	68	128,377	12,000	36,060	0	9,000	0	95,317	844,704	0
2024	69	69	132,228	12,000	37,142	0	9,000	0	98,086	802,314	0
2025	70	70	136,195	0	38,256	0	9,000	0	88,939	766,425	0
2026	71	71	140,280	0	39,404	0	9,000	0	91,877	724,982	0
2027	72	72	144,489	0	40,586	0	9,000	0	94,903	677,506	0
2028	73	73	148,824	0	41,803	0	9,000	0	98,020	623,481	0
2029	74	74	153,288	0	43,058	0	9,000	0	101,231	562,351	0
2030	75	75	157,887	0	44,349	0	9,000	0	104,538	493,519	0
2031	76	76	163,413	0	45,680	0	9,000	0	108,733	415,526	0
2032	77	77	169,132	0	47,050	0	9,000	0	113,082	327,573	0
2033	78	78	175,052	0	48,462	0	9,000	0	117,590	228,797	0
2034	79	79	181,179	0	49,915	0	9,000	0	122,263	118,270	0
2035	80	80	187,520	0	51,413	0	9,000	0	122,409	0	4,698
2036	81	81	194,083	0	52,955	0	9,000	0	0	0	132,128
2037	82	82	200,876	0	54,544	0	9,000	0	0	0	137,332
2038	83	83	207,907	0	56,180	0	9,000	0	0	0	142,727
2039	84	84	215,184	0	57,866	0	9,000	0	0	0	148,318
2040	85	85	222,715	0	59,602	0	9,000	0	0	0	154,113
2041	86	86	230,510	0	61,390	0	9,000	0	0	0	160,120
2042	87	87	238,578	0	63,231	0	9,000	0	0	0	166,347
2043	88	88	246,928	0	65,128	0	9,000	0	0	0	172,800
2044	89	89	255,571	0	67,082	0	9,000	0	0	0	178,488
2045	90	90	264,516	0	69,095	0	9,000	0	0	0	186,421
2046	91	91	273,774	0	71,168	0	9,000	0	0	0	193,606
2047	92	92	283,356	0	73,303	0	9,000	0	0	0	201,053
2048	93	93	293,273	0	75,502	0	9,000	0	0	0	208,772
2049	94	94	303,538	0	77,767	0	9,000	0	0	0	216,771
2050	95	95	314,162	0	80,100	0	9,000	0	0	0	225,062
2051	96	96	325,157	0	82,503	0	9,000	0	0	0	233,655
2052	97	97	336,538	0	84,978	0	9,000	0	0	0	242,560
2053	98	98	348,317	0	87,527	0	9,000	0	0	0	251,790
2054	99	99	360,508	0	90,153	0	9,000	0	0	0	261,355
2055	100	100	373,125	0	92,857	0	9,000	0	0	0	271,268

This analysis is based on the accuracy and consistency of the data and assumptions you have provided in items 1 through 11 and is not guaranteed. The figures shown are valid only as long as the data and assumptions remain unchanged. To maintain accuracy of this analysis, periodic updating is necessary to reflect changes as they occur.

that their lifestyle and the big expense of college for their children had precluded more wealth accumulation. Also, they had recently refinanced their mortgage which extended payments to a few years into their retirement.

"The bottom line," Ben told them, "is that if you do not start an asset accumulation plan immediately, and if you retire at age 65, then you will be broke at age 80. And current mortality tables show that if you both live to age 65, the average life expectancy of at least one of you will be around age 92."

Bob and Bev looked at the analysis and recognized that, at age 81, they would need $132,128 to maintain their current standard of living, but they would have only $61,955 ($52,955 Social Security plus $9,000 Pension). It was obvious to both of them: a $70,173 drop in their standard of living would be unacceptable.

Bob and Bev said in unison, "This is terrible. What can we do?"

Ben replied, "Let me rephrase your question. You should ask how much you need to save each year until retirement in order to make it all work." Naturally, Ben had anticipated their reaction and presented a second analysis. As he showed it to Bob and Bev, he said, "This analysis changes only one thing. On line 12, we add an annual accumulation of $31,800. Now, look at the lower right corner. It shows that you will not be broke until age 100."

Bob and Bev looked at the amount on line 12. Bev said, "That's about $2,700 per month."

"We can do it," Bob said. Bev added, "We have to do it. I want to continue our good life together no matter what it takes."

Ben explained, "As official as these analyses may look, they are just numbers based on assumptions. Furthermore, there is no possibility that every single one of our assumptions will be exactly on point." He paused to see how Bob and Bev were assimilating this important information. Then he continued, "For example, how can anyone really know what Social Security will be like in 2012, when many Baby Boomers will be retiring? What about the many years that follow 2012? How can anyone be sure the other assumptions about inflation and average investment growth rate will turn out to be true?"

At this point, Ben noted Bob and Bev beginning to look worried. He smiled at them and said, "This is why I recommend that this type of analysis be done periodically. As future changes occur, this new reality will be incorporated into the equations. Adjustments may be necessary, but with continuing reviews, such adjustments

Figure 8.4

BEV AND BOB
RETIREMENT CASH FLOW ANALYSIS #2

SIGNIFICANT ASSUMPTIONS

1.	YEAR OF RETIREMENT					2020
2.	YEAR BORN:	RETIREE 1	BOB			1955
2A.		RETIREE 2	BEV			1955

3.	ANNUAL INFLATION RATE FOR YEARS	1-10	3.0%	11-20	3.5%	THEREAFTER	3.5%
4.	SOCIAL SECURITY INFLATION RATE						3.0%
5.	AFTER-TAX RATE OF RETURN ON INVESTMENTS						7.0%
6.	PENSION INFLATION AJD:	OPT 1 = COMPOUNDED INFL RATE			0.0% BOB		0.0% BEV
6A.		OPT 2 = FLAT FIXED DOLLAR AMT			$0 BOB		$0 BEV

					2007 DOLLARS	RETIREMENT DOLLARS
7.	ANNUAL DESIRED INCOME (EXCLUDING MORTGAGE)				$80,000	$117,483
8.	ANNUAL MORTGAGE PMT (PRIN & INT ONLY)	ENDING	2024			$12,000
9.	SOCIAL SECURITY	BOB	STARTING	2020		$22,000
9A.		BEV	STARTING	2020		$11,000
10.	CAPITAL AVAILABLE FOR INVESTING				$400,000	$963,938
11.	PENSION BENEFITS	BOB	STARTING	2020		$9,000
11A.		BEV	STARTING	0		$0
12.	ADDITIONAL ANNUAL INVESTMENTS NEEDED				$32,000	$644,501

YEAR	AGE 1	AGE 2	REQUIRED INCOME	MORTGAGE PAYMENT	SOCIAL SECURITY	OTHER INC (EXPENSES)	PENSION ROBERT	PENSION BEVERLY	AMT NEEDED FROM CAPITAL	REMAINING CAPITAL	SHORTFALL
2020	65	65	117,483	12,000	33,000	0	9,000	0	87,483	1,630,485	0
2021	66	66	121,007	12,000	33,990	0	9,000	0	90,017	1,651,451	0
2022	67	67	124,637	12,000	35,010	0	9,000	0	92,628	1,671,183	0
2023	68	68	128,377	12,000	36,060	0	9,000	0	95,317	1,689,513	0
2024	69	69	132,228	12,000	37,142	0	9,000	0	98,086	1,706,260	0
2025	70	70	136,195	0	38,256	0	9,000	0	88,939	1,733,647	0
2026	71	71	140,280	0	39,404	0	9,000	0	91,877	1,759,909	0
2027	72	72	144,489	0	40,586	0	9,000	0	94,903	1,784,878	0
2028	73	73	148,824	0	41,803	0	9,000	0	98,020	1,808,369	0
2029	74	74	153,288	0	43,058	0	9,000	0	101,231	1,830,181	0
2030	75	75	157,887	0	44,349	0	9,000	0	104,538	1,850,097	0
2031	76	76	163,413	0	45,680	0	9,000	0	108,733	1,867,065	0
2032	77	77	169,132	0	47,050	0	9,000	0	113,082	1,880,719	0
2033	78	78	175,052	0	48,462	0	9,000	0	117,590	1,890,664	0
2034	79	79	181,179	0	49,915	0	9,000	0	122,263	1,896,467	0
2035	80	80	187,520	0	51,413	0	9,000	0	127,107	1,897,664	0
2036	81	81	194,083	0	52,955	0	9,000	0	132,128	1,893,748	0
2037	82	82	200,876	0	54,544	0	9,000	0	137,332	1,884,172	0
2038	83	83	207,907	0	56,180	0	9,000	0	142,727	1,868,342	0
2039	84	84	215,184	0	57,866	0	9,000	0	148,318	1,845,616	0
2040	85	85	222,715	0	59,602	0	9,000	0	154,113	1,815,302	0
2041	86	86	230,510	0	61,390	0	9,000	0	160,120	1,776,649	0
2042	87	87	238,578	0	63,231	0	9,000	0	166,347	1,728,845	0
2043	88	88	246,928	0	65,128	0	9,000	0	172,800	1,671,017	0
2044	89	89	255,571	0	67,082	0	9,000	0	179,488	1,602,217	0
2045	90	90	264,516	0	69,095	0	9,000	0	186,421	1,521,427	0
2046	91	91	273,774	0	71,168	0	9,000	0	193,606	1,427,544	0
2047	92	92	283,356	0	73,303	0	9,000	0	201,053	1,319,382	0
2048	93	93	293,273	0	75,502	0	9,000	0	208,772	1,195,660	0
2049	94	94	303,538	0	77,767	0	9,000	0	216,771	1,054,998	0
2050	95	95	314,162	0	80,100	0	9,000	0	225,062	895,909	0
2051	96	96	325,157	0	82,503	0	9,000	0	233,655	716,790	0
2052	97	97	336,538	0	84,978	0	9,000	0	242,560	515,916	0
2053	98	98	348,317	0	87,527	0	9,000	0	251,790	291,428	0
2054	99	99	360,508	0	90,153	0	9,000	0	261,355	41,325	0
2055	100	100	373,125	0	92,857	0	9,000	0	42,772	0	228,496

This analysis is based on the accuracy and consistency of the data and assumptions you have provided in items 1 through 11 and is not guaranteed. The figures shown are valid only as long as the data and assumptions remain unchanged. To maintain accuracy of this analysis, periodic updating is necessary to reflect changes as they occur.

should be relatively minor." Bob and Bev begin to relax. He continued, "So, since our assumptions seem to be reasonable and the best we can make at this time, let's proceed with the proposed accumulation plan."

The next step for Bob and Bev was to go back to their financial plan and determine in which categories the new investments should be placed. Also, they knew that a monthly investment procedure should be established and started. Ben noted that this would be the topic of their next meeting. And on this high note, the session ended.

Remember that when Boomers reach age 50, a new reality seems to take over. They say to themselves, "Wow! I'm 50. I won't be able to retire at age 55 as I had hoped, and I'm not even sure I can retire at 65. I guess I'll have to change my spending habits and make a real effort to accumulate more wealth for retirement." This new reality can suddenly propel many Boomers from a savings rate of around 5 percent to a rate up to 20 percent or more.

Bob's income of $150,000 per year permits Bob and Bev to accept a new asset accumulation plan of $32,000 – 21 percent of $150,000 – per year with little or no hesitation. The financial advisor will best serve older Baby-Boomer clients by encouraging them to look at an analysis similar to the one prepared for Bob and Bev, and to accept a significant increase in their savings rate as being the norm.

JOHN AND JIM – NON-TRADITIONAL BOOMERS

John is 51 years old and an optometrist with a semi-successful practice. Even though he is noted professionally for his outstanding ability as a diagnostician, his practice, from a financial viewpoint, has been less than spectacular. It can be said that John's lack of business sense cancels out any benefits he might gain from his professional acumen.

Jim is 44 years old and a professor at a state university. He has written several books that have sold well. He is called on extensively to lecture on his research in anthropology, and these lecture fees in combination with his teaching salary and book royalties provide Jim with a very good income.

John and Jim have been living together for more than a dozen years. They first lived in John's home, but now they are purchasing a home together. They have very strong feelings for each other and have the intent of a lifelong relationship. Without hesitation, John and Jim would marry each other if the law would permit a legal union.

During the first Fact-Finding meeting with Julie, their financial advisor, John and Jim explained how Jim's employer provides medical insurance for gay domestic partners. Since John is a sole practitioner, he wouldn't be able to get the extensive coverage as provided by the university without paying an exorbitant premium. However, Jim described the rude awakening he had last year when he discovered he would have to pay income tax on the premium paid by his employer for John's dependent coverage. He went on to explain that even though the university defines John as his dependent, the Internal Revenue Service does not.

Later at the Presentation meeting, Julie listed several issues of utmost importance for John and Jim to work on. During the discussion about medical insurance, Julie explained that first they were fortunate to have an employer who defined an unmarried domestic partner as a dependent. As they found out, the law does not accept this definition. Therefore, Jim does have to pay income tax on the cost of John's medical insurance. However, the good news is that, if and when John receives medical benefits from this insurance, the benefits payments will not be taxable.

During the discussion on ownership of their proposed residence, the advisor began to explain the potential problem John and Jim will create by listing the ownership of this new home as 50/50 joint owners with the right of survivorship, which is what they intended to do.

Jim interrupted Julie's explanation. "But if one of us dies," he said, "both of us wish for the survivor to be the full owner of the property."

"Yes, I understand," Julie replied, "and that is easy to arrange, but by the way you plan this purchase, you will create a potential tax problem. What you would do is create a large gift from John to Jim. When John sold his previous home, he received a large sum of money. Then the two of you decided that a fair arrangement would be for John to provide the down payment and for Jim, who has a much larger income but very little cash reserves, to pay the mortgage payments. So, if Jim becomes a 50 percent owner of this home without any financial input, John legally will have made a gift to Jim of one-half the down payment." John and Jim looked at each other.

"The three of us need to have a meeting with your attorney," Julie continued, "to register the property ownership as tenants-in-common. This way you each will own that portion of the property representing the amount of money contributed respectively. As far as transferring the property at death, this is also quite easy. You simply leave your individual ownership to the surviving domestic partner. It's even better tax-wise because the survivor receives a stepped-up cost basis on the portion of ownership the deceased had at death"

John was chagrined at the mistake they had almost made. He said, "Julie, I've been praised as having an outstanding ability to provide accurate diagnosis on the spot, but you just out-diagnosed me. I thank you for it."

"As do I," added Jim. "However, it just occurred to me. What's to stop John from putting the house up for sale and selling me out of a place to live? Right now, under the agreement you just described, he would own it all, since he is putting up the whole down payment and I haven't made even one mortgage payment."

Julie smiled as she replied, "You're right, Jim, that's what John could do."

At this point, John loudly interrupted. "I wouldn't do that! Jim, you know me better than that. I'm actually hurt that you would even think I would do such a thing."

"Wait, John," Julie intervened, feeling it necessary to defend Jim's inquiry. "Jim did not say you would do that. He simply asked a proper question about what could be a loop-hole in the agreement. In fact, if Jim had not asked it, then I would have brought it up."

John, beginning to calm down, said, "I'm sorry for reacting so. I do have a tendency to be too sensitive and overreacting. So, how do we take care of this?"

"The answer," said Julie, "is a buy/sell agreement which requires either of you who wishes to sell his interest in the property to first offer to the other the right to buy. This important agreement can also be prepared by your attorney." John and Jim both nodded.

"Another set of legal documents that neither of you have," Julie continued, "is called Durable Power of Attorney for medical and financial matters. These documents are important for everyone, but especially for couples who are not legally married. For example, if one of you needs to have someone admit you to a hospital or to approve a certain medical procedure, then the possession of a medical Power of Attorney will provide the authority to do so. And if you wish to authorize each other as the person along with your doctor to terminate life-sustaining equipment at a certain level of potential quality of future life, then you will be able to do so with this document. The financial durable Power of Appointment will allow each of you to transfer the authority to the other for the transaction of financial matters."

John and Jim nodded their assent. Jim spoke. "Julie, we are aware of the importance of these documents. Let's not waste any time getting them executed. Let's call our attorney right now to arrange for an appointment. And while we're there, we can also take care of the proper registration of our new home and for that buy/sell agreement, or whatever you called it."

"That's a good idea," Julie said, "but before you make the call, have the two of you also discussed the benefits of revocable trusts?"

"Yes," John replied. "I believe we have."

"Yes," Jim agreed. "John and I have talked about trusts. Maybe we should put that on our agenda as well. You will come along with us to our attorney, won't you Julie, in case we cannot explain clearly what we want?"

"Of course," Julie replied.

All of the other financial-planning items apply to non-traditional domestic partners in the same way as they do to traditional relationships. However, some legal issues, such as those discussed above, present the more difficult items and require very special handling, including the involvement of an attorney.

If the financial planner is a specialist in dealing with business management issues, then this would be an additional important topic in this financial planning case. Certainly, John has demonstrated questionable development of his practice. Professional advice could definitely improve this situation, if John agrees to seek and accept such advice. If the financial planner feels the need to bring in a specialist, then this is what the advisor should recommend. This book does not deal with the many potential issues of the proper use of business income and assets for the business owner. Obviously, where applicable, much attention to these issues is necessary, and an expert's opinion just about always pays for itself.

Chapter 9

The Boomers Are Retiring, or Are They?

A wit once said, "There are three stages of life: Childhood, Adulthood, and 'You're looking very well today.'" As with most good humor, this tells the truth with a twist and is not too different from a more serious definition of the three stages of life:

Stage 1. Childhood and Education;
Stage 2. Working, Parenting, and Continuing Education;
Stage 3. Retirement.

Over 70 million Baby Boomers are out there right now thinking about how they will fund the third stage of their life (often referred to as the Third Age). Baby Boomers have experienced the highest standard of living ever known to mankind; many have made a lot of money; and quite a few have spent most of it. Now, the oldest Boomers are moving into their 60s at a rate that could exceed 7,600 a day and will reach the height of almost 12,000 per day as the current 50 year olds become 60.

A NEW AND DIFFERENT STAGE 3

Baby Boomers have always been "different." They created "different" at every stage of their life, and no one assumes that their third stage of life will be anything other than "different." The financial advisor must be aware of how things will be different or the advisor won't be in business very long.

Throughout the 20th century, particularly after Social Security entered the scene, the concept of retirement was expanded to include more people. For most of these people, the second stage of life was to work at one job until a certain age, and then with a gold watch in hand, enter into the third stage, a time of non-work, a time of leisure, a time to swing a golf club or just sit and rock on the front porch. It was a time when the company pension and Social Security were sufficient to provide for retirement needs. However, according to a retirement preparedness survey conducted in 2003 by Merrill Lynch, only about one-third of today's retirement income is expected to come from the combination of defined benefit pensions and Social Security and this percentage is rapidly reducing.

Now, in the 21st century, retirement has begun to mean something quite different, so different that we need to create a title other than retirement to identify this stage of life. In the 20th century, we thought that, at a normal retirement age, say age 65, the body needed to slow down, to be less active. In the 21st century, this just "ain't" the way it is anymore. There is no longer an age-defined retirement "turning point."

Today, people in their 60s, 70s, 80s, and even 90s (example—Dr. Michael De-Bakey, age 98 in 2006) are actively engaged in their lives, and they possess a need and a desire to be productive. According to a 2005 Merrill Lynch retirement survey, many Boomers plan to continue working in their same careers, or begin new careers, or do volunteer work, or whatever else they may choose, enjoying "phased or cyclic retirements." In many cases, the fear of not being able to afford health insurance if they retire motivates Boomers to keep one foot in the working world. Regardless, Baby Boomers reaching traditional retirement age have the same desires as they have always had, and they no doubt will add their own unique style to whatever it is they choose to do, just as they have done all throughout their lives.

More and more, the third stage of life is a time when you can do what you want to do, not what you have to do. So, a more accurate listing of the three stages of life should be:

Stage 1. Childhood and Education;
Stage 2. Working, Parenting, and Continuing Education;
Stage 3. Your choice.

THREE STAGES OF LIFE

Because of increased longevity, this Stage 3 might be as long as or longer than either of the other two stages. Therefore, Stage 3 will require a source of income that can sustain a desirable life style, and if it is to be "your choice," then this income should come from the wealth accumulated during Stage 2.

Figure 9.1

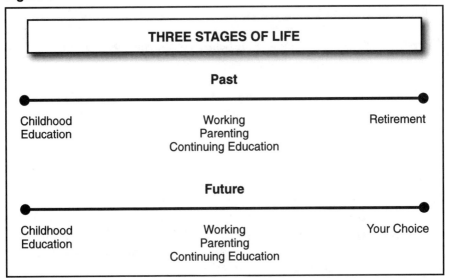

Clients Preparing for Stage 3

Just think about this new concept of the third stage of your life where you do whatever you wish. The old concept of retirement was to leave a career, separate yourself from the daily association of colleagues discussing problems and solutions, become a has-been, and accept the phasing out of your life. I think anyone would choose the new concept if given the opportunity. Wouldn't you?

Chronological aging (counting the anniversaries of your birthday) and asset accumulation are the price of admission into this wonderful third stage. What is even better is that the particular chronological age we enter the third stage and the amount of wealth we have at that time are of our own choosing.

So, how do we promulgate this third stage concept? How do we encourage our Baby Boomer clients to accumulate enough assets to be able to enjoy this better choice? Prior to their being 50, it's tough, but starting at age 50, it's a piece of cake if you are or can become their trusted financial advisor. Prior to age 50, Baby Boomers have few thoughts of retirement and the amount of accumulated assets needed. They believe that perpetual youth is their discovery. Many do feel that age 55 would be an ideal time to stop working and apply 100 percent of their time to the many varied activities of their choice. The wake-up call rings loud and clear for them when the bell tolls 50. There is a sudden realization that their employers and the government are not going to provide all of the funding for this Third Stage of life. The 50 year olds are now ready to make a necessary change. They are willing to change from a zero or maybe 5 percent accumulation rate up to a 20 percent rate. In their 50s, Baby Boomers are at or nearing their peak income levels and have more discretionary dollars. So, obtaining the benefits of the third stage of their lives is a very strong motivator for asset accumulation.

Enter the trusted financial advisor. Your assignment, if you choose to accept it, is to enhance this motivation and guide this accumulation of both qualified and non-qualified monies into proper growth investment portfolios. Your trustworthiness, experience, and knowledge are exactly what these Baby Boomers need. They will recognize your outstanding abilities, and if you place their interest first in every respect, both you and your clients will be best served.

Boomers are not a homogeneous group, and it's more than just the spread in their ages, even though this age spread does add to their differences. The most rewarding prospects for the financial advisor are those Baby Boomers who are college graduates, are married with both spouses employed full time, and have annual incomes of over $80,000 (in 2007 dollars).

This is not to say that the group just described contains the only Baby Boomers who are rewarding prospects for financial advisors willing to give the time and effort to serving them. For the most part, this service involves developing plans that will provide lifetime incomes for all the Baby Boomers among your clientele. Many financial advisors enjoy applying their knowledge and skills to the challenge of creating a tailor-made plan for each Baby Boomer, regardless of the Boomer's current state of finances.

As mentioned, early Baby Boomers are at or nearing their peak income levels. It's likely that many if not most of them will continue earning these high incomes for 15, 20, and even 25 more years. Recent surveys of Baby Boomers reveal that 80 percent of them plan on continuing to work in their later years.

The difference between working Full Time and Starting your own business is a matter of being an employee versus being an entrepreneur. The difference between "Part Time Enjoyment" and Part Time Need" is humungous. Working because you want to—choosing to work is a wonderful state compared to working because you need the money—you have to work.

Of course, it is difficult to believe that all Baby Boomers who plan to continue to work will be working voluntarily because they want to. That is, perhaps they will have to work because their earlier high-spending habits and low-accumulation rates

Figure 9.2

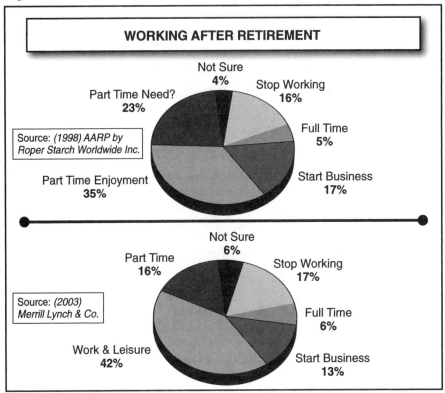

WORKING AFTER RETIREMENT

Not Sure 4%
Stop Working 16%
Part Time Need? 23%
Full Time 5%
Source: *(1998) AARP by Roper Starch Worldwide Inc.*
Part Time Enjoyment 35%
Start Business 17%

Not Sure 6%
Part Time 16%
Stop Working 17%
Source: *(2003) Merrill Lynch & Co.*
Full Time 6%
Work & Leisure 42%
Start Business 13%

have created a need for additional income. Also, defined benefit pension plans that pay a level lifetime income have either been revoked or have proven not to be sufficient to do the job, thereby creating a need to work longer and save more. When these retirement plans were developed, we had lower rates of inflation and much shorter life expectancies. Inflation has been continuous for over 50 years, and it seems that increases in life expectancy will continue forever. Hence, more money will be needed in order to sustain the standard of living to which many Baby Boomers have become accustomed.

Notice in Figure 9.3, there have been zero years of deflation since 1955, which produced an average inflation rate of 4 percent. However, by extending this analysis back to 1926, we find that the average rate from 1926 through 2005 was 3 percent. In the 1930s, one-half of the years were deflationary. Could we ever have deflationary years again? And what about double-digit inflation years as we had in the 1970s? Of course, either is possible and, of course, we hope neither will occur, but we should be prepared for such eventualities as discussed throughout this book.

Figure 9.3

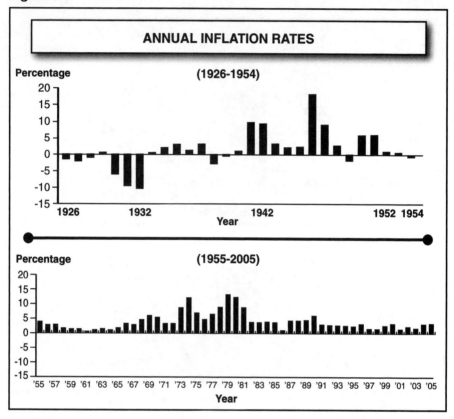

Figure 9.4 illustrates the devastation to the purchasing power of your money over time using the long-term average of 3 percent inflation.

In a period of continuous inflation, the value of your money decreases each year, and at the 24th year, it will buy only one-half of the amount with which it started. Therefore, when projecting income needs for the remainder of your life, it is imperative that inflation be included in your calculation.

When I discuss the possibility of living a very long time, some of my clients, especially those in their eighties, say, "I hope not." When I ask why, the consistent response is, "I don't want to live with pain and misery for years." When I add an important detail to my question, "What if you could live a very long time in reasonably good health and without prolonged pain and suffering?" their whole attitude changes, and they respond, "In that case, sure, I'd like to live a very long time *if my money holds out.*"

Figure 9.4

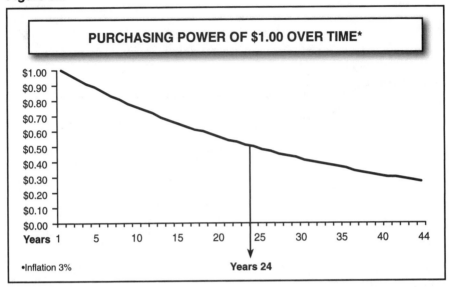

The idea of a living death—being kept barely alive by mechanical or chemical means—has never been anyone's goal, but living in a healthy state and then with a painless express check-out, the idea is totally acceptable. Is it possible? Dr Neal E. Cutler discusses this in his book ***Advising Mature Clients: The New Science of Wealth Span Planning***, with the concept of Squaring the Curve.

The "traditional" curve summarizes the general relationship between age and health that characterizes modern society for the past several decades—an especially notable decline in health in the 60s and 70s, with death (life expectancy) around age 80. Cutler uses hypothetical data to illustrate what could happen in a different kind of health-and-age scenario. Instead of a person living in a declining state of health ending in death, this graph illustrates a very healthy and fully functional person enjoying life until, at a certain time, the body just stops functioning. Of course, some might say, "Why can't we live forever?" Well, that's a different goal not obtainable at this time. However, it is not unrealistic to think that we might someday learn how to maintain our functionality without pain and suffering right up to the point of death sometime after age 120. The April 17, 2006 issue of ***Barrons*** had a front page article titled, "Live to 150," by Jay Palmer. This article stated: "A growing number of maverick scientists, doctors, researchers, biogeneticists, and nano-technologists—many with impeccable academic credentials—insist that the war against aging can be won."

Figure 9.5

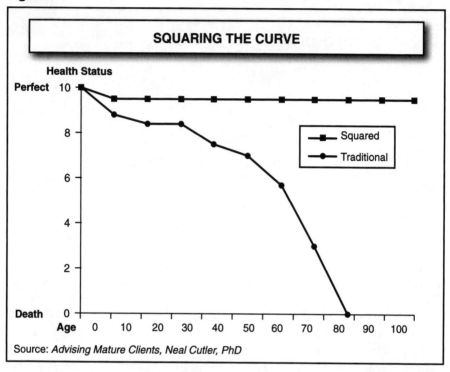

Source: *Advising Mature Clients, Neal Cutler, PhD*

In July of 2006, I attended the annual conference of the WORLD FUTURE SOCIETY, where Ray Kurzwell (award-winning inventor, author of several books, and recipient of several honorary doctorates) stated, "Within 10 to 15 years, our life expectancy will increase significantly more than one year for each year we live." The general tenor of the speakers seemed to have the consensus that 150 years will become the average. This was illustrated by one statement, "Today, a living baby girl will live to age 150."

Baby Boomers have had a tendency to live in the present. Now they are approaching the third stage of life, and they must recognize that this stage could be a very long time period. They must recognize that it requires them to make some decisions now, and that each decision made now will determine how they will live the rest of their lives. A decision not to make a decision now could generate future problems of insurmountable difficulty. As their financial advisor, you have an obligation to encourage them to recognize that how they manage their money today will have a significant effect on the quality of what might turn out to be the longest and greatest period of their lives.

Financial planning is life-long planning. It is essential for the advisor to establish with the Baby Boomer client the importance of life-long-planning, even if the client is just starting to plan at the age of 50 or 60. Professor Peter F. Drucker, philosopher and scholar, stated the concept exquisitely when he wrote, "... long-range planning does not deal with future decisions, but the future of present decisions." In more financial planner's language: What is the future value of present decisions? Convince your clients that what they do today determines what they will be in the future. It's so important to do it correctly right now, and to continue doing it into the future so that the future will be what they want it to be.

As a successful financial advisor, you must already have Baby Boomers among your clientele. You have known them and probably have been advising them for many years. Your experience with these Baby Boomer clients will help you to serve your new Baby Boomer clients. After you have secured the needed information from the new client, as discussed elsewhere in this book, you will find that, for the most part, the client will fall into one of the following three categories.

A.   Those who have more than enough money for Stage 3.
B.   Those who have just enough money for Stage 3.
C.   Those who do not have enough money for Stage 3.

We all should be so fortunate as to have every one of our new clients in category A. With these clients, the financial advisor needs only to make sure that the situation remains as privileged. The main task is to make sure inflation does not eat away at the clients' fortunes—not all that easy, but somebody has to do it.

Clients in category B also are fortunate. However, having just enough money today does not mean that it will remain that way in the future. This is what the financial advisor should attend to and assure, possibly even working to provide a more comfortable cushion.

Prospective clients in category C will be the challenge. This group often suddenly realizes that they are simply not ready for Stage 3 and are looking for some magic from a financial advisor. What they don't realize is that those in categories A and B didn't use magic to arrive at this successful state. Actually, the "magic" they seek was really the result of years of hard work on the part of both advisor and client. The advisor has a wonderful opportunity to inform this category of clients what it will take to obtain category A or B status.

After you have obtained the needed information you seek from every new client, you hope that your new category C clients are not in debt. You hope that maybe they even have some savings. But, for those clients who carry significant debt, you should administer an industrial-strength dose of the 10-percent solution. The 10-percent solution means that the clients must live on 90 percent of their take-home pay and invest or bank the other 10 percent. Industrial strength means that instead of starting with 10 percent, the amount should be increased to 15, 20, or even 30 percent, making it as much as you can without making it so tough that the clients do not return. If the clients have not been savers at all, you might start at 10 percent and raise it later as the clients discover how good they feel about what they are doing. It is important that you and your clients really agree on the percent before starting.

Whatever percent you and you clients agree upon, you should use the information you gathered about them to point out places where they can find this money. With your experience, you can more easily spot where the clients might cut back on some items and cut out entirely other items. Don't be a Scrooge, but do be a Santa Claus and tell the clients that if they are good, they will be able to spend the last 30, 40, or 50 years of their lives doing whatever they choose.

For those category C clients who have significant debt—and here debt means credit card debt mostly and not a mortgage—the 10-20-70 formula must be applied. But before you apply this solution, you must impose on your clients the first rule of getting out of debt: When you find yourself in a hole, stop digging. Ask your clients not to use their credit cards ever again, or at least until they are out of debt. Tell them that, if they don't cut them up, they should give them to you, and when they want to use them, they should call you to determine whether the purchase is necessary.

The 10-20-70 formula is the solution described by George Clason in his book *The Richest Man in Babylon.* Simply put, for every dollar clients earn, they save 10 cents, pay down their debts with 20 cents and pay all other living expenses with the remaining 70 cents. Clients who are successful in paying off all their debts will find it quite simple thereafter to save 30 percent or more of their take-home pay.

Clients Already in Stage 3

What about the Baby Boomers who have already terminated their employment? How can you, the financial advisor, be of service to those already in the third stage of their lives?

This is an easy question to answer. The financial advisor simply takes an inventory of all assets and liabilities, determines income sources and expenditures, and then calculates how long these assets will continue to fund the current standard of living. If there is sufficient cash flow to last until the client is 100 years old (100 years will be discussed later in this chapter), then the financial advisor simply assists the client in developing and managing a portfolio of investments to achieve this. If there is insufficient cash flow to do the job, then the advisor assists the client in developing and then managing a portfolio that will create assets sufficient to do the job. Sounds simple, yes? Ah, but the devil is in the details.

The financial plan may already be in place if the person has been one of your clients for many years. You should have little difficulty continuing to advise this client, given all you know about him, her, or them. But if the person is a more recent or a new client, then you must begin at the beginning by securing the needed information as you would with any new client. This means you need to take an inventory of all assets, liabilities, attitudes, goals, and resources.

If present assets are insufficient and attitudes are improper to do the job, then alternatives should be considered immediately. What part of the client's present standard of living can be lowered to accomplish the goal? What investment changes would be helpful? Are there any assets such as a summer house or an expensive boat that can be sold with the money placed in an income producing investment? What about obtaining additional income by renting part of a residence, re-entering the work force by taking a part-time or full-time job, or seeking assistance from relatives? What other information or knowledge can you impart to your client? Be upbeat as you do this review with your client. It is not the end of the world. The client still has choices even though they may be tough, and the goal of a positive Stage 3 is always possible.

One choice for the client age 62 or older who owns a house is a reverse mortgage. As the name suggests, it is like a mortgage except the payments come to the owner. There are different types of reverse mortgages, but in general they have in common these features: The current owner of the home continues as owner; the value of the reverse mortgage payout will depend on age, market-value of the home, current interest rates, and the kind of cash advances chosen. When the owner dies or sells the house, cash advances plus interest must be repaid. Admittedly this is an oversimplification as there are too many variations to discuss in detail at this point. Financial advisors who intend to suggest a reverse mortgage to their clients can get more details from the Federal Trade Commission website at www.ftc.gov and the AARP website at www.aarp.org. In both cases, simply type in "reverse mortgages" into the search box on the front page of the website.

"Almost 20 percent of American Adults have zero or less net worth" (Robert H Frank, economist, Cornell University, March 2005). However, many Baby Boomers have accumulated a small amount of the assets they will need for the future. Typically, these calculations have not included the value of the Baby Boomer's equity in their home. When including assets from a reverse mortgage, the picture changes dramatically. The combination of all assets (including home equity) could produce as much as 85 percent of the money needed to maintain in the future the owner's present standard of living. This one distribution method makes funding of the Third Stage seem much more attainable than would otherwise be the case.

When preparing a financial plan for your clients already in Stage 3, explore the Boomer's health status. Some will be in poor health—maybe the main reason they terminated work—and many will be in very good health with a long life expectancy. For many, a rocking chair doesn't seem to be the activity of choice that it once was for the *weary body* of a retiree. Today, you find this retiree's body not just chasing a golf ball but sky diving, safari hunting, and participating in all kinds of other active sports. The dancing seniors are not just standing in place holding each other up, they are creating quite a whirl on the dance floor and probably later in the bedroom. The number of years this increased activity will continue will vary among individuals. However, the general trend is for more and more years. When you are inactive, the body and the mind atrophy. When you are active, the body and mind grow and support substantial activities.

What are you, the financial advisor, recommending that is different for these new retirees? Are you still planning for a life expectancy of the late seventies or early eighties? Are you still recommending a high percentage of fixed-dollar-investment vehicles prior to the seventies and eighties? Are you aware of the Annuity Mortality Tables? If not, stop right now and look at Figure 1.4 on page 6. Your future could depend on you being familiar with this information.

When you help retirees plan for their retirement income, you should not plan on stopping this income flow when the first spouse of a couple dies. You need to keep this stream of income continuing for the survivor. And if one-half of those surviving spouses are still alive at age 92 (See Figure 1.5 on page 8), you as the financial advisor will be hard pressed to defend an assumption of a life expectancy of only into the early eighties.

I feel it to be prudent to assume that for any couple still alive at age 65, at least one of them will still be alive at age 100. Of course, if that one is still alive, healthy, and active in his or her mid-nineties, then an investment portfolio that will last longer than age 100 should be seriously considered.

We in the financial services industry have spent the past century developing various wealth-accumulation vehicles. This new century requires us to create new and equally fine wealth-distribution vehicles.

Not a new vehicle, but still unfamiliar to many financial advisors, is the immediate payout variable annuity. There are a growing number of insurance companies issuing this product. The basic concept is easy for the financial advisor to explain and for the client to understand. Clients pay or transfer a lump sum of money, qualified or non-qualified, into an immediate annuity and receive a monthly check for the remainder of their lives. Insurance agents are quite familiar with the fixed payout annuity, but not too many are familiar with how the annuity concept has been expanded to include a variable payout.

A fixed lifetime payout annuity has the same inherent problem as a level defined benefit plan payout, and that problem is inflation. If your client lives for 20 or 30 or more years in the third stage of life, even at the historically low level of inflation of 3 percent, the purchasing power of the payout shrinks significantly.

On the other hand, the purchasing power of the payout of a variable annuity is specifically designed to help solve the problem of inflation. For example, Figure 9.6 shows how the payout based on a 7 percent average annual growth rate combined with 3 percent rate of inflation not only increases, but this increase continues as long as the annuitant is alive.

Granted, the intricacies of an Immediate Variable Annuity are complicated, but so are the intricacies of a life insurance policy as well as many other financial products. It is propitious for a financial advisor to learn the pros and cons of as many products and concepts as possible. Also, make sure you dig deep enough to see more than just the surface facts. For example, with an Immediate Variable Annuity, it's proper to analyze beyond the 20th year, where many other analyses stop, in order to see the significant advantages.

Another source of payouts that requires more attention is the review and on-going management of a portfolio of qualified money. Unbelievable amounts of assets will be rolled over into self-directed IRA accounts as Baby Boomers retire. Your clients, if already in Stage 3, have probably made some decisions regarding these funds. One hopes that the clients consulted with you before making these decisions, but if they are new clients, they probably have not done so. In this case, it is important that you and your new clients review the disposition of these funds and determine how many of the roll-over decisions are irrevocable and how many resulted in funds that can be included in the financial plans you will propose. As you know, available funds can be diversified into an array of vehicles to accomplish proper growth with desired distribution either based on the Minimum Required Distribution tables or based on the individual needs of each client if this is more than the Minimum Required Distribution.

Figure 9.6

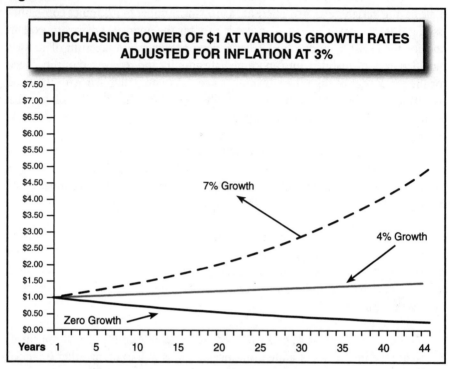

Of course, the financial advisor considers non-qualified assets at the same time as qualified assets when making financial plans for their retired clients. However, because of multiple tax considerations, non-qualified and qualified monies should be kept separate, to determine the best asset allocation. At some point, the advisor may choose to bring together the two separate accounts, at least on paper, to make sure that one is enhancing the other, to control possible overlap, and to create a composite picture for a complete understanding of how it all must work together.

The service of providing a lifetime income should be a part of all practitioners' services and, for many, will become the only service they choose to perform. In other words, there is lots of money to be managed, which means lots of earnings for the professional.

A NEW AREA OF SPECIALIZATION FOR THE FINANCIAL ADVISOR: FINANCIAL GERONTOLOGY

A specialization you may want to pursue is that of a Financial Gerontologist. This is a financial advisor additionally trained in gerontology—the study of aging; not only the study of old people—and the financial implications of the aging process.

The financial advisor's background provides the ideal fundamentals needed to help advise clients who have accumulated money and need to protect their wealth. You need to know and understand that a person's chronological age neither dominates nor determines life's functionality, but is one small factor contributing to one's remaining longevity. And you must counsel your client that, as financial gerontology research also demonstrates, it's never too late to learn and to instigate health or wealth interventions.

The important considerations for the financial advisor are: People are living longer; people are happy to be living longer, especially if it does not involve suffering; and as people are living longer, they will need more money to fund their additional life span. Hence, financial gerontology is a wonderful specialty in which financial advisors can prosper as well as provide a necessary and valuable service.

One benefit in becoming a specialist in financial gerontology is learning how to develop an intergenerational clientele. For example, many Baby Boomers discover they must learn to understand and deal with their parent's financial matters. The attitudes about money held by parents of the boomers are very different from the attitudes held by the boomers themselves. Two of three men age 65 and over in 2000 were veterans and either lived through the Depression of the 1930s or were greatly affected through their parents' experience during those terrible times. Many of these boomer parents have accumulated sizable amounts of assets—the total is estimated to be in the trillions of dollars—and because of their early experiences, they have a difficult time spending money. Remember, their culture was that of saving, not spending, and these early-learned lifetime habits are difficult to modify, let alone change.

The dynamics of what the researchers call "Family Aging" is a critical part of financial gerontology, and involves ethical as well as financial elements. For example, boomers find themselves in a position involving a conflict of interest. Do they encourage their parents to increase their standard of living, assuming there really are enough assets to do so, recognizing that this will reduce the boomers own potential inheritance? Of course, every boomer says, "It's their money; they should enjoy it." And although I strongly agree with these sentiments, I must also point out that, financially and psychologically, it is better for the boomers to just keep quiet and let their parents enjoy a lower than a newly-improved standard of living. Financially better, because the money will last longer. Psychologically better, because the parents do not have to suffer the guilt they would feel at spending more than necessary. However, it *is* possible to make everybody happy. An appropriate method is for the parent to obtain professional financial guidance from you, the advisor. Also, you can teach the boomer client how they can best deal with the situation. In either case, you would do this by providing the best management of assets while the parents are alive and developing the most efficient methods of transferring assets at their demise.

Frequently, a client who is the parent of a boomer will ask, "How can I best assist my adult children and, at the same time, not reduce their incentive to be productive and self-reliant?" Usually, the first step to recommend is that the parents pay the cost of their children becoming involved with a professional financial advisor, such as yourself. In such cases, the advisor must take great care not to violate any confidences. But this need not be all that difficult. The advisor simply seeks permission to release certain information on how one generation can best assist the other. This process can also lead to the boomers' own children becoming your third-generation clients—an easy and greatly beneficial method of prospecting.

Knowledge of financial gerontology is critical to working with clients in the huge third-stage market. A must-read in this field is *Advising Mature Clients: The New Science of Wealth Span Planning,* by Neal E. Cutler, PhD, published by John Wiley & Sons. In this book Professor Cutler, with wit and wisdom, provides a clear, concise commentary on the issues facing our aging population with appropriate suggestions for how the financial advisor can effectively advise and serve their third-stage clients.

If you would like additional information on becoming a Registered Financial Gerontologist (RFG), either contact me or go directly to the web site of the American Institute of Financial Gerontology at www.AIFG.org.

Special Considerations for Women Baby Boomers

There has been a large amount written about the potential financial problems for the female population as they age. This potential problem could be a never ending struggle for almost 30 million boomer women facing uncertain employment, financial, health care, and economic societal factors, as reported by the Global Generations Policy Institute survey in the fall/winter 2006.

"A significant number of our country's 40 million plus boomer women will not be able to afford to retire, will fall below the poverty line, and experience financial insecurity and poor health in their later years with limited aid from traditional safety nets."

This need could foster a new specialty—advising widows and pre- and post-divorce women. Certainly, the topic is too large to be properly encompassed in this book, but there is a significant need. Financial advisors might do well to team up with a psychologist to counsel this growing demographic, offering competent financial and psychological assistance.

Here Comes the Echo Generation

What is the Echo Generation? The Echo Generation is one of the terms used to describe the children of the Baby Boomers. These are the children who were born in 1976 through 1994, and, if you do the math, you see that the earliest arrivals are now in their thirties.

Why should you be interested in the Echo Generation? There are two reasons. First, they make up another large group of potential clients, numbering more than 70 million, and you already have made a contact with many of them by having their parents as your clients. Second, as mentioned elsewhere in this book, a significant number of Baby Boomers want their children informed about and involved in financial affairs. Think how exciting it will be to have a group of interested clients with a time horizon adequate to amass many fortunes.

You and their parents should make a compact to start them off properly, you working with the ones who already are adults and the parents working with the children not yet emancipated. How do you do this? You teach them the *Ten Percent Rule*.

The Ten Percent Rule is so simple to follow, it is amazing that so many people do not apply it and in doing so build up a considerable amount of wealth. All one has to do is to live on 90 percent of his or her net income. This means that you do not spend 10 percent of your income. Even children whose only income may be an allowance or money earned mowing lawns can learn to apply the 10 percent rule. They simply learn that one penny for each dime or one dime for each dollar is not theirs to spend, at least, not now. It must be put aside for the Third Stage of their lives.

The mathematics is easy: You just move the cents point one digit to the left. Even a ten-year old can comprehend this much of our money notation.

Examples: $ 2.40 net earnings = $ 0.24 accumulation

$ 45.68 net earnings = $ 4.57 accumulation

$ 750.35 net earnings = $ 75.03 accumulation

$ 2,478.57 net earnings = $ 247.86 accumulation

For some, the application of the Ten Percent Rule will be easy. For others, it will not be. Learned at an early age, such as in one's preteens, the rule is easy to apply. Learned at a later age, when bad spending habits have been adopted, the rule is not as easy to apply.

The concept of living on what you earn less 10 percent should have a universal acceptance. However, society today makes it so easy to spend what we do not have—via credit cards and via offers of zero percent financing with no payment until next year. Sometimes the voices of the media make it sound almost unpatriotic not to support our economy and spend all we have and more. Maybe the Echo Generation will be the first to overcome such bad habits. With helpful advice from their parents and their financial advisors, they have an excellent chance.

Keep This in Mind

As you develop your skills and profits in money management for 70 to 80 million Baby Boomers plus their children and their parents, you must shed any old ideas you may still harbor about the third stage of life which no longer means work cessations, short life expectancy, fixed-dollar-based life payouts, and inactive sedentary people.

Also, as do many other practitioners, you will want to plan your own work/ non-work third stage of life to include all the same principles and practices you now have learned to apply to your clients. You, the advisor, should build a clientele and a firm to properly service this clientele while building a wonderful long lifetime for everyone, including yourself.

Chapter 10

The Future

A wise uncle once told his nieces and nephews, "If you stand around waiting for the future, then one day when you're not paying attention, it'll come and just pass you right on by." So, pay attention, you who would be successful financial planners, because the future starts right now.

THE FUTURE OF FINANCIAL PLANNING

The profession of financial planning is about to blossom because it is becoming recognized more and more as a profession. True professions have a degree of standardization and a degree of regulation. They also have minimum standards of education, experience, and practice. At this time, in most states, there are no such standards or regulations governing the business of financial planning. But this is changing, and the changes can only benefit the professional planner.

Most will agree that financial planning is an art, not a science. It is true that certain aspects of financial planning are based on scientific procedures, such as the use of various calculations, but most numbers used in the calculations are assumptions. This adds a degree of subjectivity, since the value of the assumptions depends upon the skill of the person making the assumptions. In the same sense, brain surgery can be considered an art and not a science, but the educational requirements for becoming a surgeon are strict and many, and the procedures used in the operating room are standardized to a considerable degree. It is only within this standardized process that the surgeon can exercise his creativity and thereby become famous or infamous.

There is an overall process that is evolving for all financial planning engagements. Except for a few different words or combinations of activities, this basic process is becoming standardized and typically includes the following:

- Establishing and defining the relationship with the client

- Gathering client data

- Analyzing and evaluating client's financial status

- Developing and presenting financial planning recommendations

- Implementing the financial plan

- Monitoring the financial plan

This process tells *how financial planning should be done.* Whether the service is for the Baby Boomer or the non-Baby-Boomer, this degree of standardization in the service is appropriate for the industry. There will always be individual creativity which is absolutely proper as long as it is within the confines of the process.

In the 1996 Equitable Nest Egg Study, commissioned by The Equitable Life Assurance Society, it was reported that 77 percent of the Baby Boomers surveyed turned to magazines or newspaper articles when developing their financial plans, more so than any other source. Later studies as recent as 1998 continue to support the observation that many Baby Boomers feel confident in relying on their own research for investment information. However, they often do not know how much money to place in different asset categories and have no idea of how much money they will need for retirement. These Boomers can be convinced they need a well-balanced financial plan that can be prepared in consultation with a professional advisor. It is when a Boomer chooses a professional financial advisor that the advisor's credentials become important, credentials that represent specialized education and standards of practice.

The Certified Financial Planner (CFP) Board of Standards has developed a set of practice standards that will require standards of practice for all CFP® licensees. The greater probability is that, in the future, the vast majority of all who provide the services of financial planning, either, by requirement or by choice, will adhere to these standards.

There has been a developing acceptance of the CFP license, offered and administered by the CFP® Board, as the first level for financial planners. Of course, educational background is a prerequisite to licensing in all professions. As financial planning gathers more momentum toward professionalism, the CFP education and license is a logical launching pad for financial planners. Like all professions, advanced education and training adds to the professional's ability to serve and to the development of specializations. Designations that offer advanced levels of education or specializations are well represented by the following.

ChFC	Chartered Financial Consultant
CLU	Chartered Life Underwriter
CPA/PFS	Certified Public Accountant/Personal Financial Specialist

After mastering the basics of any field, and even with the earning of advanced designations and/or certifications, one *must* keep current if anything near professionalism is to be maintained. Most organizations in the field of financial planning require at least 15 credit hours of continuing education annually. In these fast changing times, should a financial planner do any less, it would almost be a breach of contract with the client.

Of course, legislating a continuing-education requirement does not necessarily produce an increase in knowledge. You can lead a professional to the classroom, but you cannot make him absorb the information. Today, however, if a professional does not absorb enough important information, it will not be long before this becomes apparent to the client, who is free to walk away at any time. So, a word to the wise should be sufficient: active participation in keeping current is a basic requirement for success.

Financial planning is ready to move up to the next level in its growth toward being recognized as a profession. This next level requires those practitioners labeling themselves as financial planners to actually have proper designations and license(s). Further, they must comply with the process of financial planning and adhere to practice standards. If they do not have the proper license, designation, and compliance with proper standards, then they should not refer to themselves as financial planners or to what they do as financial planning. No one is naive enough to believe that this utopia will occur prior to some regulations. These regulations could be imposed by either a governmental body or an industry self-regulatory organization, but even then, until there is policing, there will not be sufficient compliance.

Many practitioners have allowed themselves to fall into the trap of continuing to use outdated assumptions in their resolution of challenges and the preparation of recommendations. The life span of much professional information continues on an accelerated path of obsolescence in all fields of endeavor. Financial planning is no exception. If the financial planner does not reject outdated teachings that are no longer proper, then he will do such harm that it could set all efforts toward the acceptance of professionalism back years. There is one example of this which is of significant importance if for no other reason than the fact it is an industry-wide problem. In the development of wealth, especially that which is intended to fund the desired standard of living when a client reduces or eliminates current earnings. many practitioners are still using assumptions that were developed in the 1930s.

In the 1930s, one-half of the years were deflationary, and life expectancy was age 63. The education and training for financial advisors, therefore, emphasized the importance of a transition during a client's life to more and more conservative investing, starting a long time prior to retirement. The thinking was that one must be conservative with this important retirement money because, given the relatively short life expectancy, it was assumed a person would not have time to recover from a loss. Therefore, no risks should be taken in these investments. The thinking was correct ... *back then.* It is absolutely incorrect today, and has been incorrect for decades. Yet, it is still being taught by some institutions and is still being practiced by many financial advisors to this day.

An example comes from a survey conducted by the Society of Financial Service Professionals in July, 1997. One of the findings clearly stated that advisors serving the Baby-Boomer client were recommending the repositioning of client portfolios to make a slow transition from aggressive (more risky) to conservative (risk adverse) starting *as early as age 45.* These advisors did recommend a heavy concentration of more-risky investments up to age 45, but at that point, they followed the old 1930s saw, which is based on much shorter life expectancy and years of deflation.

Recommended Risk Exposure for Various Age Groupings			
Age	**3**	**2**	**1**
25-34	93%	5%	2%
35-44	95%	5%	0%
45-54	67%	3%	21%
55-64	23%	56%	21%
65 and older	4%	38%	58%
	3 = Risky		
	2 = Moderate Risk		
	1 = Risk Adverse		

Source: *Society of Financial Service Professionals.*

The 2000 Annuity Mortality Table indicates that a 65-year-old person has an average life expectancy of 20 more years. In these reports, average means that one-half of this group will still be alive in 20 years. Also today, there have been over five decades of consecutive years of inflation. This combination of living longer and years of inflation renders the recommendations in the above table a prescription for total disaster, even for those who die exactly on time (the half in the average that will be dead in 20 years).

A true-to-life example: I made a presentation at a regional meeting of State Farm agents in 1997. I illustrated the above thinking with statistical information on the effects of continuing long-term inflation accompanied by studies of the extensive increase in longevity of life. I concluded by stating that the old way of reducing one's equity position and increasing one's fixed dollar position (cash, bonds, etc.) a long time prior to a retirement date did not work any more, and that one's investment portfolio should be the same the day after retirement as it was the day, the year, and the decades before retirement. I did recommend that as the retirees advanced through their 70s, 80s, and 90s, their investment portfolio should *very slowly* become more conservative. I also recommended that, even at age 100, there still should be 20 percent in equities, just in case the client out lives the government pension distribution table, which illustrates distribution factors up to age 115.

The next morning, after breakfast and before I continued with the next part of my presentation, a State Farm agent approached me and said, "I want to thank you for the message you shared with us yesterday." He was shaking my hand energetically as he continued. "I've been fretting over my heavy equity position for years. I'm 63, and I'll retire in a couple of years, and I *knew* that I should be in a more conservative position, but I just hated to do so." He paused, and then continued. "My son told me a couple of weeks ago that I should just sell all those stocks and stock mutual funds and stop driving myself crazy." He looked into my eyes as I waited for him to continue. He did, his words coming in a rush. "Last night, I told my son that Haas said I do not have to get out of the market and, in fact, I should stay the same with only a very slow transition to conservative holdings that would take the remainder of my life to complete." He paused, smiled at me, and said, "Thank you, Don."

Now it is always a thrill to receive a compliment, but this was a bigger thrill than usual because I recognized what had happened. This agent had learned those outdated strategies, but in his gut, he knew they were wrong. More important to recognize is that he had taught his son the outdated concept, and this conversation with his son might possibly save the son from acting on incorrect information in the future. I was thrilled!

The future of financial planning simply could not be any brighter, for those prepared to welcome it. Of course, it will not be without a few bumps along the way as we experienced in 2000 through 2002.. An industry scandal here or a severe correction in the market there will take their toll. A few planners will fall by the wayside, but most will survive. Many of the few who do fail will blame it on luck, those few who never knew that, as Louis Pasteur said, "Chance favors only the mind that is prepared."

Becoming a successful financial planner has the same requirements as becoming successful in any business. First, get educated. If you can, find someone with a goodly amount of experience to work with you. Second, build a sturdy personal financial base – not necessarily wealthy, but sufficient – and accumulate adequate business cash reserves. Third, go into business.

The fundamentals of going into business and succeeding are always the same. They include, at the very least, the following steps: learn well and never stop learning; have a proper capital base; then go enthusiastically into business.

THE FUTURE OF THE BABY BOOMER

For a long time now, 76 million people have dominated all market places. From diapers to toys to housing to school to work – for over 60 years, Baby Boomers have been the center of attention of all major and minor marketers. The Baby Boomer's domination of the marketplace will continue through all their future stages of life into grand-parenthood and great-grand-parenthood. But the one stage of greatest importance to those who have not yet reached it is retirement. Many of the present retirees from the generation preceding the Baby Boomers represent the most affluent group of senior citizens to grace this country, but it is possible that we ain't seen nothin' yet.

Baby Boomers, even those who are already retired, will want financial counseling that reflects their values and needs as it relates to aging. The Scudder Kemper Baby Boom Generation Poll conducted a study by Dr. Christopher Hayes, Professor of Psychology at Southampton College of Long Island University. This study was by Scudder Kemper Investments, Inc., who reported findings in February 1998. The poll revealed that Boomers feel emotionally younger than their chronological age. In fact, 40 percent feel from 10 to 20 years younger. Dr. Hayes reported, "Reaching this group entails depicting Boomers as youthful – by portraying people Boomers want to relate to…. Boomers do not want to think of themselves as old, nor do they want to think of themselves as traditional retirement candidates." Financial planners have previously recognized that their older, presently-retired clients feel the same. The conclusion is obvious for the alert financial planner: do not treat retirees as if they are as old as their vital statistics say, because that is not how old they are inside their mind's eye.

The Scudder-Kemper Poll coupled with financial planner observations about how their senior-citizen clients feel about their age leads us to realize that a new paradigm has taken place. Not only do people feel younger than that described by the antiquated rules of how people act at certain ages, all people are younger, and those antiquated rules constitute another example of outdated assumptions. In fact, the old retirement planning paradigm itself must be retired. Baby Boomers plan to rewrite the book on retirement to reflect active, engaging, and productive lives.

Even though a financially secure retirement is or will be their primary goal, only a small number of Boomers have taken proper steps in this direction. Twenty percent of all Boomers say they have no intention of ever retiring. That's today. In the future that could change with far more Baby Boomers planning to retire at some point. When they do get serious about accumulating funds for retirement, Boomers have an opportunity once again to outdo all predecessors.

The amount of wealth that is about to be developed and accumulated by our 76 million Baby Boomers is beyond imagination. Inheritance information can be extremely confusing. 2004 data provided by the Federal Reserve Board's Survey of Consumer Finances on potential inheritance state that about 80 percent of Baby Boomers will receive ZERO inheritance. The 20 percent that could receive an inheritance range from $10 trillion up to $40 trillion over the next 60 years. However, the median amount received as of 2004 was $49,000 (in 2005 dollars.) This wide range of potential inheritance is due to the potentially longer life span requiring much more money. This is especially true for the significant increases in health maintenance and repair costs (including insurance) and the likelihood of even larger allocations of assets in the future. But what is left over still would be sizable for the 20 percent of recipients. Anyway, the giant portion of future wealth of Baby Boomers will come from their own efforts.

The rude awakening many Boomers experience at age 50 will not be too late with too little. Baby Boomers have always thought big, and their approach to wealth accumulation will also be of a magnitude never before seen. Remember, they have always taken the just-in-time approach to decision making all throughout their lives.

It also will not be too late because retirement will not start by their desired age of 55. It will not start by age 62, or 65, or 67 either, but at age 70 or beyond. Baby Boomers' accumulations prior to age 50 in IRAs, 401(k)s, 403(b)s, etc., will act as a launching pad to real wealth accumulation in their fifties and sixties. Any Social Security changes allowing equity investing to be a part of the plan will also add more ammunition to the money arsenal. The funds in IRAs, 401(k)s, 403(b)s, etc., with 20 more years of compounding plus an increased personal savings rate – probably 20 percent of income starting around age 50 – will produce wealth that will be the envy of the world.

A dark cloud over the future of some Baby Boomers concerns older women. As reported by the *Scudder Kemper Baby Boom Generation Poll*, as reported in fall/ winter of 2006 study by the Harvard Generations Policy Program and the Global

Generations Policy Institute: Baby Boomer women are in trouble and face years of never-ending struggle. A significant number of our country's 40 million plus boomer women will not be able to afford to retire, will fall below the poverty line, and will experience financial insecurity and poorer health.

An important element in all of this will be the emergence into prominence of the profession of financial planning. Baby Boomers are knowledgeable, and people who are in the know retain the services of the most skilled specialists in all fields. When you know, you know enough to know you cannot know it all, so you hire someone who specializes in what you need. Baby Boomers of all kinds will want and need assistance with their financial matters.

THE FUTURE OF THE FINANCIAL PLANNER

As Baby Boomers move into the wealth-accumulation phase of their lives, many will seek financial advice. The future looks to be nothing less than fantastic for financial planning and for the financial planner.

When reporting the results of the Scudder Kemper Baby Boom Generation Poll, Dr. Christopher Hayes said, "What they (Baby Boomers) really need to understand is the merits of having a complete financial plan. Those that offer an ongoing light during turbulent internal and external changes will have Baby Boomer clients for life."

James L. Greenawalt, President of Kemper Distributors, Scudder Kemper Investments, Inc., stated, "This study points out the real need among Baby Boomers to work with financial advisors who can help them create a simple, straight-forward plan that enables them to save for retirement, while at the same time meeting their other financial obligations."

The future will be demanding of the financial planner, and success will be in direct proportion to the level of professionalism developed and maintained. Baby Boomers are looking for consultants, not salespeople. Oh, they will make investments and use the facilities of those advisors that render the service of comprehensive diagnosis prior to the service of implementation. So, the planner will still sell financial products and services, but this will be done from a base of consultation. The financial planner who succeeds will be a trusted advisor acting with a strong knowledge base and whose first and only frame of reference is to provide that which places the client's interest first.

One example of products that will be in many clients' best interest is life insurance. Life insurance for the wealthy retiree, in particular, will experience a tremendous growth as in no other period in history. Clients will recognize what Ben Feldman always said, "With life insurance proceeds, you get dollars for pennies." In his field of specialization, Ben Feldman was known as The Life Insurance Agent and Mr. Life Insurance, because during his lifetime he sold more life insurance than anyone else at that time. However, even though Ben Feldman placed record amounts of life insurance, there is no doubt that financial planners of the future will surpass his performance.

Professionalism demands a high level of competence and action. The outdated methods of pressure and scare tactics simply will not work on Baby Boomers. They ignore all negative messages that attempt to scare them into action. Baby Boomers want to receive information on their own terms, and they will insist on control. However, a knowledgeable financial advisor is in a perfect position to be the sounding board and provider of advice that the Baby Boomer needs and wants.

Approximately one half of all Baby Boomers admit to being novice investors, and only 14 percent consider themselves to be experienced investors. They will have funds to allocate for the services of well-prepared consultants.

The future financial planner will be well compensated. An abundance of income will be available for those planners who offer a trained ear, well developed knowledge, thoughtful attention, and the foresight to have everything in place before the need occurs. The Baby-Boomer retirement market is just coming into existence. The need for financial advice will grow, and the rewards will be substantial for those practitioners who are prepared.

As Baby Boomers retire, the amount of qualified money that will need attention is difficult to imagine. Qualified financial planners will be in great demand for a long time to come. Those financial planners who have been or will become long time trusted advisors will easily have the wherewithal to retire themselves, but they will not be able to hide from the ongoing demand from their Baby Boomer clients for a continuation of the wonderful advice their clients have grown accustomed to receiving.

Of course there will be obstacles, but this is not new. Successful people of all times have had mountains to climb, legislation to contend with, and uncharted waters to maneuver, but they managed, prospered, and lived the good life. So it will be for financial planners who are prepared.

Appendix A

FINANCIAL PLANNING FOR

Mary and Robert Sample

Haas Financial Services Incorporated
Donald Ray Haas, CLU, ChFC, CFP®, MSFS, RFC, RFG, AEP
Registered Financial Gerontologist
1323 Fairway
Birmingham, MI 48009
(248) 645-1638

(DATE)

MARY AND ROBERT SAMPLE

PERSONAL DATA

700 Bloomfield
Birmingham, Michigan 48009

Phone:	Home - (101) 644-9999	Fax - (XXX) XXX-XXXX	E-Mail -
Robert:	Work - (102) 974-9999	Fax - (XXX) XXX-XXXX	E-Mail -
Mary:	Work - (102) 645-9999	Fax - (XXX) XXX-XXXX	E-Mail -

NAME	DATE OF BIRTH	SOCIAL SECURITY NUMBER
Robert	1-1-1962	038-00-9999
Mary	1-1-1962	383-00-9999

CHILDREN

Patricia	1-1-1994
George	1-1-1998

ASSUMPTIONS

Inflation Rate			
2007			3.0%
Long Term	Next 10 Years		3.0%
	Thereafter		3.5%

Investment Growth Rate (Long Term)	7.0%

Life Expectancy:

	Years Remaining
Robert	35.57
Mary	40.20

(DATE)

MARY AND ROBERT SAMPLE

FINANCIAL PLANNING

FINANCIAL OBJECTIVES:

Comfortable Retirement

Standard of Living

College Education

Survivorship Planning

REASONS FOR FINANCIAL

 PLANNING:

Education Funding

Estate Planning

Review Insurance

New Car (2001)

RISK TAKING PROPENSITY:

(SCALE 0 - 23)

Mary   #9

Robert   #15

MAJOR CONCERNS:

Inflation Protection

Current Income (Mary's 1st Choice)

Future Income

Tax Control

(DATE)

MARY AND ROBERT SAMPLE

NET WORTH STATEMENT

ITEM	ASSET AMOUNT	LIABILITY AMOUNT	OWNERSHIP
PRIMARY RESIDENCE	$	$	JOINT
SECONDARY RESIDENCE			ROBERT
CASH ACCOUNTS			MIXED
ACCOUNTS RECEIVABLE			JOINT
LIFE INSURANCE CASH VALUE			BOTH
STOCK MARKET			JOINT
FIXED ANNUITY			ROBERT
VARIABLE ANNUITY			ROBERT
IRA			ROBERT
IRA			MARY
LIMITED PARTNERSHIPS			JOINT
PRECIOUS METALS			JOINT
COLLECTIBLES			JOINT
PERSONAL PROPERTY			JOINT
	_____	_____	
TOTAL	$ 0	$ 0	
NET WORTH	$_____0		

(DATE)

MARY AND ROBERT SAMPLE

ITEMIZED INVESTMENTS
REAL ESTATE

TYPE	Date of Purchase	Purchase Price	Current Market Value	Ownership
		$_____	$_____	
		$____0	$____0	

CASH ACCOUNTS

TYPE/NAME	Maturity Date	Current Interest Rate	Current Value	Ownership
			$_____	
			$____0	

STOCK MARKET

NAME OF COMPANY	Shares	Date of Purchase	Purchase Price	Current Market Value	Ownership
			$_____	$_____	
			$____0	$____0	

ANNUITIES

NAME OF COMPANY	Type	Contract Date	Current Interest Rate	Purchase Price	Current Surrender Value	Owner/ Beneficiary
				$_____	$_____	
				$____0	$____0	

LIMITED PARTNERSHIPS

TYPE/NAME	Shares	Date of Purchase	Purchase Price	Current Market Value	Ownership
			$_____	$_____	
			$____0	$____0	

RETIREMENT PLANS

TYPE/NAME	Shares	Maturity Date	Current Interest Rate	Purchase Price	Current Market Value	Ownership
				$_____	$_____	
				$____0	$____0	

LIABILITIES

Balance Owed	Due Date	Current Interest Rate	Monthly Payment	
$____0			$____0	

(DATE)

MARY AND ROBERT SAMPLE

HISTORY NET WORTH STATEMENT

ITEM	2005 ASSET AMOUNT	2006 ASSET AMOUNT	2007 ASSET AMOUNT
PRIMARY RESIDENCE	$		
SECONDARY RESIDENCE			
CASH ACCOUNTS			
ACCOUNTS RECEIVABLE			
LIFE INSURANCE CASH VALUE			
STOCK MARKET			
VARIABLE ANNUITY			
LIMITED PARTNERSHIPS			
IRA - ROBERT			
IRA - MARY			
PRECIOUS METALS			
COLLECTIBLES			
PERSONAL PROPERTY			
TOTAL	$ 0	0	0

HYPOTHETICAL

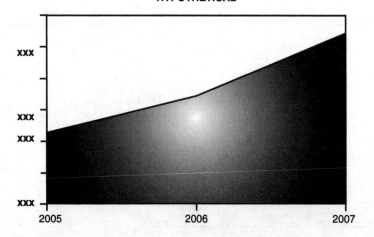

(DATE)

MARY AND ROBERT SAMPLE

<u>INCOME TAX INFORMATION</u>

<u>SOURCE OF INCOME</u>	2006	2005	2004
WAGES:			
ROBERT	$	$	$
MARY			
INTEREST			
TAX - EXEMPT INTEREST			
DIVIDENDS			
CAPITAL GAIN (LOSS)			
PENSIONS			
PARTNERSHIPS			
SOCIAL SECURITY			
OTHER			
	_____	_____	_____
	$ **0**	$ **0**	$ **0**
IRA	$	$	$
401(k)			
403(b)			
SEP/KEOGH			
<u>**TAX**</u>			
FEDERAL	$	$	$
MICHIGAN			
CITY			
	_____	_____	_____
	$ **0**	$ **0**	$ **0**
SOCIAL SECURITY - ROBERT			
MARY			
	_____	_____	_____
	$ **0**	$ **0**	$ **0**
TOTAL TAX	$ **0**	$ **0**	$ **0**
MARG. FEDERAL TAX	%	%	%
SUSPENDED LOSS			
CARRY-OVER	$	$	$

(DATE)

MARY AND ROBERT SAMPLE

INCOME SOURCES

	YEAR	2007	2008	2009
PENSION		$	$	$
ROBERT				
MARY				
SOCIAL SECURITY				
ROBERT				
MARY				
ANNUITY				
WAGES				
TOTAL BASIC INCOME		$ 0	$ 0	$ 0

ADDITIONAL INCOME SOURCES

CASH $
STOCK MARKET
ANNUITIES
IRA/401(k)/403(b)

      TOTAL $ _____ @ 6% =

(DATE)

MARY AND ROBERT SAMPLE

CASH MANAGEMENT STATEMENT

ANNUAL EXPENDITURES: FIXED   **YEAR**
HOUSING (MORTGAGE/RENT) $_____
PROPERTY TAXES   _____
HOUSE UPKEEP/REPAIRS/MAINTENANCE   _____

UTILITIES & TELEPHONE   _____
FOOD/GROCERIES   _____
CLOTHING & CLEANING   _____

INCOME & SOCIAL SECURITY TAXES   _____
DEBT REPAYMENT   _____
TRANSPORTATION   (AUTO/COMMUTING)   _____

AUTO, HOME AND LIABILITY INSURANCE   _____
MEDICAL/DENTAL/DRUGS/HEALTH INSURANCE   _____
DISABILITY INCOME INSURANCE   _____

LIFE INSURANCE   _____
EDUCATION EXPENSES   _____

TOTAL FIXED EXPENDITURES $_____

ANNUAL EXPENDITURES: DISCRETIONARY
VACATION/TRAVEL $_____
RECREATION/ENTERTAINMENT   _____
CONTRIBUTIONS   _____
GIFTS   _____

HOUSEHOLD FURNISHINGS   _____
EDUCATION FUND   _____
PERSONAL CARE   _____
OTHER   _____

TOTAL DISCRETIONARY EXPENDITURES $_____

TOTAL ANNUAL EXPENDITURES $_____

SAVINGS $_____
INVESTMENTS   _____
     _____

TOTAL ANNUAL EXPENDITURES & ACCUMULATIONS $_____

ESTIMATED INCOME $_____

(DATE)

MARY AND ROBERT SAMPLE

PROPERTY AND LIABILITY INSURANCE

HOMEOWNERS

		EXPIRATION
COMPANY	POLICY NUMBER	DATE
DWELLING		$
PERSONAL PROPERTY		
LIABILITY		
REPLACEMENT COST		
DEDUCTIBLE		

ANNUAL PREMIUM $ 0

AUTO

		EXPIRATION
COMPANY	POLICY NUMBER	DATE

	CAR 1	CAR 2
BODILY INJURY LIABILITY	$	$
PROPERTY DAMAGE LIABILITY		
COMPREHENSIVE DEDUCTIBLE		
COLLISION (BROAD) DEDUCTIBLE		
PERSONAL INJURY PROTECTION		
ANNUAL PREMIUM	$ 0	$ 0

TOTAL ANNUAL PREMIUM $ 0

EXCESS LIABILITY

		EXPIRATION
COMPANY	POLICY NUMBER	DATE
AMOUNT	$	

REQUIRED UNDERLYING COVERAGE

	BODILY INJURY	PROPERTY DAMAGE	SINGLE LIMIT
AUTO	$	$	$
HOME			
OTHER			

ANNUAL PREMIUM $_____0

TOTAL ANNUAL PREMIUM $ 0

(DATE)

MARY AND ROBERT SAMPLE

MEDICAL INSURANCE

COMPANY   _____

POLICY NUMBER   _____

POLICY DATE   _____

TYPE   _____

HOSPITAL

ROOM AND BOARD   _____

MISCELLANEOUS EXPENSE   _____

SURGERY   _____

SECOND SURGICAL OPINION   _____

PRE-CERTIFICATION   _____

PRESCRIPTION DRUGS   _____

HOME HEALTH CARE   _____

MAJOR MEDICAL

MAXIMUM $_____

DEDUCTIBLE   _____

CO-INSURANCE %   _____

$ OUT OF POCKET   _____

TOTAL OUT OF POCKET   _____

DENTAL/VISION

MAXIMUM $_____

DEDUCTIBLE   _____

BENEFITS:

ANNUAL PREMIUM $_____ 0

(DATE)

MARY AND ROBERT SAMPLE

DISABILITY INCOME INSURANCE

COMPANY	_____
POLICY NUMBER	_____
POLICY DATE	_____
TYPE	_____

BENEFITS

MONTHLY $_____

SOCIAL SECURITY SUBSTITUTE   _____

COST OF LIVING RIDER   _____

PARTIAL DISABILITY (RESIDUAL)   _____

ELIMINATION PERIOD   _____

REHABILITATION EXPENSE   _____

TREATMENT OF INJURY   _____

BENEFIT PERIOD

ACCIDENT   _____

SICKNESS   _____

PREMIUMS

BASIC $_____

SOCIAL SECURITY SUBSTITUTE   _____

COST OF LIVING   _____
PARTIAL DISABILITY

TOTAL MONTHLY BENEFIT $_____ 0

TOTAL ANNUAL PREMIUM $_____ 0

(DATE)

MARY AND ROBERT SAMPLE

LONG TERM CARE INSURANCE

COMPANY   _____

POLICY NUMBER   _____

POLICY DATE   _____

TYPE   _____

DAILY BENEFIT

NURSING HOME CARE $ _____

HOME CARE   _____

INFLATION ADJUSTMENT RIDER 5% - COMPOUNDED

ELIMINATION PERIOD
NURSING HOME CARE
HOME HEALTH CARE

PRE-EXISTING CONDITION   _____ (1)

CAN POLICY BE CANCELLED?   _____

PRIOR HOSPITAL STAY REQUIRED

SKILLED NURSING CARE   _____

INTERMEDIATE NURSING CARE   _____

CUSTODIAL NURSING CARE   _____

PRIOR SKILLED NURSING CARE REQUIRED

INTERMEDIATE NURSING CARE   _____

CUSTODIAL NURSING CARE   _____

PRIOR NURSING HOME CARE REQUIRED

HOME HEALTH CARE   _____

INFLATION ADJUSTED

ANNUALLY (5%)   SIMPLE   _____

                          COMPOUND   _____

ANNUAL PREMIUM $_____0

(1) IF REPORTED ON APPLICATION COVERED IMMEDIATELY

(DATE)

MARY AND ROBERT SAMPLE

LIFE INSURANCE

COMPANY/ NUMBER	DATE ISSUED	AGE AT ISSUE	DEATH BENEFIT	TYPE OF POLICY	ANNUAL PREMIUM	OWNER/ BENEF.	WAIVER PREM
ROBERT			$ _____		$ _____		
			$ 0		$ 0		
MARY			$ _____		$ _____		
			$ 0		$ 0		

NOTES: _____

_____

A: OWNER:_____

PRIMARY BENEFICIARY:_____

CONTINGENT BENEFICIARY: _____

B: OWNER:_____

PRIMARY BENEFICIARY:_____

CONTINGENT BENEFICIARY: _____

(DATE)

MARY AND ROBERT SAMPLE

LIFE INSURANCE

COMPANY/ NUMBER	BASE POLICY CASH VALUE	PAID UP INS. CASH VALUE	ACCUMULATED DIVIDENDS	LOAN	LOAN INTEREST RATE
ROBERT					
	$_____	$_____	$_____	$_____	
	$_____ 0	$_____ 0	$_____ 0	$_____ 0	
MARY	$_____	$_____	$_____	$_____	
	$_____ 0	$_____ 0	$_____ 0	$_____ 0	

(DATE)

MARY AND ROBERT SAMPLE

PROTECTION RECOMMENDATIONS

EXCESS LIABILITY

HOMEOWNERS

AUTO

MEDICAL

DISABILITY/LONG TERM CARE

LIFE INSURANCE

(DATE)

MARY AND ROBERT SAMPLE

EMERGENCY FUND

    PRESENT

        CASH ACCOUNTS $
        LIFE INSURANCE CASH VALUE

                                           $_____

    PROPER
        CURRENT BUDGET - INCOME &
        SOCIAL SECURITY TAXES x .25 = $_____

RECOMMENDATIONS

(DATE)

MARY AND ROBERT SAMPLE

INVESTMENT PORTFOLIO

Investments	Thousands	Percent	Generic Range	Recommended Percent
CASH	$		10 - 20%	10%
STOCK MARKET			15 - 25%	25
REAL ESTATE			20 - 25%	25
PRECIOUS METALS			1 - 4%	1
TAX FAVORED			20 - 38%	38
COLLECTIBLES			0 - 5%	1
	————	————	————	————
TOTAL	$ 0.0	0%	100%	100%

CASH   **STOCK MARKET**

          $_____ $_____

          $ 0.0 $ 0.0

REAL ESTATE   **PRECIOUS METALS**

          $ _____ $ _____

          $ 0.0 $ 0.0

TAX FAVORED   **COLLECTIBLES**

          $ _____ $ _____

          $ 0.0 $ 0.0

(DATE)

MARY AND ROBERT SAMPLE

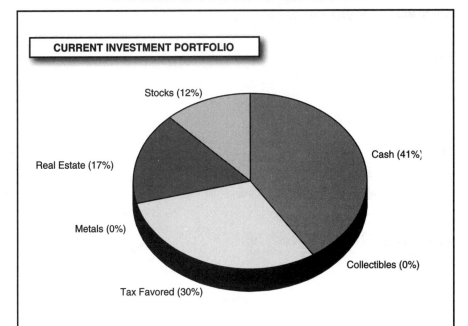

CURRENT INVESTMENT PORTFOLIO

Stocks (12%)

Real Estate (17%)

Metals (0%)

Tax Favored (30%)

Cash (41%)

Collectibles (0%)

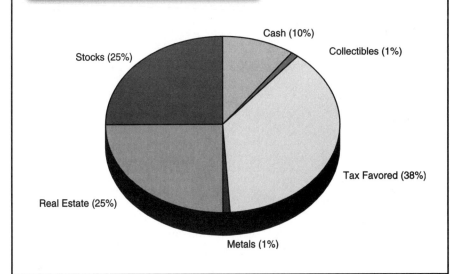

SPECIFIC RECOMMENDED PERCENTAGE

Cash (10%)

Collectibles (1%)

Stocks (25%)

Real Estate (25%)

Tax Favored (38%)

Metals (1%)

(DATE)

MARY AND ROBERT SAMPLE

INVESTMENT RECOMMENDATIONS

CASH

STOCK MARKET

REAL ESTATE

PRECIOUS METALS

TAX FAVORED

COLLECTIBLES

(DATE)

MARY AND ROBERT SAMPLE

ESTATE ANALYSIS

1) ASSET	ROBERT	MARY	JOINT
PRIMARY RESIDENCE	$	$	$
SECONDARY RESIDENCE			
CASH ACCOUNTS			
STOCK MARKET			
FIXED ANNUITY			
VARIABLE ANNUITY			
LIMITED PARTNERSHIPS			
IRA			
PRECIOUS METALS			
COLLECTIBLES			
PERSONAL PROPERTY			
LIFE INSURANCE			
TOTAL	$ 0	$ 0	$ 0	$ 0

2) There would be zero death taxes at either death (one death)

3) The following taxation would occur when both of you have died:

ESTATE TAXATION
Assumes First to Die is:

	PRESENT	PROPOSED	2009
GROSS ESTATE	$	$	$
EXPENSES			
TAXABLE ESTATE	$	$	$
GROSS TAX	$	$	$
FEDERAL CREDIT	(780,800)	(780,800)	(1,455,800)
TOTAL TAX	$	$	$

*Plus Income Tax on All Retirement Plans

RECOMMENDATIONS

MARY AND ROBERT SAMPLE

RETIREMENT PLAN ASSET ALLOCATION
CASH

$ _____
                              $ 0.0

BONDS

$ _____
                              $ 0.0

STOCK MARKET

$ _____
                              $ 0.0

REAL ESTATE

$ _____
                              $ 0.0

                              $ 0.0

	PRESENT			PROPOSED	
CASH	$ 0.0	0%	$	0.0	0%
BONDS	0.0	0		0.0	0
STOCK MARKET	0.0	0		0.0	0
REAL ESTATE	0.0	0		0.0	0
TOTAL	$ 0.0	0%	$	0.0	0%

RECOMMENDATIONS

(DATE)

MARY AND ROBERT SAMPLE

RETIREMENT CASH FLOW ANALYSIS

ASSUMPTIONS

1.	YEAR OF RETIREMENT				2020
2.	YEAR BORN:	*RETIREE 1*	*ROBERT*		1953
2A.		*RETIREE 2*	*MARY*		1953

3. ANNUAL INFLATION
   RATE FOR YEARS *1-10* 3.5% *11-20* 4.0% *THEREAFTER* 4.0%
4. SOCIAL SECURITY INFLATION RATE 3.0%
5. AFTER-TAX RATE OF RETURN ON INVESTMENTS 8.0%
6. PENSION
   INFLATION AJD: *OPT 1 = COMPOUNDED INFL RATE* 0.0% *ROBERT* 0.0% *MARY*
6A. *OPT 2 = FLAT FIXED DOLLAR AMT* $0 *ROBERT* $0 *MARY*

					1998 DOLLARS	RETIREMENT DOLLARS
7.	ANNUAL DESIRED INCOME (EXCLUDING MORTGAGE)				$55,000	$105,386
8.	ANNUAL MORTGAGE PMT (PRIN & INT ONLY)		*ENDING*	0		0
9.	SOCIAL SECURITY	*ROBERT*	*STARTING*	2020		$19,000
9A.		*MARY*	*STARTING*	2020		$9,500
10.	CAPITAL AVAILABLE FOR INVESTING				$324,000	$1,761,439
11.	PENSION BENEFITS	*ROBERT*	*STARTING*	0		$0
11A.		*MARY*	*STARTING*	0		$0
12.	ADDITIONAL ANNUAL INVESTMENTS NEEDED				$0	$0

YEAR	AGE 1	AGE 2	REQUIRED INCOME	MORTGAGE PAYMENT	SOCIAL SECURITY	OTHER INC (EXPENSES)	PENSION ROBERT	PENSION MARY	AMT NEEDED FROM CAPITAL	REMAINING CAPITAL	SHORTFALL
2020	67	67	105,386	0	28,500	0	0	0	76,886	1,822,393	0
2021	68	68	109,074	0	29,355	0	0	0	79,719	1,885,277	0
2022	69	69	112,892	0	30,236	0	0	0	82,656	1,950,136	0
2023	70	70	116,843	0	31,143	0	0	0	85,700	2,017,019	0
2024	71	71	120,933	0	32,077	0	0	0	88,855	2,085,971	0
2025	72	72	125,165	0	33,039	0	0	0	92,126	2,157,038	0
2026	73	73	129,546	0	34,030	0	0	0	95,515	2,230,265	0
2027	74	74	134,080	0	35,051	0	0	0	99,029	2,305,696	0
2028	75	75	138,773	0	36,103	0	0	0	102,670	2,383,375	0
2029	76	76	143,630	0	37,186	0	0	0	106,444	2,463,343	0
2030	77	77	148,657	0	38,302	0	0	0	110,355	2,545,641	0
2031	78	78	154,603	0	39,451	0	0	0	115,153	2,629,534	0
2032	79	79	160,787	0	40,634	0	0	0	120,153	2,714,937	0
2033	80	80	167,219	0	41,853	0	0	0	125,366	2,801,752	0
2034	81	81	173,908	0	43,109	0	0	0	130,799	2,889,862	0
2035	82	82	180,864	0	44,402	0	0	0	136,462	2,979,130	0
2036	83	83	188,098	0	45,734	0	0	0	142,364	3,069,402	0
2037	84	84	195,622	0	47,106	0	0	0	148,516	3,160,497	0
2038	85	85	203,447	0	48,519	0	0	0	154,928	3,252,212	0
2039	86	86	211,585	0	49,975	0	0	0	161,610	3,344,314	0
2040	87	87	220,049	0	51,474	0	0	0	168,574	3,436,542	0
2041	88	88	228,850	0	53,018	0	0	0	175,832	3,528,600	0
2042	89	89	238,005	0	54,609	0	0	0	183,396	3,620,157	0

(DATE)

MARY AND ROBERT SAMPLE

RETIREMENT CASH FLOW ANALYSIS (cont'd)

YEAR	AGE 1	2	REQUIRED INCOME	MORTGAGE PAYMENT	SOCIAL SECURITY	OTHER INC (EXPENSES)	PENSION ROBERT	PENSION MARY	AMT NEEDED FROM CAPITAL	REMAINING CAPITAL	SHORTFALL
2043	90	90	247,525	0	56,247	0	0	0	191,277	3,710,840	0
2044	91	91	257,426	0	57,935	0	0	0	199,491	3,800,237	0
2045	92	92	267,723	0	59,673	0	0	0	208,050	3,887,884	0
2046	93	93	278,432	0	61,463	0	0	0	216,969	3,973,267	0
2047	94	94	289,569	0	63,307	0	0	0	226,262	4,055,816	0
2048	95	95	301,152	0	65,206	0	0	0	235,946	4,134,898	0
2049	96	96	313,198	0	67,162	0	0	0	246,036	4,209,812	0
2050	97	97	325,726	0	69,177	0	0	0	256,549	4,279,787	0
2051	98	98	338,755	0	71,252	0	0	0	267,502	4,343,967	0
2052	99	99	352,305	0	73,390	0	0	0	278,915	4,401,413	0
2053	100	100	366,397	0	75,592	0	0	0	290,805	4,451,088	0

This analysis is based on the accuracy and consistency of the data and assumptions you have provided in items 1 through 11 and is not guaranteed. The figures shown are valid only as long as the data and assumptions remain unchanged. To maintain accuracy of this analysis, periodic updating is necessary to reflect changes as they occur.

(DATE)

MARY AND ROBERT SAMPLE

RETIREMENT CASH FLOW ANALYSIS

ASSUMPTIONS

1.	YEAR OF RETIREMENT				2020
2.	YEAR BORN:	**RETIREE 1**	**ROBERT**		1953
2A.		**RETIREE 2**	**MARY**		1953

3. ANNUAL INFLATION
   RATE FOR YEARS **1-10** 3.5% **11-20** 4.0% **THEREAFTER** 4.0%
4. SOCIAL SECURITY INFLATION RATE 3.0%
5. AFTER-TAX RATE OF RETURN ON INVESTMENTS 8.0%
6. PENSION
   INFLATION AJD: **OPT 1 = COMPOUNDED INFL RATE** 0.0% **ROBERT** 0.0% **MARY**
6A. **OPT 2 = FLAT FIXED DOLLAR AMT** $0 **ROBERT** $0 **MARY**

		1998 DOLLARS	RETIREMENT DOLLARS
7.	ANNUAL DESIRED INCOME (EXCLUDING MORTGAGE)	$65,000	$124,547
8.	ANNUAL MORTGAGE PMT (PRIN & INT ONLY) **ENDING** 0		0
9.	SOCIAL SECURITY **ROBERT STARTING** 2020		$19,000
9A.	**MARY STARTING** 2020		$9,500
10.	CAPITAL AVAILABLE FOR INVESTING	$324,000	$1,761,439
11.	PENSION BENEFITS **RROBERT STARTING** 0		$0
11A.	**MARY STARTING** 0		$0
12.	ADDITIONAL ANNUAL INVESTMENTS NEEDED	$0	$0

YEAR	AGE 1	AGE 2	REQUIRED INCOME	MORTGAGE PAYMENT	SOCIAL SECURITY	OTHER INC (EXPENSES)	PENSION ROBERT	PENSION MARY	AMT NEEDED FROM CAPITAL	REMAINING CAPITAL	SHORTFALL
2020	67	67	124,547	0	28,500	0	0	0	96,047	1,802,466	0
2021	68	68	128,906	0	29,355	0	0	0	99,551	1,843,130	0
2022	69	69	133,418	0	30,236	0	0	0	103,182	1,883,271	0
2023	70	70	138,087	0	31,143	0	0	0	106,944	1,922,711	0
2024	71	71	142,920	0	32,077	0	0	0	110,843	1,961,251	0
2025	72	72	147,922	0	33,039	0	0	0	114,883	1,998,672	0
2026	73	73	153,100	0	34,030	0	0	0	119,069	2,034,734	0
2027	74	74	158,458	0	35,051	0	0	0	123,407	2,069,170	0
2028	75	75	164,004	0	36,103	0	0	0	127,901	2,101,686	0
2029	76	76	169,744	0	37,186	0	0	0	132,558	2,131,960	0
2030	77	77	175,685	0	38,302	0	0	0	137,384	2,159,638	0
2031	78	78	182,713	0	39,451	0	0	0	143,262	2,183,416	0
2032	79	79	190,021	0	40,634	0	0	0	149,387	2,202,726	0
2033	80	80	197,622	0	41,853	0	0	0	155,769	2,216,945	0
2034	81	81	205,527	0	43,109	0	0	0	162,418	2,225,385	0
2035	82	82	213,748	0	44,402	0	0	0	169,346	2,227,296	0
2036	83	83	222,298	0	45,734	0	0	0	176,564	2,221,853	0
2037	84	84	231,190	0	47,106	0	0	0	184,084	2,208,154	0
2038	85	85	240,438	0	48,519	0	0	0	191,918	2,185,212	0
2039	86	86	250,055	0	49,975	0	0	0	200,080	2,151,945	0
2040	87	87	260,057	0	51,474	0	0	0	208,583	2,107,174	0
2041	88	88	270,460	0	53,018	0	0	0	217,441	2,049,609	0
2042	89	89	281,278	0	54,609	0	0	0	226,669	1,977,842	0

MARY AND ROBERT SAMPLE

RETIREMENT CASH FLOW ANALYSIS (cont'd)

YEAR	AGE 1	AGE 2	REQUIRED INCOME	MORTGAGE PAYMENT	SOCIAL SECURITY	OTHER INC (EXPENSES)	PENSION ROBERT	PENSION MARY	AMT NEEDED FROM CAPITAL	REMAINING CAPITAL	SHORTFALL
2043	90	90	292,529	0	56,247	0	0	0	236,282	1,890,336	0
2044	91	91	304,230	0	57,935	0	0	0	246,296	1,785,415	0
2045	92	92	316,400	0	59,673	0	0	0	256,727	1,661,253	0
2046	93	93	329,056	0	61,463	0	0	0	267,593	1,515,856	0
2047	94	94	342,218	0	63,307	0	0	0	278,911	1,347,057	0
2048	95	95	355,906	0	65,206	0	0	0	290,701	1,152,493	0
2049	96	96	370,143	0	67,162	0	0	0	302,981	929,593	0
2050	97	97	384,948	0	69,177	0	0	0	315,771	675,558	0
2051	98	98	400,346	0	71,252	0	0	0	329,094	387,345	0
2052	99	99	416,360	0	73,390	0	0	0	342,970	61,643	0
2053	100	100	433,015	0	75,592	0	0	0	64,109	0	293,314

This Analysis Is Based On The Accuracy And Consistency Of The Data And Assumptions You Have Provided In Items 1 Through 11 And Is Not Guaranteed. The Figures Shown Are Valid Only As Long As The Data And Assumptions Remain Unchanged. To Maintain Accuracy Of This Analysis, Periodic Updating Is Necessary To Reflect Changes As They Occur.

MARY AND ROBERT SAMPLE

<u>MISCELLANEOUS</u>

1.

2.

3.

4.

5.

6.

7.

(DATE)

MARY AND ROBERT SAMPLE

MORTGAGE REFINANCING CONSIDERATIONS

PROPER SIZE OF MORTGAGE

$ _____ (Value of House) x .80   = $ _____

$ _____ (Total Investments) x .25   = $ _____

                                               = $ _____

PROPER MONTHLY PAYMENT

MAXIMUM $ _____ (Income) x .25 ÷ 12   = $ _____
IDEAL $ _____ (Income) x .15 ÷ 12   = $ _____

CONSIDERATIONS

   1.   Refinance Mortgage $ _____

		MONTHLY	**ANNUAL**
2.	Mortgage Payments 15 years @ 8%	$ _____	$ _____

USE OF FUNDS

      Pay Off Present Mortgage $ _____
      Cost Of New Mortgage
      Cash Reserves
      Investments

(DATE)

MARY AND ROBERT SAMPLE

EDUCATIONAL FUNDING

PATRICIA AGE 13

Year	Starting Balance	Net Growth	Annual Deposit	Withdrawal	Fund(s) Ending Balance
2007	$5,300	$371	$8,660	$0	$14,331
2008	14,331	1,003	8,660	0	23,994
2009	23,994	1,680	8,660	0	34,334
2010	34,334	2,403	8,660	0	45,397
2011	45,397	3,178	6,791	0	57,235
2012	57,235	4,006	8,660	0	69,901
2013	69,901	4,893	8,660	12,044	71,410
2014	71,410	4,999	8,660	24,811	60,258
2015	60,258	4,218	8,660	26,299	46,837
2016	46,837	3,279	8,660	27,877	30,899
2017	30,899	2,163	0	15,205	17,856
TOTAL			$86,600	$106,237	

GEORGE AGE 9

Year	Starting Balance	Net Growth	Annual Deposit	Withdrawal	Fund(s) Ending Balance
2007	$1,900	$133	$6,881	$0	$8,914
2008	8,914	624	6,881	0	16,419
2009	16,419	1,149	6,881	0	24,449
2010	24,449	1,711	6,881	0	33,042
2011	33,042	2,313	6,881	0	42,236
2012	42,236	2,956	6,881	0	52,073
2013	52,073	3,645	6,881	0	62,559
2014	62,599	4,382	6,881	0	73,862
2015	73,862	5,170	6,881	0	85,914
2016	85,914	6,014	6,881	15,205	83,603
2017	83,603	5,852	6,881	31,323	65,014
2018	65,014	4,551	6,881	33,202	43,243
2019	43,243	3,027	6,881	35,194	17,957
2020	17,957	1,257	0	19,196	17
TOTAL			$89,453	$134,121	

ASSUMPTIONS

2007 ANNUAL COST	$18,000
EDUCATION INFLATION RATE	6.00%
AFTER - TAX GROWTH RATE IS	7.00%

(DATE)

MARY AND ROBERT SAMPLE

<u>ACTION ITEMS</u>

<u>COMMENTS</u>   <u>ITEM</u>

1.

2.

3.

4.

5.

6.

7.

8.

FINANCIAL PLAN UPDATE

Name   **Today's Date**

Appointment: Call for an appointment as soon as you
                        have mailed this information to me

Review with:

❏ **Advisor's Name** *(Hourly Fee: $)*   ❏ **Advisor's Name** *(Hourly Fee: $)*

🖅 **MAIL** the following information:

1. Enclosed pages with current information *(1)*

2. Brokerage Account Statements *(if NOT purchased through our office)*

3. **Anniversary Statements** for Life Insurance and Annuities *(All policies)*

4. List newly acquired assets or liabilities (if any) on the reverse side of this page

5. Mortgage Balance $ [   ]   Interest Rate   [   ]
   Monthly Payment $ [   ]   Date of Final Payment [   ]
   (Principal & Interest Only)

6. Current Income

7. Completed Financial Planning Update forms *(enclosed)*

8. Please provide copy of driver's license and expiration date *(for each of you)*

📁 **BRING** the following to the meeting:

9. 2004, 2005, and 2006 income tax returns

10. All current homeowners, automobile, and excess liability insurance policies

Please call me if you have any questions ((XXX) XXX-XXXX).

Sincerely,

Lori Gilbert
Financial Plan Coordinator
Technology Specialist

(1) These pages do NOT show products purchased through this office. I will update these for you.

FINANCIAL PLAN UPDATE

NAME   DATE

FINANCIAL OBJECTIVES

RANK IN ORDER FROM 1 (HIGHEST) TO 9 (LOWEST).

Use Each Number ONLY Once!

PRIORITY
NUMBER   ITEM
_____   Maintain/Expand Standard of Living
_____   Enjoy A Comfortable Retirement
_____   Take Care Of Self and Family During A Long Term Disability

_____   Invest And Accumulate Wealth
_____   Reduce Tax Burden
_____   Provide College Education For All Children

_____   Take Care of Family In The Event of Death
_____   Develop An Estate Plan
_____   Any Others Important To You (Specify)

INVESTMENT OBJECTIVES

RANK IN ORDER FROM 1 (HIGHEST) TO 6 (LOWEST).

Use Each Number ONLY Once!

_____   Liquidity
_____   Safety Of Principal
_____   Current Income From Investments
_____   Appreciation
_____   Protection From Inflation
_____   Tax Reduction Or Deferral

CURRENT ATTITUDE

Allocate eight points among these four investment characteristics. **A maximum of four points** may be allocated to any one characteristic. Points may be allocated in units of one-half point.

What is your allocation for YOUR IDEAL INVESTMENT?

Remember: No more than 4 points in any one category.
                       No more than 8 points for the TOTAL of all categories.

Tax Benefits		Current Cash Flow		Appreciation		Safety		
	+		+		+		=	8

BIG TICKET ITEMS DURING THE NEXT 5 YEARS

ITEM	WHEN	COST
		$

LIST OF ITEMS TO DISCUSS

Haas Financial Services, Inc.
29600 Northwestern Hwy, Suite 114
Southfield, Michigan 48034

Financial Planning is an
ongoing activity which
requires periodic updating.
Many factors are constantly
changing that affect your
personal considerations.
Now, **it's your move!** Just
call **(248) 213-0101** to schedule
an appointment.

We'll do the rest!

Index

TOOLS & TECHNIQUES

Brought to you by the publisher of Tax Facts

ROAD TO SUCCESS

Begins with Tools & Techniques

The Disciplined Approach for Today's Professional.
Discover more at www.NUCOstore.com/TandT

▼ Trust the Series designed to turn your ideas into saleable, profitable actions

▼ Discover value at any knowledge level—introductory, overview & review